Realism and Anti-Realism

Central Problems of Philosophy
Series Editor: John Shand

This series of books presents concise, clear, and rigorous analyses of the core problems that preoccupy philosophers across all approaches to the discipline. Each book encapsulates the essential arguments and debates, providing an authoritative guide to the subject while also introducing original perspectives. This series of books by an international team of authors aims to cover those fundamental topics that, taken together, constitute the full breadth of philosophy.

Published titles

Forthcoming titles

Realism and Anti-Realism

Stuart Brock and Edwin Mares

McGill-Queen's University Press
Montreal & Kingston • Ithaca

© Stuart Brock and Edwin Mares 2007

ISBN 978-0-7735-3238-0 (bound)
ISBN 978-0-7735-3239-7 (paper)

Legal deposit first quarter 2007
Bibliothèque nationale du Québec

Published simultaneously outside North America
by Acumen Publishing Limited

McGill-Queen's University Press acknowledges the financial support of
the Government of Canada through the Book Publishing Development
Program (BPIDP) for its activities.

Library and Archives Canada Cataloguing in Publication

Brock, Stuart, 1968-

Realism and anti-realism / Stuart Ross Brock, Edwin David Mares.

Includes bibliographical references and index.
ISBN 978-0-7735-3238-0 (bound)
ISBN 978-0-7735-3239-7 (pbk.)

1. Realism. I. Mares, Edwin David II. Title.

B835.B73 2007   149'.2   C2006-905546-7

Designed and typeset by Kate Williams, Swansea.

Contents

Acknowledgements

In writing this book we have benefited from the comments of others. In particular, we should like to thank Nicholas Agar, Jean-Paul van Bendegem, John Brock, Ramon Das, Joshua Glasgow, Rob Goldblatt, Seahwa Kim, Neil Leslie, Alex Miller, Cei Maslen, Zoe Prebble, Kate Williams and two referees for Acumen. Special thanks are due to our editor, Steven Gerrard. Without his help, patience and encouragement this book would never have been real. It would have existed in our minds only.

In writing this book, we have also tested the patience of many. And so we should like to give special thanks to our loved ones: Nalayini, Julian, Jonathan, Emma and Sue. We dedicate this book to them.

Some material from Stuart Brock, "Fictionalism about Fictional Characters", Noûs 36 (2002), 1–21, appears in Chapter 12 with the kind permission of Blackwell Publishers.

1 Introduction

Questions about the ultimate reality of things sometimes seem like silly questions to non-philosophers, but to philosophers they are questions of the utmost importance and deepest significance. It is not easy or straightforward to know when some contentious realm of entities is real, or to understand and appreciate what is at issue between those on each side of the dispute. Thus, the questions posed by those who originally framed the realist–anti-realist debate centuries ago – most notably, the nominalists and idealists – have dominated the attention of philosophers ever since. Indeed, questions about the plausibility and character of realism and its alternatives are at the heart of all metaphysical disputes today.

Our aim in this book is to make clear to any intelligent reader what is really at stake in the contemporary realism debate. As far as we know, no other work has really succeeded in doing that. This is unfortunate, because the primary literature is notoriously difficult to grapple with. Consequently, anyone confronting this literature for the first time is likely to be deterred by the abundance of jargon and the almost universal presupposition that the reader has significant background knowledge of the main issues. The uninitiated could be forgiven for giving up quickly after forming the impression that they are somehow uninvited guests at an exclusive club. It is hoped this book might succeed in making the club a little more ecumenical. This book is for those who want to direct their attention squarely towards questions of realism and anti-realism for the first time. It is meant as a substantial introduction to the realism debate, and a good springboard to the most important technical papers on the topic. With this goal in mind, let us move directly to our main question.

1.1 What is realism?

Perhaps the most striking feature of the realism literature is its lack of agreement over what the basic terms "realism" and "anti-realism" mean. Let us start therefore by stipulating what *we* mean by "realism". Realism about a particular domain is the conjunction of the following two theses: (i) there are facts or entities distinctive of that domain, and (ii) their existence and nature is in some important sense objective and mind-independent. Let us call the first thesis the "existence thesis" and the second thesis the "independence thesis".

Some further elaboration is necessary. Notice that our characterization of the existence thesis involves quantification over entities *and* facts. (There is a difference: entities are the referents of the singular terms in a language, while facts are aspects of the world represented by whole declarative sentences in a language.) This is awkward, to say the least. And this awkwardness explains why many who have attempted to explain the existence thesis – and distinguish it from the independence thesis – have quantified only over individuals. But to ignore the realist's commitment to facts is to miss something very important about the realist's distinctive claim. For it is possible to be a realist about some domain without thinking that there are any special entities distinctive of that domain. And the facts in question are not just trivial negative facts to the effect that such things do not exist. One might believe it is a fact that everything that goes up must come down without believing in gravitational fields; one might believe it is a fact that, in the novel *Wuthering Heights*, Heathcliff is haunted by a ghost on the windy moors without believing in Heathcliff or ghosts; one might believe it is a fact that Senator John Kerry could have won the US presidential election without believing there is a possible world in which (something appropriately related to) Kerry does win; one might believe it is a fact that one ought to assist people in need without believing that such actions have the property of being morally good. In our view, those who believe such things (without believing that such facts depend on us) count as realists about the relevant domain – scientific realists, realists about fiction, modal realists and moral realists – but they *do not* count as realists about scientific *entities*, fictional *objects*, possible *worlds* or moral *properties*.

Notice also that our brief description of the independence thesis alludes to an important sense in which a domain is objective and mind-independent. But what sense is the important sense? The sense-data of the phenomenalists, the ideas of the idealists, the monads of the Leibnizian, the phenomenal world of the Kantian and the verifiable world of the logical positivists have all been alleged to exist. But such entities are all, to a greater or lesser extent, subjective and mind-dependent, and so lack reality in our fundamental sense. For a domain to be objective and mind-independent in our sense it must not exist in any of these ways. Facts about the domain must be out there to be discovered rather than constructed; entities within the domain will be detected rather than constituted by our mental states. This is, very roughly, what it means for a realm of facts and things to exist objectively and mind independently.

We started this section by noting that there is a lack of consensus about the right characterization of realism. Consequently, the reader should be unsurprised to discover that many philosophers have qualms about our particular account. Nonetheless, our understanding of the notion has a fine pedigree, and we think every philosopher working in the field would agree that ours is at least one way legitimately to unpack the notion, even if they disagree about whether it is the best way. To be sure, consider what others have said about the issue.

> Realism [is] a claim about what entities exist and a claim about their independent nature. (Devitt [1984] 1991: 14)

> To assert that something is somehow mind-independent is to move in the realist direction; to deny it is to move in the opposite direction ... Many philosophical questions have the following general form: Is such-and-such mind-independent in so-and-so way? Given specifications of such-and-such and so-and-so, one may call someone who answers "Yes" a realist.
> (Williamson 1995: 746)

> There are two general aspects to realism, illustrated by looking at realism about the everyday world of macroscopic objects

and properties. First, there is a claim about *existence*. Tables, rocks, the moon, and so on, all exist, as do the following facts: the table's being square, the rock's being made of granite, and the moon's being spherical and yellow. The second aspect of realism about the everyday world of macroscopic objects and their properties concerns *independence*. The fact that the moon exists and is spherical is independent of anything anyone happens to say or think about the matter. (Miller 2002: 1)

So our construal of realism represents one well-established tradition. But our characterization was chosen not only because of its lineage, but also because we believe it is the most useful way to represent realism and anti-realism. It unifies realist debates across different domains, and allows us to represent clearly contemporary positions commonly held to be opposed to realism. To illustrate, consider Figure 1.1, showing the various salient positions, each of which will be explained in the chapters to come.

Realism is the shaded region in the first quadrant, the upper-right-hand region bounded by the existence and independence axes. Anti-realist positions – positions opposed to realism – include error theory, fictionalism, instrumentalism, non-factualism, idealism, verificationism, social constructivism and response-dependent theories. Each anti-realist position is located in either the second or fourth quadrants. As Figure 1.1 makes clear, idealism, verificationism, social constructivism and response-dependence on the one

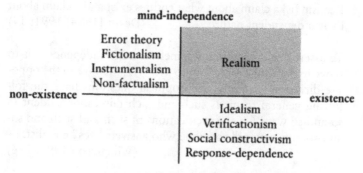

Figure 1.1

hand, and the other forms of anti-realism on the other, have less in common with one another than they do with the realist theories they oppose. According to idealism, verificationism, social constructivists and response-dependence theorists, there are positive facts about the relevant domain; individuals of the relevant kind exist, but they are not objective – they depend on us. According to other forms of anti-realism, however, there are no individuals or facts of the relevant kind, and their non-existence does not depend on us; they would still fail to exist even if there were no minds at all. Finally, it is important to note that there is no territory to be staked out in the third quadrant. Why? The existence thesis and the mind-independence thesis are not independent of one another. In order for an individual or fact to be dependent on our minds, it must exist; *mind-dependence* therefore guarantees *existence*.

Of course, this characterization of realism and its alternatives is more than just a little metaphorical. We shall attempt to make precise our understanding of the two theses that constitute realism – and evaluate them – in Part I. Before we do that, however, it is important to contrast our characterization of realism with some alternatives.

1.2 Supplementing and modifying the canonical characterization

Some philosophers will take issue with our account of realism (and, conversely, anti-realism) on the grounds that it is either incomplete or mischaracterized. Realism, as they conceive of it, is not just a claim about the existence and independence of a certain sort of fact or entity. The account, it is maintained, must at best be expanded and supplemented to include further theses, or at worst be completely recast.

Sometimes it is said that realism is partly an issue about our potential for knowledge. This epistemic constraint on our account of realism might be spelt out in a number of different, non-equivalent, ways. For example, a number of philosophers suggest that the following thesis should be a component of any satisfactory elucidation of realism.

- *The confidence thesis.* Although it may in some circumstances be difficult, we are always capable of coming to know about the existence and nature of the domain we are realists about. That domain is epistemically accessible to us (cf. Wright 1992: 2; Haldane & Wright 1993: 4).

This thesis sets the realist in direct opposition to the sceptic. Realism, on this conception, is the optimistic alternative to a sceptical position. More commonly, though, realism is given a pessimistic epistemic gloss. Jack Smart, David Papineau, Philip Pettit and Amie Thomasson (among others) thus partially characterize realism by way of the following thesis.

- *The insecurity thesis.* It is possible to be in ignorance or error about the domain we are realists about. In order to avoid such mistakes, one must make appropriate contact with the domain in question, and there is no guarantee that anyone will succeed in doing that.

The confidence and insecurity theses are not, despite initial appearances, contrary to one another (indeed, many philosophers embrace them both), for while the insecurity thesis may provide succour to the sceptic, it does not automatically pave the way to scepticism. It cannot do so without also denying the confidence thesis.

Nothing in our characterization of realism is inconsistent with these claims. We believe each thesis is plausible in its own right. And often anti-realist arguments will assume that the realist is committed to one or other of the two claims. Nonetheless, philosophers inclined to supplement the account with either of these theses will find the map of the terrain provided in this book frustratingly incomplete. Some explanation for this lacuna is therefore necessary.

While introducing an epistemic component to an account of realism is not uncommon, it is still controversial (cf. Lewis 1984; Devitt 1991). Reasons to avoid including such an element in our characterization of realism are not hard to find. If we could know incorrigibly and infallibly of our own existence, as Descartes supposed we could, would this undermine our very reality? That sounds silly, but the insecurity thesis seems to entail as much. If there were objects existing outside the light cone – objects that cannot be observed, and hence cannot be known about – would this undermine their reality? Again, that sounds silly, but the confidence thesis seems to entail as much. Another reason for the controversy is that these epistemic theses do not fit well with the independence thesis. For the confidence and insecurity theses make claims not just about an independent reality, but also about our minds. The worse our mental capacities become – the closer our minds approximate that of a scallop – the less plausible the confidence thesis becomes. And the better our mental capacities become – the closer our minds approximate that of an omniscient being – the less plausible the insecurity thesis becomes. For this reason, we thought it wise to dodge trouble by not including these tenets in the canonical account of the realist–anti-realist divide. For those readers who seek more, we hope that this partial map still proves useful.

Another common amendment to the canonical characterization is to scrap completely the existence and independence theses in favour of a semantic thesis (or cluster of theses). Such a move became popular in the twentieth century, when analytic philosophy took a linguistic turn. This was not so much because it was thought that the two canonical theses were incorrect, but rather because it was felt that providing an emphasis on truth (and meaning) would be a more illuminating way of understanding the dispute between realists and anti-realists.

Philosophers such as Michael Dummett who attempt such a re-characterization of the traditional divide, suggest that realists about a domain will claim that distinctive statements about that domain are either true or false, independent of our means for coming to know which. This way of marking the boundaries of any realist–anti-realist dispute suggests that realists and anti-realists have different conceptions of *truth* itself. Realists, for example, tend to embrace a correspondence theory of truth, according to which a proposition is true if and only if it corresponds to the facts. Anti-realists, on the other hand, are thought to hold a contrary theory: perhaps a theory that equates truth with warranted assertability, practical utility or something else altogether.

This contemporary reconstruction of the debate is very interesting indeed, and we take some time to consider its merits in Chapters 4–6. Whatever its merits, though, we resist giving any sort of semantic spin on our official account of realism and anti-realism for two reasons. First, to do so would be to prejudice the issue. The semantic gloss is at least as controversial as the epistemic glosses considered earlier. While contemporary philosophers such as Thomas Kuhn, Hilary Putnam, Dummett and Crispin Wright all give an account with a semantic spin, other equally important figures working in the area, such as David Lewis, Michael Devitt and Paul Horwich, vigorously deny any connection between the problem of realism and the problems of truth and meaning. Secondly, we think the questions "How should a theory of truth affect one's stand on the problem of realism?" and "How should one's stance on the realism issue affect ones accepted theory of truth?" are very interesting questions indeed. Answers to these question are not, and should not, be trivial. But they would be – or at least would be more likely to be – if we insisted on *defining* realism in terms of a theory of truth.[1]

1.3 Looking ahead

This book is split into two parts. Part I is an examination of the realist and anti-realist debate abstracted away from any particular application of it. In Chapters 2 and 3 we explain in more detail *local* realism and anti-realism and look at the motivations that might support one position over the other with regard to a particular subject matter. In Chapter 2 we look specifically at the existence thesis and in Chapter 3 we consider the independence thesis, explaining, motivating and challenging each thesis in detail. In Chapters 4, 5 and 6 we examine particular types of global anti-realism: idealism, Kantianism and verificationism. We will see that each of these is motivated by intricate combinations of semantic, epistemological and metaphysical reasons.

In Part II we look at how the ideas outlined in Part I can and have been applied to different subject matters. This has proved a very difficult undertaking, because for almost every sub-discipline within philosophy there is a corresponding realist–anti-realist debate about the distinctive posits of that sub-discipline. We could not hope to do justice to them all, so we have picked what we take to be a representative sample. In particular, we examine the respective cases for realism and anti-realism about colours, morality, science, mathematics, modality and fiction. We devote a chapter to each topic. We could have written a lot more on each sub-field, but we hope to have said enough to illustrate a number of important points.

The first point is that the realism and anti-realism debates within various different domains are much more unified than we are often led to believe. Although the details vary from subject matter to subject matter, local realist arguments are invariably indispensability arguments; and local anti-realist arguments either tend to rely on appeals to Ockham's razor or take the form of what we call an "attitude problem" (cf. §2.2). Noticing this much is informative, for we can get a better appreciation of the issues in one domain by seeing how the same issues arise in other domains.

The second point is that a comparison of the realism debates in different areas can give us an appreciation of the need for a kind of consistency in our views that is often lacking. Our thinking about the metaphysical issues in various different domains tends to be modularized. Why is it that we so often take indispensability arguments for mathematical entities so seriously and yet are incredulous when faced with parallel arguments for *possibilia*? Why is it that so many of us are prepared to take apparent quantification over other times at face value, but insist on paraphrasing away any apparent quantification over other possibilities? One hope we have is that Part II will serve as an aid for avoiding this kind of double-think, or at least force us to think about, justify and explain away any seeming incoherence in our overall metaphysical picture.

Thirdly, our attitudes in one domain should inform our attitudes in others, and it is hoped that Part II will help make these connections perspicuous. For example, David Hume's discussion of the "tertiary" qualities can only be appreciated when contrasted with the secondary qualities. Hume here points to analogies between moral and evaluative concepts on the one hand, and colour concepts and their cognates on the other. An appreciation of the analogy should show us how tenuous it would be to embrace a realist position about moral properties while embracing an anti-realist position about colours. Here is another example. *Fictionalism* about a given area of discourse is often thought to be a variety of anti-realism. Very roughly, the fictionalist asserts (i) that the distinctive posits of the relevant discourse are not real, and (ii) that they are instead merely fictional entities. Such a position is unstable if we accept a commonly held position about fictional objects. Perhaps most philosophers writing on fictional objects today are *realists* about such things. But if we accept the arguments in favour of realism about fictional objects, we must reject at least one of the fictionalist's two characteristic theses.

Finally, consideration of how the realist debates play out in different domains helps us see not only connections and points of similarity between the debates, but also important points of difference. For example, it is interesting to note that (as far as we know) no one has defended a fictionalist, instrumentalist, or non-factualist view of secondary quality concepts; no one has seriously defended a constructivist theory of modality; no one has defended a response-dependent account of fictional characters. Sometimes there are good reasons why this is the case, but sometimes this gap is inexplicable. It would be nice if by making these differences salient we encourage others to defend the relevant position in print.

Local realism and anti-realism: 2 the existence axis

Very few of us are global anti-realists. Most of us believe that there are concrete particulars that exist independently of our minds and our conceptual schemes. But very few of us are global realists either. Whether or not some entities – entities such as colours, quarks, moral qualities, numbers, possible worlds, and fictional characters – are real is a controversial matter. To borrow a slogan from a famous philosopher,[1] when it comes to questions about whether such entities are real, most of us are pickers and choosers, some-but-only someists – that is, most of us are local realists about some entities, but local anti-realists about others.

In Chapters 2 and 3 we shall examine the various considerations that might motivate one to be a realist or anti-realist about a particular domain, without requiring that one be a realist or anti-realist globally. Realists about a realm of Fs will motivate their position first by demonstrating that Fs exist, and will only then proceed to argue that Fs are not merely objects of our own manufacture. Let us therefore call someone who argues that Fs exist a "minimal realist" about Fs. And let us call someone who also argues that such entities exist independently of us a "robust realist" about Fs. In this chapter we examine the existence axis, and therefore aim to evaluate minimal realism and the anti-realist alternatives to it. Consequently, whenever we talk simply of realism or anti-realism in *this* chapter, we shall be talking about minimal realism and anti-minimal realism. Dropping the qualifier is intended as a terminological convenience for both authors and readers.

2.1 Motivating realism

It is sometimes suggested that realism is the default position. Common sense tells us that colours and odours, tables and chairs, atoms and electrons, good things and bad things all exist. The onus of proof, therefore, always rests with the anti-realist to demonstrate that such things do not exist, or so it has sometimes been maintained. Such presumptions, though, are dangerous, for common sense does *not* side unequivocally with the realist about everything. Ordinary folk, like philosophers, are also pickers and choosers. They are realists about some things, and anti-realists about others. For example, most people tend to be unbelievers in square circles, phlogiston, Greek gods and fictional characters. Realism about a controversial domain, therefore, must be motivated. Realists and anti-realists alike must provide some argument for their respective positions.

Realist arguments for the existence of the domain of entities are often abductive arguments. An abductive argument is an argument of the following form:

(P1) The best available explanation of certain phenomena is theory T.
(P2) We should accept the best available explanation of the observed phenomena.
(C) Therefore, we should accept theory T.

The second premise is what is known as an "abductive premise". It merely states the method of abduction, which is to accept the best available explanation. Sometimes, for this reason, abduction is called "inference to the best explanation". The best explanation is one that has the best combination of "theoretical virtues". The theoretical virtues include (but are not exhausted by) simplicity, strength (i.e. being able to explain more data), elegance and ease of use.[2]

So far, we have an argument for the belief in a particular theory, T. What we need is to link this belief with the belief in the existence of a particular sort of entity. This link is provided by the doctrine of ontological commitment. "Ontological commitment" is a term of art. The phrase was coined by W. V. Quine, who tells us that, strictly speaking, it is *persons* who make ontological commitments. According to Quine, we can determine the ontological commitments of an individual by ascertaining which theories she accepts. Once we have done that, we must regiment those theories by translating them (and all of the statements that follow logically from them) into the language of first-order logic (the predicate logic that is usually taught to undergraduates in philosophy),[3] while giving each of the symbols of this artificial language their standard interpretation. Then we must examine the sentences of the formal language and isolate those beginning with an existential quantifier.[4] These sentences express the ontological commitments of the individual and, in a derivative sense, of the theories she accepts.[5] Having spelt out the doctrine of ontological commitment, we are now in a position to complete the realist's argument thus:

The Quinean argument for minimal realism
(P1) We should believe that Fs exist if our accepted theories are ontologically committed to Fs.
(P2) The theories we accept are ontologically committed to Fs.
(C) Therefore, we should believe that Fs exist.

But there is a wrinkle. On many occasions we say things – and embrace theories that say things – that have unwanted or unintended ontological commitments. What should someone who finds herself in such a predicament do? Quine famously makes three suggestions:

(i) Eliminate those aspects of our accepted theories that entail the existence of such objects. And, most importantly, demonstrate that such talk is superfluous to our theoretical needs. So, for example, if we can fully explain consciousness, apparent miracles, mystical experiences and so forth in terms of physical phenomena, we can and should eliminate all talk of spirits and souls.

(ii) Alternatively, one may insist on retaining those problematic aspects of our accepted theories, but suggest that such statements should not be taken at face value. So, for example, on the basis of accepted science, we may continue to say things such as "There is nothing in a void", despite disavowing the existence of a genuinely spooky kind of entity (namely, those things with the property of being nothing). Quine, however, insists that in such cases we show how it is possible, at least in principle, to paraphrase away sentences that lead to such unsavoury ontological commitments. That is easy to do in this instance. When we say "There is nothing in a void", what we really mean is "It is not the case that there is something in a void".

(iii) Finally, if every attempt to dispense with such entities fails, one should capitulate, and give up all resistance to such commitments. Any rational person who straightforwardly accepts a theory should also accept the whole theory. And that means accepting the entailments of the theory, *including the existential entailments*. So, for example, if we accept current physical theory, and such theories are ineluctably committed to entities such as quarks and electrons, one should embrace these commitments, no matter how bizarre such entities might seem to us now.

Now it is important to note that this list does not exhaust the possible escape routes available to those caught in the unfortunate predicament Quine envisages. But all alternatives involve, in one way or another, embracing a "deviant" or "non-classical" logic. Some contemporary apostles of Alexius Meinong (see Chapter 12), for example, suggest that we should recognize a new quantifier not acknowledged by most logicians. In addition to standard existential quantification, there is also "particular" quantification. Existential quantification is ontologically loaded, but particular quantification is neutral. Everything that exists also has being in the particular sense, but there are some things that have being but do not exist. Which things? Perhaps all and only those we are uncomfortable committing ourselves to (cf. Routley 1980; Lewis 1990).

Alternatively one could admit just one basic quantifier, but reject the classical inferences that lead to the uncomfortable commitments. Puff is a magic dragon, but do not conclude from this that there are any dragons. To draw such a conclusion we need an additional premise, often left implicit, to the effect that Puff exists. Some of those who dodge Quine's predicament in this way embrace what is now called a "free logic" (cf. Lambert 2002). Or one could allow only one basic quantifier, embrace the claim that Puff is a dragon, endorse any inference from this premise to the conclusion that dragons exist, but give the existential quantifier a substitutional rather than an objectual gloss. According to this proposal, "$\exists x$" and its natural language analogue are to be understood to mean not "There is an object such that ..." but rather "There is a true substitution instance of ...". A substitution instance is just a sentence. Thus, we can allow "∃x (x is a magic dragon)" but this will just be because we allow "Puff is a magic dragon". An adherent of such a proposal can therefore deny that existential generalizations carry with them any serious ontological commitment (cf. Marcus 1962; Kripke 1976; Haack 1978).[6] But the philosophical orthodoxy disapproves of avoiding commitment by way of such strange contortions, and as a consequence any anti-realism exploiting one of these latter strategies is unlikely to gain widespread acceptance. We shall therefore investigate such strategies no further.

So the realist's success will depend on how compelling her argument is to those not already strongly inclined towards a realism about Fs. She will therefore have to justify (P2). But to do that, she will have to demonstrate that those caught in Quine's predicament are unable to dodge such commitments by embracing option (i) or (ii). This will require her to show that Fs are indispensable to our accepted theories.

2.2 Motivating anti-realism

Anti-realism about Fs is the view that Fs do not exist. The anti-realist must therefore undermine one of the premises of the realist's argument. She must either show that our accepted theories are not ontologically committed to Fs – that they are dispensable entities – or alternatively show that even if our accepted theories are committed to Fs, this is no reason to believe that Fs exist. But this is merely the first step in motivating anti-realism, for merely demonstrating that there is a fallacy in one argument to a certain conclusion does not establish that the conclusion is false. Anti-realism, just like realism, therefore needs to be independently motivated.

Anti-realists often seem to have in mind something like the following argument in support of their position. If Fs exist, they must be either *sui generis* properties or reducible to some other kind of property. These are, after all, the only alternatives. But either way, the realist is in trouble. She faces a dilemma. If she chooses to impale herself on the first horn, by suggesting that Fs are *sui generis* properties, she will violate the principle of parsimony (better known as Ockham's razor). If, on the other hand, she chooses to impale herself on the second horn, she will face an "attitude problem". Either way, it is maintained, realism stands refuted. The anti-realist's dilemma for the realist is represented in Figure 2.1. Now it is important to realize that this dilemma for the realist is not universally applicable. Despite appearances to the contrary, this general schema does not form the basis for an argument in support of global anti-realism. There must be something special about the purported domain of *F*s that gives rise to the problem. In order to see exactly why, let us deal with each horn of the dilemma in turn.

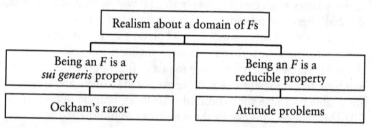

Figure 2.1

2.2.1 Ockham's razor

Ockham's razor,[7] or the principle of parsimony, is not a controversial thesis. Most philosophers and scientists accept some version or other of the razor. There is, however, much disagreement about exactly what the principle is and what it counsels us to do. For those who like slogans, the thesis is often expressed somewhat loosely as follows: entities should not be multiplied beyond necessity. But do not misunderstand this. The razor is not a practical injunction against exerting oneself on the production line, nor is it a moral prohibition in contrast to the biblical prescription to "be fruitful and multiply". The razor is instead a principle guiding our choices between competing theories. The razor tells us that if one theory is more parsimonious than any other, then, *ceterus paribus*, it is a better theory than the others and more likely to be true.

Ockham's razor thus seems to favour anti-realism over realism, for it challenges the realist's thesis along the existence axis. A realist about *F*s claims that *F*s exist because our accepted theories are ontologically committed to *F*s. The anti-realist challenges this claim by asserting that there is an alternative theory that is not committed to *F*s that is at least as serviceable in all other relevant respects and is committed to nothing not already postulated by the accepted theory. Then, *after making an appeal to Ockham's razor*, she concludes that we should believe that there are no *F*s.

In order for Ockham's razor to perform this bridging function in the anti-realist's argument, however, it must be articulated precisely. This turns out to be a little trickier than one might expect, for the razor is an ambiguous principle. Some versions of the razor pose no threat to a realist position. One disambiguation though – the one all anti-realists either implicitly or explicitly have in mind – presents the realist with a very real challenge. It is the aim of this section to articulate that version of Ockham's principle, distinguish it from some other less-threatening beasts, and then to reconstruct the first part of the anti-realist's argument in light of this discussion.

Philosophers who discuss Ockham's razor typically make a distinction between qualitative and quantitative parsimony. The distinction is famously expressed by Lewis as follows:

> Distinguish two kinds of parsimony ... qualitative and quantitative. A doctrine is qualitatively parsimonious if it keeps down the number of different *kinds* of entity ... A doctrine is quantitatively parsimonious if it keeps down the number of instances of the kinds it posits.   (Lewis 1973: 87)

Thus, a theory that postulates vampires and demons might be thought to be qualitatively less parsimonious than a theory that postulates vampires alone. A theory that postulates 600 billion human beings might be thought to be quantitatively less parsimonious than a theory that postulates a mere 6 billion human beings.

Those who discuss the distinction in any great detail tend to take it for granted that qualitative parsimony is indeed a theoretical virtue, and focus instead on quantitative parsimony. Such philosophers ask such questions as: (i) how should we understand and explicate the quantitative principle; (ii) is it desirable in a philosophical or scientific theory; and (iii) if it is a theoretical virtue, is it a primitive virtue or can it be derived from other more basic virtues (cf. Nolan 1997; Baker 2003)? Such questions, while interesting in their own right, need not concern us here, for it is the qualitative rather than the quantitative version of the razor that is at work in the anti-realist's argument.

To see why, keep in mind that the aim of metaphysics is to carve reality into its basic categories or kinds. (It is then up to the empirical scientist to do the relevant *a posteriori* investigations to determine how many entities of a particular kind there are – or so we think.) Metaphysical debate, therefore, will be about whether or not to include a certain category in our ultimate account of reality or, to put it another way, whether or not there really are any entities of a certain kind. Those who say there are count as realists *about that kind*; those who say there are not count as anti-realists *about that kind*. Clearly, therefore, considerations of qualitative parsimony express a preference for anti-realist theories over realist theories so conceived. The same cannot be said of quantitative parsimony. Anyone who believes in angels is a realist about angels, even though some realists believe in fewer angels than others.

Elliot Sober (1981) highlights a rather different ambiguity in Ockham's slogan "entities should not be multiplied beyond necessity". This principle is often interpreted as the maxim that in contexts where we have no reason for believing something exists, we thereby have a reason for believing that it *does not* exist. There is, however, an alternative weaker interpretation of the razor. According to this weaker principle, if there is no necessity to postulate an entity, we should – if we are rational – *suspend judgement* about its existence. Sober distinguishes between the two versions of the razor as follows:

> The principle of parsimony has typically been described and defended as if it were a deletion rule, counseling agnosticism … But agnostic formulations of the methodological maxim belie the way in which the razor is employed to atheistic effect. The razor [according to this alternative stronger interpretation] counsels removal and replacement. A claim of existence is excised from a theory, only to be replaced with its own negation.
>
> (Sober 1981: 145–6)

Let us therefore call the stronger version of the principle the "replacement rule", and the weaker version the "deletion rule". Quite clearly, support for the deletion rule is easier to find than support for the replacement rule, for the probability of any conjunction is never higher than the probability of either of the conjuncts. But unfortunately, while both versions of the razor counsel a rejection of realism, only the replacement rule supports an anti-realist position. Only the replacement rule can provide the logical bridge from premise to conclusion in the anti-realist's argument. When we use the term "Ockham's razor" (or "the principle of parsimony") from now on, then, it should be understood both as a principle of qualitative parsimony and as a replacement rule. The principle we have in mind might therefore be given something like the following gloss: if kind F is superfluous to our explanatory needs, then Fs do not exist or, at least, we should believe they do not rather than simply suspending judgement on the issue.

Because the razor plays such a crucial role in the anti-realist's argument, it would behove the anti-realist to provide some sort of meta-justification for accepting it. After all, the realist is not required to accept Ockham's principle and, even if she does, she is unlikely to accept the formulation of the principle outlined here without some compelling reason. What kinds of justifications are available to the anti-realist?

Perhaps the anti-realist can simply appeal to intuition and common sense here. We have no evidence to confirm or disconfirm the hypothesis that there are tiny invisible elves pushing every electron in every atom, ensuring (and perhaps overdetermining) that the electrons orbit the nucleus of the atom. As a consequence, we firmly believe that the tiny invisible elves do not exist. And we are justified in doing so, the anti-realist will maintain, because something like the razor is correct. Others have proffered more philosophical considerations in support of the principle of parsimony. Some justify it on aesthetic grounds, others on pragmatic grounds, and others argue that it can be grounded in the more general virtue of simplicity. To our minds, though, the best independent justification of the razor is to be found elsewhere.

Sober (1981) suggests that Ockham's razor must be embraced if inductive generalizations are sound.[8] Most philosophers accept that the following non-deductive inference is good (although they have some difficulty explaining why):

An inductive generalization
(P1) Every emerald observed thus far has been green.
(C) Therefore, every emerald is green.

Now, of course, such inferences must be constrained in certain ways if they are to count as inductively strong; for example, the sample size must be large enough, the sample must be representative, the predicates must be projectable and so on. But so long as the premises are accepted and these constraints are met, we should give credence to the conclusion.

One such constraint is particularly relevant in the present context: in order for an inductive generalization to be good, *the premises must represent all of the available relevant evidence*. Call this the "total relevant evidence constraint", or TRE for short. Notice that if TRE is not met, we cannot be sure that the hypothesis is probable given the data. To illustrate, imagine that you have recently read the latest issue of the journal *Geology*, a special issue devoted to the orange emerald. In it, you find numerous papers describing the various geological properties of this rare kind of emerald. Imagine further that while you find many of the papers speculative and inconclusive, you are in no doubt about the existence of such emeralds, even though you have never seen one. Clearly, such a view is justified. Testimony from experts in the field of geology, after all, carries a lot of weight. This thought experiment, therefore, illustrates one way in which inductive generalizations can go wrong. In order to make good inferences from a piece of evidence, we must be confident that TRE is true.

Sober suggests that inductive generalizations are of a kind with parsimony arguments. To illustrate, consider the following trivial variant of the above inductive argument:

A transformation of an inductive generalization
(P1*) Nothing observed thus far is a non-green emerald.
(C*) Therefore, nothing is a non-green emerald.

Here, the premises and conclusion of the original argument have been replaced by logical equivalents. Moreover, the observational evidence here, as before, must represent all of the available relevant evidence. Now notice that the conjunction of (P1*) and TRE entails that we have no reason at all for believing that there are non-green emeralds, and from this we are invited to conclude that non-green emeralds do not exist. Why should we do that? Presumably only because we believe the further conditional premise: if we have no reason for believing in non-green emeralds, then such emeralds do not exist. But this premise looks like a simple variation of the principle of parsimony. So, if inductive generalizations are good inferences, a lack of evidence in support of the existence of some kind counts as evidence for its non-existence. Induction itself, it seems, presupposes the razor.

Having explained and justified the principle of parsimony in this way, stating the first part of the anti-realist's argument is a fairly straightforward affair. An idealized version of the argument runs basically as follows.

The argument from parsimony
(P1) *F*s are superfluous to our explanatory needs.
(P2) *Ockham's razor.* If *F*s are superfluous to our explanatory needs, then *F*s do not exist.
(C) Therefore, *F*s do not exist.

2.2.2 Reductionism and attitude problems

At this point it will be instructive to consider a spurious objection to the anti-realist argument outlined above. The objection is levelled against the second premise; it is an objection to the view that parsimony, *so conceived*, is really something we desire in our theorizing. Why? The thought is that such a principle will some-times counsel us to reject one theory in favour of another when the two are merely notational variants of one another. To illustrate the worry, suppose Ed and Stu draw up an inventory of the various kinds of things they each believe exist. At the end of the process, Stu's list is longer than Ed's. On Ed's list there are, *inter alia*, pep-pers, zucchinis, eggplants and cantaloupes. All of the items on Ed's list appear on Stu's, but in addition to these, Stu has included four more: capsicums, courgettes, aubergines and rock melons. Is Ed's account of reality more likely to be true than Stu's? The principle of parsimony *seems* to imply as much. (After all, Stu postulates four kinds of things Ed does not, and in every other respect, the two lists are the same.) But intuitively this seems just plain wrong. Perhaps Ed's list is to be preferred because it fits more snugly into our pockets. But it could hardly be a better account of the kinds of things there are. For according to Stu, capsicums and peppers are the same kind of thing, courgettes are identical to zucchinis and so on. Ed has saved time and paper when writing his list, but his view of the world is not really more economical.

What this objection draws our attention to is that reduction and elimination have a common goal: theoretical economy of a certain kind. The difference between the two approaches is that the reductionist about *F*s keeps this ontology intact; she continues to maintain that *F*s exist, but identifies the *F*s with something else. The eliminativist, on the other hand, eliminates *F*s from her ontology altogether. The problem with the principle of parsimony, at least as it is articulated above, is that it seems to favour eliminativist over reductionist approaches. But no such preference is justified. Reducing numbers to sets, possibilities to actualities, or minds to bodies are ways of economizing on a par with eliminating numbers, possibilities and minds altogether.

We agree with the intuition that elimination is not in any sense better than reduction. But we disagree that this poses any serious challenge to those who accept the principle of parsimony. At worst, a small amendment is called for. Perhaps when constructing our theories of the world, we should not aim to keep the number of superfluous kinds to a minimum; we should instead keep the number of superfluous *and irreducibly distinct* kinds of things to a minimum. Some have argued that it is this latter constraint on our theory selection that properly deserves the name Ockham's razor (cf. Thomasson 1999: ch. 9). Alternatively, one might suggest – plausibly, we think – that no amendment is called for at all, because if a reduction is successful the reduced property cannot be *superfluous* unless its reductive base is superfluous. If *G*s are essential to our explanation, and *F*s are reduced to *G*s, then the *F*s are *just as* essential to our explanation: they play exactly the same explanatory role. We should therefore, according to the razor, eliminate both or neither. But under no circumstances should we eliminate one and not the other (cf. Barnes 2000).

Once such a concession has been made, however, the anti-realist faces a rather different problem. The parsimony argument for anti-realism considered in the previous section will only have force against the non-reductive realist. The anti-realist therefore needs a *further* argument against realists about *F*s who maintain that *F*s are not *sui generis* properties, but reducible to something else.

One way to resolve the difficulty would be to amend the definition of "realism" to match our potential amendment to the razor. Just as the principle of parsimony counsels us to economize on irreducibly distinct kinds of things, so too realism about a subject matter might be taken *inter alia* to be the view that the kinds of "entities posited are distinctive in the sense that they are not *a priori* identifiable with, or otherwise replaceable by, entities independently posited" (Pettit 1991: 589). It would thus be maintained that locating the realist in a quartered region between the existence axis and the mind-independence axis gives, at best, an incomplete characterization of realism. But, as we have seen in Chapter 1, such a stipulation is at odds with most current conceptions of the term "realism". Theories that advertise themselves as realist – modal realism, moral realism, fictional realism and mathematical realism – are often varieties of reductionism.

A very closely related solution to the problem denies that any amendment to the canonical definition of realism is necessary, but maintains that "reductive realism" is an oxymoron. Any reduction *covertly* involves a kind of elimination, and thus fails to fall on the right side of the existence axis. So any form of reductionism *cannot* count as a form of realism. Of course, reductionists will often *say* that entities distinctive of the relevant domain exist, and in some sense what they say is true. But such talk is not to be taken at face value, for a reduction counts as a kind of *paraphrase* of a kind with a nominalist construal of mathematics. The only difference is that, in cases of a reduction, the paraphrase is much easier to provide. This disguised elimination is easy enough to see in proposed reductions such as "witches are merely strange women" and "ghosts are simply illusions". According to those who embrace disappearance versions of reductionism, all reductions should be viewed along the same model. All apparent commitment to reduced properties is deceptive; the genuine commitments are uncovered by the reduction (cf. Rorty 1965). Such a solution to the problem at hand is, however, somewhat implausible, for disappearance theories tell us that talk of reduced properties is not to be taken at face value. That seems right in *some* contexts (when, for example, someone says "My ex-wife is a witch"), but surely not in all contexts. When avowed reductionists about *F*s tell us explicitly that *F*s really exist, they are usually asking to be taken literally, and we have a *prima facie* obligation to take them at face value.

A more common strategy among anti-realists is not to rule out reductions across the board, but to attack instead reductions only of the kind under dispute. There is something special, it will be maintained, about the domain in question that makes it impossible to reduce facts about it to facts about some other domain. Arguments of this kind almost invariably involve pointing out that we have conflicting attitudes towards the reduced properties on the one hand, and the proposed reductive base on the other. Consequently, we call this style of objection to reductionist proposals an "attitude problem". Attitude problems are arguments with the following basic structure.

The basic form of an attitude problem
(P1) Subjects have a certain attitude towards the A-facts.
(P2) Subjects do not have that same attitude towards the B-facts.
(C) Therefore, the A-facts are not reducible to the B-facts.

It is perhaps surprising that attitude problems have been thought to pose such a threat to reductionists, for it is well known that arguments of this kind are *not* deductively valid. This is because attitude contexts are opaque contexts. It is not only possible but relatively common to have two different attitudes to the very same set of facts presented under different guises or different descriptions. Ed believes that Gerald Ford was the thirty-eighth president of the United States; Ed does *not* believe that Leslie King was the thirty-eighth president of the United States. And this is all perfectly consistent with the fact that Gerald Ford really is Leslie King.

Objections of this kind, then, are never decisive against the reductionist. But such arguments *can be* powerful inductive considerations against reductionism and, with supplementary premises, can support anti-realism. For arguments like this fail to provide support for their conclusions only when subjects fail to recognize something important about the two sets of facts. In Ed's case, the inference is not good because Ed does not know enough about Ford; he has not yet figured out that Ford is King. But once he does figure it out, not only will his beliefs about Ford and King harmonize, but so too will his other attitudes; after learning that Ford and King are identical, there will be no asymmetry in Ed's desires, admiration, concern and so on for Ford on the one hand, and his desires, admiration, concern and so on for King on the other. Such considerations suggest that all attitude problems contain an implicit premise: *if the A-facts were reducible to the B-facts, subjects would know as much*. The cogency of the argument will thus depend (in part) on the plausibility of this premise.

The plausibility of this premise in the context of the Ford–King argument is very low indeed. But in other contexts, this kind of premise can appear much more likely. As a consequence, attitude problems find ubiquitous expression in the literature.

To illustrate, consider one of the most famous attitude problems: an argument first presented by Frank Jackson against physicalism. Physicalism is the view that all facts, including mental facts, can be reduced to physical facts. According to Jackson, any physicalist theory about the mind is bound to be incomplete, for it will not be able to account for facts about *qualia*, that is, it will not be able to fully explain *what it is like* to have a certain experience. And so, according to Jackson, mental states are not reducible to physical states.

In order to motivate his distinctive attitude problem – a problem he calls "the knowledge argument" – Jackson outlines the following thought experiment:

> Mary is a brilliant scientist who is, for whatever reason, forced to investigate the world from a black and white room via a black and white television monitor. She specializes in the neurophysiology of vision and acquires, let us suppose, all the physical information there is to obtain about what goes on when we see ripe tomatoes, or the sky, and use terms like "red," "blue," and so on. She discovers, for example, just which wavelength combinations from the sky stimulate the retina, and exactly how this produces via the central nervous system the contraction of the vocal chords and expulsion of air from the lungs that result in the uttering of the sentence "The sky is blue".   (Jackson 1982: 128)

Jackson thinks it is obvious that Mary does not know *everything* there is to know about seeing colours, despite knowing everything *physical* there is to know about such things, for after Mary is freed from the black and white room, and sees a ripe tomato for the first time, she learns something completely new: namely, what it is like to see something red. We might express Jackson's problem for the physicalist in standard argument form as follows:

The knowledge argument
(P1) Before her release, Mary knows everything *physical* there is to know about colour experience.

(P2) Before her release, Mary does *not* know everything there is to know about colour experience.

(C) Therefore, facts about colour experience cannot be reduced to the physical facts (and so physicalism is false).

The knowledge argument is interesting, in part because it poses a serious challenge to a philosophical dogma of the twentieth century. As a consequence, it has spawned a vast literature of replies and counter-responses. But an evaluation of the argument is not our concern here. Instead we want to point to certain features of the argument that make it paradigmatic of attitude problems, and then say something about the role such arguments play in anti-realist attacks on realism.

Notice first that the two premises of the argument point to an asymmetry in the attitudes of a subject towards two related domains. In this case the subject is Mary, and the attitude under consideration is (propositional) knowledge. Notice secondly that Jackson gives us a *special reason* for thinking that mental facts cannot be reduced to physical facts. There is no problem, as far as Jackson is concerned, for theories that reduce the chemical facts, the geological facts or the botanical facts to the physical facts. It is *only* psychological facts that elude physicalist reductions. Notice finally that Jackson stipulates that Mary acquires "all the physical information there is to obtain" about colour experience. And so, if the psychological facts really were reducible to the physical facts, Mary would know it. These three features are essential to any successful attitude problem.

It is important to keep in mind that arguments of this kind do not provide *direct* support for an anti-realist conclusion. Jackson himself is a *realist* about the mental in general, and *qualia* in particular. Instead, attitude problems play a role in an extended argument against the realist. The anti-realist must show (i) that *qualia* cannot be reduced to some other property already included in her ontology – this is where attitude problems come into play – and (ii) that *qualia*, taken as *sui generis* properties, play no explanatory role at all. *Qualia* would thus be dispensable, so, after wielding Ockham's razor, the anti-realist will be justified in eliminating them altogether. (A realist such as Jackson will, of course, deny that *qualia* are superfluous in this way, but Jackson himself has trouble explaining why, given that he believes *qualia* are epiphenomenal states – states that have no causal consequences.)

Any anti-realist who employs an attitude problem in her extended argument against the realist, however, must address one rather delicate issue: how is it that subjects can have an attitude towards a set of controversial "facts" if there are no such facts at all. This question is particularly pressing for anyone who uses Jackson's knowledge argument to partially justify an anti-realist position about *qualia*. For if there are no *qualia* at all, what could possibly justify acceptance of (P2) of this argument? A plausible answer to this question is unlikely to be forthcoming in this case, but it can be in others. Just how good this answer is will depend on the attitude problem under consideration and, perhaps more importantly, on the variety of anti-realism being advanced.

2.3 Alternatives to realism

Anti-realism is not simply a denial of realism, for one can attack the realist from many different angles. One way to appreciate the prospects of anti-realism, then, is by way of a taxonomy. It is to this task we now turn.

2.3.1 Error theory

Recall that the realist about a disputed domain of Fs maintains that there are Fs and, consequently, there are non-trivial facts about the domain of Fs. Furthermore, the realist claims that we have at least some knowledge of the nature of Fs. Our beliefs about this domain are not infallible – we can make mistakes – but they are, for the most part, reliable.

An error theorist, by contrast, will claim that there are no Fs. Furthermore, error theorists tell us that most of us are guilty of making systematic mistakes about this alleged domain. For while it is commonly believed that Fs exist, there are good reasons for denying that they do. Justifying this distinctive thesis may involve reporting an empirical discovery (as one might after engaging in a thorough search for the Loch Ness Monster), deriving an inconsistency in the realist's view (as Zeno attempted to do against those who thought there were moving objects), or simply uncovering something deeply mysterious about the domain in question (as Gilbert Ryle attempted to do against those who thought there were inner experiences).

Error theory is perhaps the most straightforward variety of anti-realism. Error theorists take claims about Fs at face value. According to the error theorist, statements of the form "There are Fs" are truth-apt: that is, the statements have a truth-value. Moreover, they are commonly used to make assertions and express beliefs. Nonetheless, such statements, assertions and beliefs are straightforwardly false. Error theorists therefore deny (P1) of the Quinean argument for minimal realism, for while many of us accept such theories – and indeed believe them – such beliefs are unjustified. There is a gap, the error theorist tells us, between what we actually believe and what we should believe.

2.3.2 Prefix fictionalism

Prefix fictionalism is one of two related anti-realist positions that go by the name "fictionalism". It is a general strategy for paraphrasing away aspects of our accepted theories that have unwanted ontological commitments. Like the realist, the prefix fictionalist will make claims apparently about a domain of Fs. Such claims, it will be maintained, are not only truth-apt, but are also true. Consequently, they will be believed, asserted and assented to. Unlike the realist, though, the prefix fictionalist will not take such claims at face value. Instead, they should be understood as elliptical for longer statements about the content of a theory. In other words, according to this variety of fictionalism, every claim apparently committing the speaker to a domain of Fs contains an *implicit prefix*: "according to such-and-such theory". Sincere utterances of such statements do not (usually) express a subject's beliefs about a domain of Fs; but they do express a subject's beliefs about the content of a theory purportedly about Fs. A prefix fictionalist is thus committed to the view that such a theory is a fiction, and therefore the entities postulated by the fiction are only fictitious entities. More precisely, when we make sincere assertoric utterances of the form "$\exists x F x$" what we really mean is something of the form, "*According to the realist's fiction, $\exists x F x$*". And because the latter does not entail the former, ontological commitment to Fs is dodged.

Prefix fictionalists claim not only that the realist's theory is a fiction, but that it is a *useful* fiction. The prefix fictionalist can see that realism has a certain utility, but her hope is to inherit many, if not all, of the benefits of realist talk without the ontology associated with such talk. Whether or not the prefix fictionalist succeeds in this goal will depend on two things: how she fleshes out the details of her theory, and what purpose she puts the theory to. As we shall see, prefix fictionalist theories can vary significantly in both ways.

The prefix fictionalist will, of course, reject the conclusion of the Quinean argument. But which premise of the argument will she challenge? She will challenge (P2). The theories she accepts are *not* ontologically committed to Fs. Why? Because any *apparent* commitments of this kind can be systematically paraphrased away – by adding a prefix – so as to avoid the unsavoury commitments.

2.3.3 Instrumentalism/non-cognitive fictionalism

Instumentalists, like realists, claim that sincere utterances about a controversial category will be either true or false: they are truth-apt. Unlike the realist, though, the instrumentalist claims that such utterances are straightforwardly false. But, it is maintained, this is not a defect, because the aim of discourse about this domain is not truth but something else. So, for example, Bas van Fraassen (1980) argues that the aim of science is simply empirical adequacy (cf. Chapter 9); Hartry Field (1980) contends that mathematics is valuable because it is conservative (cf. Chapter 10). Whatever basic theoretical virtues a hypothesis has, however, an instrumentalist maintains they can be had without the theory being true, and without the posits of the hypothesis existing.

Instrumentalism is often called "fictionalism", but it is important to recognize the differences between instrumentalism and the conception of fictionalism articulated above. Unlike the fictionalist, the instrumentalist tells us that discourse in the relevant area *is* to be taken at face value. There is no ellipsis; paraphrase is unnecessary to uncover the true meaning of what is said. The instrumentalist's distinctive thesis, though, is that there is a difference in kind between *acceptance* of what is said on the one hand, and *belief* in what is said on the other. A theory can be fully acceptable for certain purposes without being true, and without being believed. As a consequence, sincere utterances in the area are not assertoric if assertions are expressions of one's beliefs. Instead, statements about Fs will be used to perform some other kind of speech act: to quasi-assert, where quasi-assertions serve to express propositions that one accepts. Consequently, the instrumentalist, or non-cognitive fictionalist, will deny (P1) of the Quinean argument. (P1) *can* be denied because a conceptual wedge is driven between assertion and quasi-assertion and, more importantly, between belief and acceptance. And because the aim of belief is to get at the truth, while the aim of acceptance is something else altogether, the instrumentalist/non-cognitive fictionalist *must* deny (P1).

But what exactly is involved in accepting a proposition (or set of propositions)? According to Jonathan Cohen:

> to accept that *p* is to have or adopt a policy of deeming, positing, or postulating that *p* – that is, of going along with that proposition (either for the long term or for immediate purposes only) as a premise in some or all contexts for one's own or others' proofs, argumentations, inferences, deliberations, etc.
>
> (Cohen 1989: 368)

Although acceptance of *p* bears some similarity to belief that *p*, it differs from belief in the same way that supposition does. Clearly one can suppose that *p* without believing it; one might even suppose what one strongly disbelieves. But acceptance is not quite the same thing as supposition either. Acceptance of *p* involves a kind of commitment to *p* that is not there when we simply suppose that *p*. How so? Unlike supposition, acceptance involves a belief that what is accepted is useful in some way; that is why we go along with it. Moreover, what a person accepts, unlike what a person supposes, is reflected in her linguistic practices; when one accepts that *p* one is likely to assent to utterances expressing *p*.

2.3.4 Non-factualism

The final anti-realist position we shall consider is a position called "non-factualism". Sometimes this position goes by the name "non-cognitivism" because, according to the non-factualist, sincere utterances of statements apparently about a disputed domain do not express a subject's beliefs about that domain. Nonetheless, "non-cognitivism" is a misleading label, because it does not effectively distinguish this position from that of the non-cognitive fictionalist.

The non-factualist's distinctive claim is that utterances within the disputed area of discourse are not representations of the facts. Against the realist, she suggests that such statements are not truth-apt, and so cannot sensibly be said to be true. (But nor can they be false either.) Unlike the non-cognitive fictionalist, the non-factualist claims that the utterances under consideration should not be taken at face value, but not because they use metaphorical devices or contain hidden prefixes. Instead, it will be claimed that the surface grammatical form of such utterances does not reflect their logical form, for such utterances are grammatically declarative sentences. Declarative sentences can be used to express propositions. And propositions are representations; they are truth-apt and can be believed. All this is denied by the non-factualist. Instead, she claims that sincere utterances of such statements are not assertoric; they are used instead to perform another speech act: perhaps to express one's attitudes of approval or disapproval, to prescribe a course of action, or perhaps to do something else.

Because the non-factualist makes no distinction between acceptance and belief, she has no basis on which to challenge (P1) of the Quinean argument. Instead she takes issue with (P2). Because utterances within the disputed area of discourse are not representational, they cannot properly be said to be a part of any theory, let alone our accepted theories. And if it is only these utterances that are supposed to commit us to a domain of Fs, (P2) of the argument is false.

2.3.5 Hermeneutic and revolutionary conceptions of the anti-realist's project

We do not pretend to have given a full menu of the anti-realist's options here; nor do we claim to have given a complete characterization of the options mentioned. But we do hope to have given readers at least a sample of the most popular flavours on offer. In order to appreciate these flavours, though, it is important to draw attention to a distinction that stems back to John Burgess and Gideon Rosen (1997).[9] Apart from error theory, the anti-realist strategies outlined above give us a way of construing thought and talk with apparent yet unwanted ontological commitments. But how does this construal help us achieve this aim? Burgess and Rosen consider two suggestions: perhaps the reconstructions are *descriptive* analyses of discourse within the disputed area; perhaps they are theories of what such thought and talk *in fact* amounts to. These theories, then, are intended to capture and explain our current metaphysical commitments and linguistic practices. Following Burgess and Rosen, let us call this kind of anti-realism "hermeneutic".

Hermeneutic varieties of anti-realism are genuine competitors to error theories. But fictionalists, instrumentalists and non-factualists alike need not be hermeneutic anti-realists, and their positions may complement rather than clash with error theory. For suppose it was discovered that most of us have made an epistemic blunder; our beliefs about some controversial domain are in fact all false. Once this discovery has been made, we face the following pressing question: what should be done in light of this discovery? One natural suggestion would be to eliminate all talk of the relevant kind, except perhaps when reproaching others who have not yet revised the way they think about the disgraced domain. But this is not the only possible response. One might instead recommend that we continue to talk as we have all along, but revise our interpretation of such talk. While we have all been realists about Fs in the past, we should now replace this conception: we should become fictionalists, instrumentalists or non-factualists about Fs. Following Burgess and Rosen, let us call this kind of anti-realism "revolutionary". According to the revolutionary anti-realist, then, the analyses are *prescriptive* reinterpretations of discourse within the disputed area.

Anti-realists must be careful to distinguish between these two very different approaches and make clear which construal they have in mind. And this is true for *any* anti-realist, including those who challenge realism not along the existence axis, but instead along the independence axis.

Further reading

The literature on ontological commitment is prolific. For those new to the topic, but who want to delve further, we recommend the following accessible and important papers: William Alston, "Ontological Commitments", *Philosophical Studies* 9 (1958), 8–17; Frank Jackson, "Ontological Commitment and Paraphrase", *Philosophy* 55 (1980), 303–15, and "A Puzzle About Ontological Commitment", in *Cause, Mind, and Reality: Essays Honouring C. B. Martin*, John Heil (ed.), 191–9 (Dordrecht:

Kluwer, 1989); David Lewis and Stephanie Lewis, "Holes", *Australasian Journal of Philosophy* **48** (1970), 206–12; Amie Thomasson, "Parsimony and Ontological Commitment", in *Ordinary Objects* (Oxford: Oxford University Press, forthcoming); and Peter van Inwagen, "Meta-Ontology", *Erkenntnis* **48** (1998), 233–50.

Local realism and anti-realism:
3 the independence axis

To say that something is real is to say more than simply that it exists: it must exist *objectively*. Objective existence, in the relevant sense, has nothing to do with impartiality. An official government inquiry into the state of the economy may be unbiased and disinterested, and so objective in one perfectly respectable sense, but this is not enough to secure any sort of realism about the economy. It must also be shown that the economy exists independently of us: independently of our minds and our mental states. It is this dimension of realism that we hope to explore in the remaining chapters of Part I. In this chapter we explain some senses of mind-dependence that are inimical to realism.

3.1 Answering the quietist's challenge

What it takes for something to exist mind-independently should be intuitively easy to grasp. But articulating clearly and precisely what mind-independence amounts to, on the other hand, is a delicate matter. To some extent this task is straightforward. It is certainly easy to come up with slogans associated with this aspect of realist doctrine. A realist about a domain of *F*s typically claims that the *F*s exist "outside our minds", and that is why we "discover" or "detect" the *F*s rather than "constructing them", "inventing them" or "projecting them on to the world". And all of this goes some way towards explaining what it means to say that the realm of *F*s exists mind-independently. An anti-realist, of course, rejects this characterization.

It would be a mistake, however, to think that there is just a single notion of mind-dependence in play here. One of the most important things we want to emphasize is that there is a rich diversity of notions that can be mapped along the vertical "dependence" axis. Berkelean idealism, Kantian idealism and verificationism are all very different theories at odds with a comprehensive realism. Each theory, in its own way, tells us that there are mind-dependent objects. Because these views have shaped the realism debate over the past 300 years, and because the arguments in their support are subtle and often persuasive, we shall explore each view separately in later chapters. Nonetheless, it is interesting to note that each of these views is naturally construed as a kind of *global* anti-realism. And as a consequence, perhaps, the theories have almost no adherents today.

Despite this rare alliance among contemporary philosophers, many still maintain that some things are less than fully real. They suggest that there is a mind-dependent realm. It is a limited portion of what there is, but it is a significant portion nonetheless. Entities that belong to this realm are mind-dependent in a way that does not presuppose idealism or verificationism, or so it is claimed. But what could *this* kind of diluted mind-dependence amount to? Can we explicate the idea in a precise and informative way?

Some have had doubts. Quietists claim that, when all is said and done, any serious attempt to articulate the distinction between realism and anti-realism is bound to fail, for it will either make one side of the dispute seem simply incredible, or will amount to nothing but an enumeration of superficial synonyms. Rosen formulates the basic idea as follows:

> We *sense* that there is a heady metaphysical thesis at stake in these debates over realism – a question on a par in point of depth with the issues Kant first raised about the status of nature. But after a point, when every attempt to say just what the issue is has come up empty, we have no real choice but to conclude that despite all the wonderful, suggestive imagery, there is ultimately nothing in the neighbourhood to discuss.
>
> (Rosen 1994: 279)

Quietists can motivate their position in one of two ways. They might proffer an in-principle objection to any attempt to articulate a plausible version of the mind-dependence thesis precisely. One way this might be done is by identifying a presupposition of both realism and anti-realism that can be demonstrated to be false, or at least unjustified (cf. McDowell 1994; Smith 2002). Alternatively, quietists might proffer a more piecemeal argument. The quietist might lie in wait, critiquing every proposed distinction and speculating (for whatever reason) that no adequate alternatives will be given (cf. Rosen 1994). Rather than look at the details of each kind of argument, we propose here to attempt to do what the quietist tells us we cannot do. We aim to unpack the notion of mind-dependence in a way that we hope will be inoffensive to contemporary metaphysicians. To the extent that we succeed, we respond to both kinds of argument in one fell swoop. We leave it up to the reader to decide how successful our attempt is.

Before proceeding, though, a few preliminary remarks are in order. First, our approach will be to identify two different kinds of mind-dependence that might underwrite a restricted anti-realism. We do not claim these exhaust the ways something might fail to be objectively real. But robust realists about any domain tend to deny – either implicitly or explicitly – that the entities distinctive of that domain are mind-dependent in either of these two ways.

Secondly, in both cases there is a surprising amount of disagreement about how best to articulate the notion we are all reaching for. We do not want to claim that our endorsed proposal in each case is the best; we leave it open that a better account might be given. But we do hope that in each case our presentation is clear enough to at least give a flavour of the family of views in the vicinity. Moreover, we also hope that our account will not make it a trivial matter whether or not some kind of entity is real. Our definition should not rule out by *fiat* a version of realism or anti-realism about any domain. That, we maintain, requires further argument.

Finally, we recognize that in each case considered below, it is controversial to suggest that anything depending on us in these ways would not be a *bone fide* citizen of the robustly real world. We hope to go some way towards motivating this claim. If we succeed, we will have silenced the quietist.

3.2 Social constructivism

One way something might depend on us, and hence be less than fully real, is by being socially constructed. Social constructivism about any domain is always a fashionable option. Indeed, Ian Hacking opens his monograph on the topic, *The Social Construction of What?* (1999), by giving an incomplete list of an enormously diverse range of things that have been said to be socially constructed. (The list takes up almost the whole of the first page of his book!) Indeed, the list contains such a miscellaneous assortment of phenomena that it is hard to see what could unify the items on the list.

Hacking suggests that in order to understand what theories under the "social constructivist" umbrella have in common, we should not look for an analysis of the concept. Instead, we should look for the purpose of describing a theory thus. In response to this challenge, Hacking famously suggests that:

> Social constructionists about X tend to hold that:
> 0. In the present state of affairs, X is taken for granted; X appears to be inevitable.
> 1. X need not have existed, or need not be at all as it is. X, or X as it is at present, is not determined by the nature of things; it is not inevitable.
> 2. X is quite bad as it is.
> 3. We would be much better off if X were done away with, or at least radically transformed.
> (reconstructed from Hacking 1999: 6, 9)

So, for example, those who claim that gender, race or sexual orientation are socially constructed tend to claim that there is a prejudice against women, blacks and homosexuals within our culture, that such prejudices have all sorts of bad effects on those who form a part of these minority groups, that these categories are not forced on us, and that if we choose to reject them such prejudices will disappear or diminish.

We are sympathetic to Hacking's account of the pragmatic aim of social constructivists, but we are interested here in giving an elucidation of the idiom "social construction" itself. If it is possible, we hope to give a full-blown analysis of the concept. Hacking is sceptical that any sort of conceptual explication is possible, but it is interesting to note that his account of the use such phrases are put to is a partial analysis of the concept. Certainly, something might be socially constructed without clauses 0, 2 or 3 applying to it. Our local bridge club, for example, is a paradigm case of a socially constructed entity. No one would claim that it is inevitable. Occasionally, its membership has dropped enough to threaten its continued existence. But it gives a lot of pleasure to its constituents, and so is, at least to that extent, a good thing. And it would make those who enjoy the game worse off if it were disbanded. Clause 1, though, seems like a necessary condition for an entity counting as socially constructed. Let us see if we can flesh out and expand on clause 1 in order to explain exactly what social constructivism amounts to.

If socially constructed entities are "not determined by the nature of things", that is, if they are not biologically determined, the question arises: what are they determined by? Such entities are determined by or depend on *us*: they depend on the intentions of human beings. And because intentions are compound mental states – states composed of, *inter alia*, beliefs and desires – socially constructed entities are mind-dependent entities.

The next question that should occur to the attentive reader is: what exactly do these notions of "dependence" and "determination" amount to? Often when social scientists claim that a realm of objects is constructed, they mean only that such objects *causally* depend on us. We might explicate this notion of dependence as follows:

> *Causal dependence*: A domain of Fs *causally* depends on us if and only if we play an essential causal role in bringing the Fs into existence; that is, the Fs would not have come into existence in the first place had human beings, and our concomitant actions, intentions and mental states not existed.

But social constructivism of this variety poses no threat to realism. It may well be that global warming and US troop fatalities in the Middle East are socially constructed in this sense. But George Bush could not justify either his failure to sign the Kyoto Protocol or the war in Iraq on the grounds that global warming and US deaths are not real. That simply would not wash. Just a little reflection shows that causally constructed entities are as real as anything else. Artifacts, such as tables and chairs, televisions and computers, tins and

cans, are all socially constructed in so far as they depend causally
on us, but they are also real entities *par excellence*.

In his monograph *Social Constructivism and the Philosophy of
Science* (2000), André Kukla recognizes the compatibility of realism
and this species of constructivism. But he thinks there is another
variety of constructivism – a variety that appeals to a different
kind of dependence relation – that is incompatible with realism.
He writes:

> constructed objects [like artifacts] need humans to come into
> existence; but they share with natural objects the property
> that their *continued* existence doesn't depend on the contin-
> ued existence of humans. If all of humanity suddenly ceased
> to exist, there would still be lasers … Constructivisms begin
> to get interesting when they assert that features of reality have
> this stronger form of human dependency – that they would
> cease to exist without the continued presence (and appropriate
> behaviour) of human agents.   (*Ibid.*: 21)

The kind of social constructivism relevant to the realism debate
tells us that there are things that depend on us in just this way. And
if we make the further plausible assumption that we are essentially
psychological kinds,[1] we can make this notion of dependence precise as follows:

> *Metaphysical dependence*: A domain of Fs *metaphysically*
> depends on us if and only if the continued existence of our
> minds is required for the continued existence of the Fs.

Paradigm cases of constructed entities of this kind include: money,
state laws, clubs, economies, nations, kings, presidents and prime
ministers. Let us call social constructions that metaphysically depend
on us "psychological" constructions.[2] Arguably, our world contains
an abundance of psychological constructions. Were humanity to be
wiped out tomorrow all of these psychologically constructed kinds
would disappear with us. The same claim could not be made on
behalf of entities that merely causally depend on us. Tinned tuna
and cauliflower cheese might well survive the annihilation of the
human race, at least for a short time.

However, we have not said enough yet about psychological constructions to appreciate why they might be disqualified from any claim to objectivity. To see why, consider minds and mental states themselves. Minds are trivially mind-dependent in the metaphysical sense. But it should be fairly uncontroversial that minds can be as robustly real as rocks are. Pointing out that minds, like everything else, depend on themselves for their continued existence should not undermine our confidence that such entities exist objectively. Moreover, it should be just as uncontroversial that human minds are not socially constructed entities: not even psychological constructions. They are not constructed at all.

In order to understand what it takes for something to be a psychological construction, then, we need to specify what more is required for something to qualify over and above its metaphysically depending on us. And to do that, we need to look more closely at the differences between things such as currencies, states and monarchs on the one hand, and minds and mental states on the other. Two salient differences seem relevant here.

First, it is trivially true that the mental facts supervene on the mental facts. The same cannot be said for psychological constructions. While every psychologically constructed entity would go out of existence if we did, this is not always because facts about psychologically constructed entities supervene on the mental facts. One could hold fixed all the facts about minds, without holding fixed the facts about currencies, states and monarchs. And that is because socially constructed entities can have properties none of us have ever been aware of. The money in my pocket might be discoloured, the average temperature in New Zealand may have just risen and the Queen may have a prime number of hairs on her head, but no one could know these things solely on the basis of knowing everything there is to know about our minds.

The second observation is related. Arguably, socially constructed entities are at least partially composed of natural, non-constructed entities. Countries are composed of land masses, money is composed of coloured paper and parliaments are composed of human beings. And facts about land masses, paper and human beings do not supervene on facts about the mental. But each of these natural objects (or collection of objects) serves a social function. And they have this social function because we, as members of a community, have *decided* that they will. We could have made different choices in this regard and, if we had, the constructed entities might not have come into existence. It is in virtue of this possibility that Hacking tells us that socially constructed entities "need not have existed" and are "not inevitable". Moreover, if the constructed entities metaphysically depend on us, we could all change our minds at any point and, in virtue of that decision alone, the constructed entities would go out of existence. No further action need be taken. No deliberate process of extermination needs to be embarked on. So, for example, if everyone (and especially those in government) simply decided not to accept paper as a form of currency and decided they would only accept clam shells instead, the pieces of paper in our pockets would no longer be money. The government would not have to take the gratuitous additional step of burning the paper that had previously been legal tender. And this explains why all psychological constructions metaphysically depend on us.

Notice that the same cannot be said for natural objects. Thus, we find Catherine MacKinnon lamenting that men and the male world in general are not constructs. Her words illustrate the contrast nicely. She writes:

> women know the male world is out there because it hits them in the face. No matter how they think about it, try to think it out of existence or into a different shape, it remains independently real ... No matter what they think or do, they cannot get out of it.   (MacKinnon 1989: 123)

Minds and mental states are less like money and more like MacKinnon's conception of the male world. We cannot simply wish our minds out of existence, we cannot simply will not to believe, or desire or to feel something. Although we have some control over our mental states – and might even be able to bring it about that there are no minds at all (say, by detonating enough nuclear weapons) – such consequences require more than simply a thought or hope that it be so.

And so, if something is psychologically constructed this is one innocent way in which something might be mind-dependent. Such entities are not merely metaphysically dependent on us. Their continued existence requires that we have an appropriate intention: an intention that they continue to exist. This layered variety of mind-dependence conflicts with realism, but it is not the only modest variety of mind dependence that has this property.

3.3 Response dependence

An alternative way of specifying how something might be mind-dependent – and hence compromise realism – without leading ineluctably to idealism appeals to the traditional distinction between primary qualities (like being square) and secondary qualities (like being red). According to many, secondary qualities, unlike primary qualities, are dispositions to produce experiences of a certain kind in us. Red things, loud things, pungent things and smooth things all produce sensations in us, although in each case the sensory modality is different.

Mark Johnston, Wright and Pettit, in several different and important papers,[3] extend this idea to introduce the notion of a "response-dependent concept". Response-dependent concepts are concepts whose extensions depend in a very special way on us and our mental responses. This "dependence on us" is not a form of metaphysical dependence. It is, however, a plausible form of mind-dependence that seems to conflict with realism. The idea can be expressed roughly as follows:

> *Response dependence*: A concept F is response-dependent if and only if there is a bi-conditional – or *basic equation* – of the form "x is F if and only if x is disposed to produce response R in subjects S in conditions C" that is knowable *a priori*.[4]

Secondary qualities are not the only candidates for the extension of response-dependent concepts. Other properties more obviously fit the bill. Humorous things rouse laughter, disgusting things provoke disgust, shocking things produce surprise and addictive things provoke desire in those who come in contact with them. Arguably, none of these concepts are secondary-quality concepts, but they are all conspicuously response-dependent.

In order fully to appreciate the idea, four points need to be made about the basic equation. The last three are qualifications; but the first is a point of clarification. It is of the utmost importance that the truth of the biconditional be knowable *a priori*, for *any* concept might coincidentally provoke a response in subjects like us. For example, it may be true that something has a mass if and only if we would be disposed to believe that it does. This basic equation is plausibly true, but this is not enough to ensure that mass is a response-dependent concept. It is not! And that is because the connection between mass and our response is too fortuitous. We must further demonstrate that there is an *a priori* connection between the concept of having a mass and that of judging that it does.[5]

Secondly, not any old collection of things will count as subjects in the relevant sense. It is *a priori* knowable that glasses are fragile if and only if they are disposed to shatter when dropped. But fragility is not a response-dependent concept. For, *inter alia*, the subject of the disposition is not a subject of the right kind. The subjects must be human beings, or at least individuals like us who possess a mind. Thirdly, not any old reaction in a subject will count as a response of the relevant kind. It might be *a priori* knowable that something is a carcinogen if and only if it is disposed to cause uncontrolled division of cells in subjects like us. But being a carcinogen is not a response-dependent concept, despite the fact that carcinogens typically provoke responses in human beings, for the response is not of the right kind. A germane response will be a mental process: a change of mental state. The mental state we come to find ourselves in after becoming acquainted with the object need not be a sensation like those characteristically associated with the secondary qualities. It might instead be an affective, conative or cognitive state of some kind. Indeed, both Johnston and Wright believe one of the most interesting species of response-dependent concept is the judgement-dependent concept: a concept whose extensions are determined by our judgements or beliefs employing that concept.

Finally, and perhaps most importantly, the conditions specified in a basic equation will identify any restrictions on the subjects and environment that need to be in place in order for the basic equation to be knowable *a priori*. So, for example, it is *not a priori* that something is red if and only if it causes red sensations in people like us. For unconscious, blind and colour blind people will not have this kind of experience in the presence of red things. And nor will normal subjects when the object is covered in a blanket, or in the subject's peripheral vision, or in a dark room. All such caveats are stated explicitly in the C-conditions. They inform us of the kind of subject and environment required to produce the relevant response. But a basic equation can only help us determine which concepts are response-dependent if the C-conditions are not stated in a trivial "whatever-it-takes" kind of way. Wright points out that for *every* concept there is a basic equation associated with the concept that is knowable *a priori*. So, for example, for any concept F, the following biconditionals are *a priori* knowable:

(i) x is F if and only if an omniscient god would judge that x is F;
(ii) x is F if and only if subjects who are accurate at identifying Fs would believe that x is F in a favourable environment;
(iii) x is F if and only if subjects who always felt queasy in the presence of Fs and only felt queasy in the presence of Fs were such as to feel queasy in the presence of Fs.

So a basic equation can inform us of something interesting about the main concept it explicates. But only if the C-conditions are spelt out in a *substantial* way that ensures that the biconditional is *a priori* knowable. The C-conditions of a response-dependent concept, then, must always be non-trivial.

We believe it is at least *prima facie* plausible that the extensions of response-dependent concepts are not objective properties. If this is right, it is not because such properties are social constructs. Response-dependent concepts pick out dispositional properties, and dispositional properties are intrinsic. As such, they do not metaphysically depend on us. Nor, for that matter, do they causally depend on us. To illustrate, recall that "addictiveness" is a response-dependent concept. Tobacco is addictive. It would continue to be addictive even if we went out of existence. Indeed, it *would* cause addiction in people like us even if we never existed in the first place.

While these observations serve to distinguish sharply between response-dependent concepts and social constructs, they also undermine our confidence in the claim that response-dependence is a form of anti-realism, for the intrinsic nature of such properties makes the rhetoric of invention and projection seem particularly inappropriate here. Any crisis of confidence we might have, though, should be relieved by the following observations about the extent of the compromise with a realist required when we insist that a given concept is response-dependent. Let us outline just three such compromises highlighted by Pettit (1991):[6]

(i) Response-dependent concepts "implicate the subject" in a way that response-independent concepts do not. According to the response-dependent theorist, there are non-empty concepts *essentially* connected to our mental states: our sensations and emotions, our beliefs and our desires. And it should make us uncomfortable to suggest that objective reality is subject-involving in this way. And this, it seems to us, is good reason to think that response-dependence is an interesting form of mind-dependence in conflict with realism.

(ii) It is natural to think that an independent objective reality will contain properties that can be recognized and appreciated by different cultures and species. But the extensions of response-dependent concepts do not obviously meet this constraint of "ontic neutrality", as Pettit calls it. Concepts about dispositions to produce sensations in appropriately situated human beings seem just too parochial. There is no reason to think that other species will recognize or appreciate them.

(iii) Recall the insecurity thesis, a non-compulsory but commonly embraced aspect of the realist doctrine. It tells us that it is always possible to be in ignorance or error about any domain we are realists about. But, according to Pettit, "the responses involved in any response-dependent area of discourse cannot lead [appropriately situated] subjects astray" (1991: 622). Whether or not Pettit is right to suggest that *every* response-dependent area of discourse is like this, it is certainly true of many. Interestingness, for example, is a response-dependent concept. It is *a priori* that something is interesting if and only if normal subjects would judge that it is interesting in appropriate circumstances. This implies that normal subjects in appropriate circumstances will be almost infallible in their judgements about what is interesting. And this fact conflicts with the insecurity thesis.

There is, however, a more substantial reason to be sceptical of the claim that response-dependent discourse is inherently anti-realist in nature. The worry is raised, and considered in detail, by Wright. It parallels a spurious problem for the social constructivist considered in the previous section. Recall that any account of mind-dependence that is going to pose a threat to realism had better not entail that minds and mental states themselves are dependent in this way. But Wright suggests that there is a *prima facie* reason for thinking that our account of response-dependence cannot meet this basic desideratum. Following the lead of Wright, we will consider the case of intention (although we could say the same thing, *mutatis mutandis*, for any mental state). It is *a priori* that x intends to φ if and only if x is disposed to believe that she intends to φ in situations where she is not self-deceived. It therefore seems that intentions (and other mental concepts) are response-dependent concepts. And if they are, response-dependent theories cannot give us the kind of contrast to realism we require.

Despite the seductive appearance to the contrary, though, Wright suggests that perhaps mental concepts are not response-dependent after all. To see why, he asks us to consider the basic equation without the self-deception clause. The biconditional then reads: x intends to φ if and only if x is disposed to believe that she intends to φ. But this is not *a priori* because, for all we know, x might be self-deceived. That is why we need to include the caveat "in situations where she is not self-deceived". But what does this clause mean? Presumably it means little more than "in situations where she gets it right". And that means the C-conditions contained within this basic equation are trivial. Ruling out cases of self-deception is a "whatever-it-takes" condition of the unacceptable kind.[7]

We started this chapter with a dilemma, posed in part by the quietist. The dilemma was this: any attempt to unpack a notion of mind-dependence that conflicts with realism will make anti-realism seem either preposterous or empty. The preposterous hypotheses, we were told, are idealism and verificationism. Our challenge, then, was to come up with a substantial account of mind-dependence that conflicted with realism and yet did not force us to embrace either of the outrageous alternatives. We came up with two. In the remaining chapters of Part I, we want to examine the prospects for answering this challenge in a different way. Perhaps idealism and verificationism are not so preposterous after all.

Further reading

The following are excellent book-length discussions of social constructivism: Paul Boghossian, *Fear of Knowledge* (Oxford: Oxford University Press, 2006); Ian Hacking, *The Social Construction of What?* (Cambridge, MA: Harvard University Press, 1999); and André Kukla, *Social Constructivism and the Philosophy of Science* (London: Routledge, 2000). For those interested in books and collections on response-dependent concepts, we suggest starting with: Roberto Casati and Christine Tappolet (eds), *European Review of Philosophy: Response-Dependence*, volume 3 (Stanford, CA: CSLI Publications, 1998); Peter Menzies (ed.), *Secondary Qualities Generalised*, Monist, special issue, 81(1) (1998); Christopher Norris, *Truth Matters: Realism, Anti-Realism, and Response-Dependence* (New York: Columbia University Press, 2002); and Crispin Wright, *Truth and Objectivity* (Cambridge, MA: Harvard University Press, 1992).

4 Idealism

4.1 Overview

Idealism is the theory that nothing exists except minds and ideas in minds. Thus, in terms of the mind-independence axis, idealism is a paradigm form of anti-realism. There are two sorts of idealism: subjective idealism and absolute idealism. According to *subjective idealism*, human minds directly perceive nothing but themselves and their own ideas. The existence of other minds is inferred from one's own perceptual ideas. According to *absolute idealism*, everything including one's own mind is a part of a greater mind: the mind of God. The most famous subjective idealists are George Berkeley and John Stuart Mill. The best known absolute idealists are G. W. F. Hegel, F. H. Bradley, and J. M. E. McTaggart.

Idealism is sometimes thought to be akin to scepticism, but it is in fact a radical form of anti-scepticism. Idealists typically do not hold that we can know everything, but they do hold that what exists can be thoroughly understood. The view underlying both absolute idealism and subjective idealism is that the universe is (at least in principle) completely intelligible. There is nothing that cannot be comprehended. An extreme version of this thesis is held by Hegel. He says that "what is rational is actual and what is actual is rational" (1952: 10). By this he means that whatever exists can be understood and whatever we derive from intellectual considerations alone must be true. Berkeley and Bradley both hold that there is some contradiction in thinking that there are things that cannot be perceived or even things that temporarily are not perceived. Idealists thus oppose the realist claim that there are things that exist independently of the mind.

In this chapter we shall look at Berkeley's arguments for idealism. We begin, however, by describing the theories of perception and ideas of John Locke, since Berkeley's views arise in opposition to Locke's.

4.2 Locke

In this section we present a brief description of Locke's views, as they were understood by Berkeley. These are not Locke's views as most modern Locke scholars understand them.[1] Locke believes in the existence of mind-independent physical objects. But, according to Locke when we have sensory experiences, we are not directly aware of physical objects; rather, we are aware of ideas. These ideas are caused by physical objects and ideas represent the objects that cause them. Although ideas represent physical things, they are in some ways rather unlike those things.

Locke distinguishes between two sorts of properties that things can have: primary and secondary properties. Primary properties, such as size, shape, movement and solidity, are properties that physical objects have in and of themselves. Secondary qualities, such as colour, odour and taste, on the other hand, are properties only of our sensations (which Locke calls "ideas") of things. Secondary qualities are not qualities that inhere in the material objects themselves. We shall discuss secondary qualities at greater length in Chapter 10, in our examination of the nature of colour.

For our purposes, Locke's philosophy has two salient features. First, it is a form of representational realism. We are not directly aware of physical objects, but only of representations of physical objects. Secondly, it holds that physical objects are rather unlike our representations of them.

4.3 Berkeley's theory of ideas

All of Berkeley's arguments that we shall consider here depend heavily on his theory of what it is to understand or conceive of something. What we present here goes slightly beyond the texts, but the view we attribute to Berkeley seems a plausible one for him to hold and makes sense of his various arguments.

First, Berkeley rejects abstract ideas. An abstract idea is an idea of a kind of thing, rather than an idea about a particular thing.

For Berkeley, to have an idea of something is to have the idea of a particular thing. Here too we find that Berkeley attacks Locke's view. Locke and Berkeley both hold that abstract ideas cannot be mental images. Consider the general idea of a triangle. If we had an image that represented triangles in general it would be an image of a triangle that is neither right angled nor oblique, and so on (Locke 1959: IV ch. 7 §9; Berkeley 1965: introduction, §13). But Locke, unlike Berkeley, thinks that the mind has some faculty that allows us to move from images of particular things to abstract general ideas (1959: IV ch. 7 §9). Berkeley, however, is an *imagist*. He thinks that all ideas are mental images. Thus, if there can be no image that represents triangles in general, there can be no general idea of triangularity.

Thus, we have the following argument:

(P1) Abstract ideas are indeterminate; they are ideas of things without being determined in all their properties.
(P2) All ideas are mental images.
(P3) We cannot have mental images of things that are not fully determinate.
(C) We do not have any abstract ideas.

Let us examine Berkeley's imagism further. It seems clear in Berkeley's writings that to understand a statement is to imagine or perceive some state of affairs that would make that statement true. For example, to understand the sentence "Zermela is in the garden" one needs to conjure up an image of a dog in a garden. It also seems that Berkeley thinks that to understand sentences with existential quantifiers, such as "Some dogs are in the garden", one needs to construct a mental image of a dog (or more than one dog) in a garden.

This brings us to what we think is a very important part of Berkeley's theory of meaning. He thinks that in order to understand sentences of the form "There is something that has the property P" we need to be able to imagine a particular thing with the property P. Thus, in order to understand the sentence "There is a dog in the garden" we need to be able to imagine a particular dog in the garden. We call this the "principle of specification", since we are required to conjure up a specific entity every time we understand a sentence of this form.

At first glance, the principle of specification looks like a *scope error*. To understand what a scope error is, consider the following story. After work Stu goes to the car park to fetch his car. When he arrives at his parking space, there is no car there. He then believes that his car has been stolen, but he has no idea who has stolen it. Thus, it is true that

(1) Stu believes that someone has stolen his car

but it is false that

(2) There is someone of whom Stu believes that he stole Stu's car.

The phrase "someone" is a quantifier phrase. In sentence (1) the quantifier phrase comes within the scope of the phrase "Stu believes that" and in sentence (2) it occurs outside the scope of this sentence. In logical notation, we can formalize the first sentence as saying "Bel(Stu, $\exists x S(x)$)", where "$S(x)$" means "x has stolen Stu's car". The second sentence can be formalized as "$\exists x$ Bel(Stu, $S(x)$)". The point is that we cannot derive sentence (2) from sentence (1) in any standard logical system.

The specification principle seems to say that, in contexts concerning imagination, we can derive sentences like (2) from sentences like (1). That is from sentences that say that "y imagines that something is P" we can derive sentences that say that "There is something that y imagines to be P". In logical notation, it would seem that we are asked to derive sentences of the form "$\exists y$ Imag(x, $P(y)$)" from sentences of the form "$\exists y$ Imag(x, $P(y)$)". Again, in standard logical systems this inference is a fallacy.

But we think that the principle of specification can be saved within the framework of Berkeley's imagism. Consider the following example. Suppose that Stu is asked to understand the sentence "There is a llama in the garden". Stu does not know any llamas personally. So he imagines a llama that has features cobbled together from the various llamas that he has seen on television and in zoos. Thus he imagines a llama, but no particular llama. If he imagined this amalgam wandering around the garden, it would seem that he understands the sentence reasonably well.

We can save the principle of specification merely by stipulating that any object that has the properties that are being imagined, in this case, any llama that has all the properties that Stu has cobbled together in his mind, is being imagined by Stu. Thus, it might be the case that, unknown to Stu, he is thinking about several particular llamas.[2]

What if there are no llamas that have all the properties that Stu has combined in his imagination? As we shall see in §4.6.1, it will not matter whether there are any actual things that fit with our imaginings, but rather it need only be the case that it be possible for there to be such objects. To use the parlance of possible worlds (see Chapter 11), there need only be some possible world in which there is an object that matches one's imaginings.

4.4 Berkeley on primary and secondary qualities

Berkeley uses his theory of understanding to attack Locke's view of the physical world. As we have seen, Locke claims that the physical world in itself has no colour, taste, odour and so on. This, Berkeley thinks, is a meaningless assertion.

For Berkeley, the statement "The physical world in itself contains no secondary properties" is meaningful (i.e. we can understand it) if and only if we can imagine a world in which things have no secondary properties. Berkeley maintains that we cannot imagine a world of things with shape, size and so on, without having colour, taste or any other secondary quality. Thus, he claims that this statement is meaningless.

It might seem that there is an equivocation here. On Locke's view, we can represent to ourselves objects that have in themselves no secondary properties. We do this all the time, whenever we perceive or imagine physical things. The *objects* of these representations have no secondary properties. But the *ways in which these objects are represented* do include secondary properties. Thus, there is a sense in which it would seem that we can represent objects without secondary properties, even if the representations themselves use or contain secondary properties.

But it is clear that Berkeley demands something more from our imagining a world without secondary properties. He seems to be claiming that we need to know what such a world *is like* in and of itself. We can represent things using properties that these things do not really have. We do so all the time. When we remember our childhoods we often exaggerate the size of things, for example. But then we are not representing to ourselves what these things were really like. Berkeley seems to require that in order for us to understand a statement "x is P" we need to be able to imagine what it would be like for x to have the property P. And Berkeley is right to say that we cannot imagine what a world in which there are no secondary qualities is really like in and of itself.

On the other hand, Berkeley's requirement that we understand what things are like in and of themselves seems very strong. Consider something that Berkeley does believe exists: God. According to Berkeley, God is a mind, just as every human being is a mind. But God's mind is much more powerful than our own. It has the power, for example, to create other minds. Berkeley thinks that we come to understand what God's mind is like by reflecting on our own minds and what our own minds would be like without their imperfections (Berkeley 1965: §§151–4). One would expect that any understanding of God that comes about through this process would be far from perfect. But if an imperfect understanding of God will be good enough for us to understand talk about God as an omnipotent, omniscient and all-good being, why is an imperfect understanding of matter as colourless and so on, not good enough to understand talk about it?

Berkeley's argument against Locke has the following structure:

(P1) The statement "The physical world in itself contains no secondary properties" is meaningless.
(P2) We cannot accept any theory that contains meaningless statements.
(C) We cannot accept any theory that contains "The physical world in itself contains no secondary properties".

4.5 Conceptual realism and idealism

Berkeley holds a position that we call "conceptual realism".[3] According to conceptual realism, things are as we conceive them to be. This does not mean that everything is as we imagine it to be, but rather that the limits of how things can be are set by the limits of what we can imagine them to be like. For Berkeley, as we have seen, it is unintelligible to say that things are otherwise than as we can conceive them, for to understand this assertion we would have to be able to imagine things in ways in which we cannot imagine them.

As we saw in the previous section, Berkeley thinks that we cannot conceive of things except as having what Locke deemed to be secondary qualities. Moreover, Berkeley holds that these secondary qualities cannot exist except in minds. Therefore, we have the following argument for idealism:

(P1) Things are as we conceive them to be.   (conceptual realism)
(P2) We cannot conceive things except as having
      secondary qualities.   (by introspection)
(P3) Therefore, no physical object exists without
      having secondary qualities.   (1, 2)
(P4) Secondary qualities cannot exist except in minds.
(C) Things cannot exist outside minds.   (3, 4)

In order to see the force of this argument, we need to ask about the support for (P4).

Berkeley supports (P4) with his "argument from relativity". We follow Margaret Wilson (1999: ch. 16) in dividing this argument into three stages. First, Berkeley argues that a thing can have different secondary qualities depending on the distance one is from that thing. For example, a shirt can look pink from a distance, but from much nearer it can be seen to have red and white stripes. Secondly, different species perceive things to have different secondary qualities. There is much more variability of how species perceive, say, colour than Berkeley knew. It seems, for example, that some insects are sensitive to the ultraviolet part of the light spectrum. Dogs, on the other hand, see fewer colours than people do. Thirdly, there is variability in the secondary properties we individually perceive objects to have. As Locke pointed out, if a person puts one hand in a bucket of hot water and his other hand in a bucket of cold water, then places both hands in a bucket of lukewarm water, he will perceive the lukewarm water to be both hot and cold at the same time. Berkeley claims that to explain the relativity of the perception of secondary qualities one must say that they are not in things themselves, but rather in our minds.

Unfortunately for Berkeley, it would seem that we can deny (P4) without rejecting any of the phenomena that he uses as evidence for it. We can admit that our perceptions of so-called secondary qualities are not consistent, either between individuals (of the same or different species), from moment to moment in one individual, or even at a single time within one individual. But we still might maintain that these qualities are in real things by saying that some of these perceptions are inaccurate. Perhaps we have no way of knowing which perceptions are accurate, but this is an epistemological problem; it does not show that the qualities in question have no independent existence.

4.6 Berkeley's master argument

At various points in his writings, Berkeley gives an argument that André Gallois (1974) has called Berkeley's "master argument". The master argument purports to show that it makes no sense to talk of things that are not being conceived. Our reconstructions of this argument have it attempting to show that the sentence "There are things that are unconceived" is meaningless. Our reconstruction borrows from George Pitcher (1977: 111–14), Kenneth Winkler (1989) and George Pappas, (2000: 66–8).

The argument purports to show that there are no objects that are not conceived by any person. In other words, the conclusion is that every object is conceived of by at least one mind. Thus, this is an anti-realist argument: it attempts to show that there is nothing that is completely mind-independent. Like many of Berkeley's arguments, the master argument is a *reductio ad absurdum*. It starts with the hypothesis that there are things that are mind-independent and purports to derive a contradiction. The hypothesis is supposed to entail that there are objects that are both conceived and not conceived.

Here is the passage from Berkeley that contains the argument. It is part of a dialogue between two fictional characters: Philonous, who represents Berkeley's views, and Hylas, who, roughy, puts forward the views of John Locke.

> Philonous: ... If you can conceive it possible for any mixture or combination of qualities, or any sensible object whatever, to exist without the mind, then I will grant it actually to be so.
> Hylas: If it comes to that the point will soon be decided. What more easy to conceive of a tree or a house existing by itself, independent of, and unperceived by any mind whatsoever? I do at this moment conceive of them existing after that manner.

Philonous: How say you Hylas, can you see a thing which is at the same time unseen.

Hylas: No, that were a contradiction.

Philonous: Is it not as great a contradiction to talk of conceiving a thing that is unconceived?

Hylas: It is.

Philonous: The tree or house therefore which you think of is conceived by you.

Hylas: How should it be otherwise?

Philonous: And what is conceived by you is surely in the mind?

Hylas: Without question, that which is conceived is in the mind.

Philonous: How then came you to say, you conceived of a house or a tree existing independent, and out of all minds whatsoever?

Hylas: That was I own an oversight, but stay, let me consider what led into it. – It is a pleasant mistake enough. As I was thinking of a tree in a solitary place where no one was present to see it, methought that was to conceive a tree as existing unperceived or unthought of, not considering that I myself conceived of it all the while. (1965: 140f.)

The conclusion is that Hylas cannot think that there are things that are not conceived. What we have said so far will allow us to reconstruct this argument thus far:

> Hylas is thinking that there are things that
> are unconceived. (hypothesis)

Now we need to figure out how Berkeley gets from here to his conclusion:

> Hylas is conceiving of something as being both
> conceived and unconceived. (conclusion)

The principle of specificity allows us to get some of the way. That is, it allows us to infer the following from the hypothesis: "There is some object x such that Hylas is conceiving of x as being unconceived". This is still a far cry from the conclusion.

To understand how far this is from the conclusion, we need to distinguish between the content of representation and the way we represent that content. Ed, for example, could conceive of his dog as not being loved. His conception of his dog in this way is a loving conception, since it would be coloured by his pain at thinking about his dog abandoned and unloved. Although his conception is a loving one, the content of that representation has his dog not being loved. He is not thereby representing his dog as being both loved and unloved. Here we have a distinction between the *way a thing is represented* and the *content* of that representation. The way Ed is representing his dog is connected with his feelings for that dog, but his love for his dog is not part of the content of that representation. On the surface, it looks as though Berkeley is confusing the two in his master argument.

Is Berkeley committing this simple fallacy? We are not sure. We are not scholars of the history of philosophy and so we shy away from saying what was in Berkeley's mind when he wrote this passage. But we think there might be more to this argument than a simple fallacy, as we hope to show in §4.6.1.

4.6.1 A modal version of the master argument

We reconstruct the argument using Berkeley's theory of understanding with the addition of the concept of a *possible world*. We explain this concept at some length in Chapter 11, so we will only say a few brief words about it here. A possible world is a universe (or the representation of a universe) like our own. A statement is said to represent a possibility (or be "possibly true" or merely "possible") if and only if that statement is true in some possible world. We put this together with a view that is implicit in Berkeley (as it is implicit in the works of many philosophers): if a statement S can be understood, it is possible that S be true. Putting these two claims together with Berkeley's theory of understanding (§4.3), we have the principle of possibility: *If it is possible to conceive that a particular statement S is true, then there is a possible world in which S is true.*

The crux of our reconstruction is the idea that people can conceive of things in other possible worlds. This seems to be a reasonable assumption. When we imagine things that are possible but do not happen in our universe, such as when we read stories, we conceive of things that happen in other possible worlds. So we have the principle of trans-world conceivability: *People can represent things in other possible worlds.*

We now have enough to reconstruct the master argument. We begin with the hypothesis that Hylas is thinking that there are things that are unconceived. By the principle of specification, this entails that there is some particular object that he is conceiving as being unconceived. Let us call this object "x". Thus, we have Hylas thinking that the statement "x is unconceived" is true. If this is possible, then by the principle of possibility there must be a possible world in which that object is unconceived. Let us call this world "w". Thus, we have: "x is unconceived" is true at w.

So, we now have Hylas in one possible world and the object in another. Hylas is conceiving that object, but it is true at that second world that the object is unconceived. By the principle of trans-world conceivability, if "x is not conceived" is true at w, then there is no one in any possible world who conceives of x. But Hylas is in a possible world and conceiving of x. This is a contradiction. Thus, our original hypothesis must be false. In other words, Hylas is not really thinking that there are things that are not conceived.

Here is a more rigorous rendering of the argument:

(1) Hylas is thinking that there are things that are unconceived. (hypothesis)
(2) There is some x such that Hylas conceives of x as being unconceived. (by 1 and the principle of specification)
(3) If it is intelligible to hold that x is unconceived, there is some possible world w at which x exists and x is unconceived. (principle of possibility)
(4) There is some possible world w at which x exists and is unconceived. (2, 3)
(5) If it is true in w that x is unconceived, then there is no thing y in any possible world such that y conceives of x as it is at w. (principle of trans-world conceivability)
(6) There is no thing y in any possible world such that y conceives of x as it is at w. (4, 5)
(7) Hylas is in some possible world.
(8) Hylas does not conceive of x. (6, 7)
(9) Hylas does conceive of x. (2, contradicting 8)
(C) Hylas is not really thinking that there are unconceived things. (1–9, *reductio ad absurdum*)

Some philosophers have taken issue with the principle of possibility. They think that we can think about impossible things. To show that we can understand contradictions, they point to the fact that we seem sometimes to understand stories that contain contradiction or even that we sometimes have contradictory beliefs (see Priest 1987, 2003).

An even more controversial principle is the principle of specification. It is crucial to the master argument. Without using this principle, the argument cannot get off the ground. The reason Berkeley holds this principle is that he thinks that in order to conceive of some state of affairs we have to imagine that state of affairs. And, as we have seen, according to Berkeley, our imaginations are very specific. We can only imagine specific things. One way to avoid the conclusion of the master argument is to hold that our powers of abstraction allow us to think of a proposition of the form "there is something that is such and such" without actually imagining a thing that is such and such. Realists typically have rejected imagism, and so they have no reason to accept the principle of specification.

Further reading

On absolute idealism, the works of Hegel, Bradley and McTaggart are all extremely difficult, but there are some good secondary sources, at least on Hegel and Bradley: Terry Pinkard, *German Philosophy 1760–1860: The Legacy of Idealism* (Cambridge: Cambridge University Press, 2002); Charles Taylor, *Hegel* (Cambridge: Cambridge University Press, 1975); and Richard Wollheim, *F. H. Bradley* (Harmondsworth: Penguin, 1959). On Berkeley, see: George S. Pappas, *Berkeley's Thought* (Ithaca, NY: Cornell University Press, 2000); George Pitcher, *Berkeley* (London: Routledge, 1977); I. C. Tipton, *Berkeley: The Philosophy of Immaterialism* (London: Methuen, 1974); Margaret Dauler Wilson, *Ideas and Mechanism: Essays on Early Modern Philosophy* (Princeton, NJ: Princeton University Press, 1999); and Kenneth P. Winkler, *Berkeley: An Interpretation* (Oxford: Oxford University Press, 1989).

5 Kantianism

5.1 Introduction

Kantianism is another form of global anti-realism, although Kantians tend to call themselves realists. Kantians accept all of the entities of the common-sense and scientific worldviews. They accept the existence of tables, chairs, cats, dogs, matter, forces such as gravity and so on. But they claim that all of these entities are in a sense mind-dependent and it is because of this that we classify Kantians as anti-realists.

The key distinction for Kantians is between the world as it appears to us and the world as it is in itself. The world as it is in itself is often called the "noumenal world" and things as they are apart from the way in which we perceive and understand them are called "noumena". Kantians claim that the nature of noumena cannot be known; only the world as it appears to us – the so-called "phenomenal world" – can be discovered.

In this chapter we shall look briefly at Kantianism as it was presented by Kant himself and then provide a closer examination of the work of a modern Kantian, Hilary Putnam.

5.2 Kant

Immanuel Kant holds that we must be born with rather complex innate mental structures that allow us to interpret the world. Moreover, these structures do not mirror the nature of the world as it really is.

As we have said, Kant distinguished between the world as it is in itself – the "noumenal" world – and the world as we perceive it

– the "phenomenal" world. The phenomenal world is both spatial and temporal, but according to Kant space and time themselves are merely mental structures. Thus, the noumenal world is neither spatial nor temporal. Kant argued that if we take space and time to be real, rather than mental, we commit ourselves to a series of paradoxes. So he concluded that space and time must be ways we have of perceiving the world, but not real entities (CPR A405–567/B432–595).[1] In addition, there are several innate conceptual structures – "categories" – that Kant thinks we impose on the world. These are divided into four groups: categories of quantity; categories of quality; categories of relation; and categories of modality. We shall examine some of these categories.

Among the categories of quantity are the concepts of unity and plurality. Kant thinks that we could not have learned the concept of a unit (a single thing) from experience. Rather, we impose that notion on our experiences. Thus, when Ed sees a collection of light-coloured shapes in front of him as a single computer, he is (among other things) imposing the concept of unity on his experience.

Among the categories of relation is the category of cause and effect. According to Kant, we do not learn what a cause is from experience, but rather we have the innate tendency to see certain events as causes of or effects of other events. Kant argues that we need the concept of cause and effect to have the experience of an *objective time series*. When we experience the world, we perceive things in a certain order, but we do not always think that this order corresponds to the real order of events. For example, Ed is looking at his dog right now. First he sees her tail, then her torso, and finally her head. Ed does not think that her tail comes into being first, then her torso, and that lastly her head pops into existence. Rather, he thinks that they all coexist. That they appear at different times during times in the subjective time series is caused by the movement of his head (which he experiences in his kinaesthetic sensations).

The argument that the concept of cause and effect is used to construct an objective time series is called a "transcendental argument". A transcendental argument is an argument that starts with a premise that describes a feature of our experience. Here the premise is that we construct an objective time series that is in certain ways different from the subjective time series. The argument then attempts to show that a certain innate structure is needed to produce that feature of experience.

Kant's philosophy is designed to thwart a certain sort of scepticism. This might seem odd, because Kant is certainly sceptical that we can have knowledge about the nature of the noumenal world. But he did think that we can have knowledge about the phenomenal world. The natural sciences are just this: physics, biology and so on are about the phenomenal world. Kant wants to protect the natural sciences against scepticism. For example, Hume had raised grave doubts about the reasonableness of cause and effect reasoning, which reasoning Kant believes is central to doing physics. Kant is attempting to show that we can defend natural science without engaging in speculation about the world beyond our experience.

One of the most important elements of Kant's defence of science is his position on the use of Euclidean geometry in natural science. In *The Elements*, Euclid produced a set of axioms (or basic statements) that are supposed to describe space.[2] Kant raised the question of how we know these axioms to be true. If we were to justify the axioms on the basis of our experiences of things in space, then our knowledge of them would be empirical. Kant, however, thought that we have *a priori* knowledge of the axioms of geometry and that we know these axioms to be necessarily true. If our knowledge of the axioms were empirical, we could not tell whether they are necessarily or merely contingently true of space. Kant claimed that we know the axioms of geometry to be true of space, because we can reflect on the nature of space itself. Space is not something that really contains us, but instead is internal to our minds. We have direct cognitive access to space as a whole and we can know its nature directly.

5.2.1 The problem of non-Euclidian geometry

Kant's claim that we can know that the geometry of space satisfies the axioms of Euclidean geometry *a priori* became problematic in the early twentieth century. In formulating his general theory of relativity, Albert Einstein used a non-Euclidean geometry. The problem concerns one of the axioms of Euclidean geometry called the "parallel postulate". Suppose that we have a straight line (that goes on in both directions forever) and a point not on that line (on a

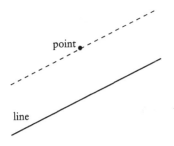

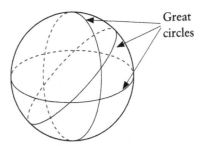

Figure 5.1

Figure 5.2

plane) (Fig. 5.1). According to the parallel postulate, there is exactly one line parallel to the original line that can be drawn through this point. The parallel postulate might seem obvious – Kant certainly thought so – but there is a problem with it.

If we accept the parallel postulate, in effect we say that space is "flat". But Einstein's general theory of relativity holds that bodies curve space around them. The usual illustration of this idea is placing heavy objects on a rubber sheet. The sheet dips at the place where each object is located. If we think about lines on a curved surface, we can see that they behave differently from lines on a flat surface. Consider a simple curved surface: the surface of a sphere. We define a straight line to be the shortest distance between two points. The shortest distance between any two points on a sphere follows the path of a *great circle*. Figure 5.2 shows great circles on a sphere. Thus, on a sphere, a straight line is a great circle. But no two great circles are parallel. So, if we have a straight line on a sphere (i.e. a great circle) and a point not on that line, we cannot draw a line thought that point parallel to the first straight line. In other words, if the geometry of space is curved, then the parallel postulate is false, and this is what Einstein's general theory of relativity implies.

Kantians are left with a dilemma. Either they must abandon Kant's theory of space or claim that one of our best scientific theories is false. Kantians have been reluctant to reject the general theory of relativity, since Kant's views were born of a desire to protect modern science against scepticism. So, by and large, Kantians have abandoned his theory of space.

Most modern Kantians have gone even further. They reject Kant's quest for *necessary* structures of experience and thought that can be known *a priori*. For example, Kuhn says of himself that "I am a Kantian with moveable categories" (2000a: 264). Michael Friedman is a Kantian who investigates the "relative *a priori*", that is, he claims that scientific theories have necessary presuppositions – these presuppositions are *a priori* relative to the theories – but when our theories change radically (during scientific revolutions) so do our presuppositions (Friedman 2001). Thus, Friedman too is a Kantian with categories that can change.[3]

In what follows, we shall examine the Kantian theory of Putnam. Putnam thinks, like Kant, that our worldview has a conceptual structure and that this conceptual structure need not give us an accurate picture of the noumenal world.

5.3 Putnam's relativism

According to Putnam, there are many different *conceptual schemes* that are equally legitimate. A conceptual scheme is just a set of concepts that we use to categorize objects in the world. Our conceptual scheme, for example, includes concepts such as the concept of cats, dogs, planets, eggs and so on. This might seem like a common-sense conceptual scheme, but according to Putnam it only seems so because we hold it. There are other schemes that are just as reasonable. Putnam (1987: 33–40) gives us the following example. There are people who believe in *mereology*. Mereology is a form of mathematics that deals with objects, as does our normal mathematics, but with some important differences.[4] Mereologists hold that (i) every part of an object is an object and (ii) any two or more objects are parts of a single object, the *fusion* of those objects. Thus, for example, the fusion of Ed's left leg and his dog Zermela's nose is an object.

Putnam asks us to consider a possible world[5] with two "normal" objects in it. Here we will use the dogs, Lola and Zermela. A person with our conceptual scheme will count two objects there, or perhaps those two objects plus all of the molecules in Lola and Zermela, all of the atoms in those molecules and all of the particles in those atoms. The mereologist will count all of those objects plus any parts of those objects (Zermela's nose, Lola's ears and so on) and the fusions of any other objects. So we have the fusion of Lola and Zermela, the fusion of their noses and so on.

The point of this example is that the mereologist and the person with our conceptual scheme carve up the world into different objects. Moreover, there is no way to say that one of these people is right and the other is wrong. There are no facts that make the mereologist's way of counting things incorrect and the other person's way correct or vice versa. Thus, according to Putnam, there are various equally legitimate ways the world can be conceptualized.

5.3.1 Model theory: an introduction

The key argument for Putnam's relativism is his so-called *model-theoretic argument*. In order to understand the model-theoretic argument, we need first to understand some model theory. This section is a brief and non-technical introduction to this branch of logic.

Model theory came into being with Alfred Tarski's article, "The Concept of Truth in Formalized Languages" ([1931] 1983). There Tarski sets out a *compositional* theory of truth. A theory of truth is compositional if it lets us build up our understanding of what makes a complicated sentence true by knowing about what makes its component sentences true.

Here we shall examine not Tarski's original theory, but a modernization of it. The core idea of the theory is that of a *model*. A model (for the sort of languages we shall be interested in here) contains a domain of objects and a value assignment. Here we shall use "v" for our value assignment. A value assignment is, in effect, a reference relation. Consider the names "Zermela" and "Lola" and a domain that includes just the dogs Zermela and Lola. The value assignment that seems most natural to us is the one that assigns to the name "Zermela" the referent Zermela and assigns to the name "Lola" the referent Lola, but other value assignment are possible. There is the value assignment that makes the name "Zermela" refer to Lola and the name "Lola" refer to Zermela, the value assignment that makes both names refer to Zermela, and the value assignment that makes both names refer to Lola.

In addition to making names in our language refer, the value assignment assigns *extensions* to *predicates*. A simple sentence (sometimes called an "atomic sentence") in logic has the form "i is F". Here "i" stands for a name and "is F" stands for a predicate. A predicate in English is a verb phrase such as "is a dog", "likes to eat hamburgers" and so on. A value assignment assigns to a predicate a collection of individuals. This is the collection of individuals of which the predicate is true according to the value assignment. Consider again the domain that contains just the dogs Zermela and Lola. This time we shall look at the predicates "is a collie" and "is a chihuahua". According to one value assignment, "is a collie" is true of just Zermela and "is a chihuahua" is true of just Lola, but on another value assignment, "is a collie" is true of Lola and "is a chihuahua" is true of Zermela; on a third value assignment, "is a collie" is true of both dogs and "is a chihuahua" is true of neither; and on a fourth "is a collie" is true of neither and "is a Chihuaha" is true of both. More value assignments are possible here. On a fifth value assignment, both predicates are true of both dogs, and on a sixth value assignment both predicates are true of neither dog and so on. One might ask how a dog can be both a collie and a chihuahua,[6] but formal model theory alone does not make distinctions between basic predicates that are compatible with one another and those that are not compatible.

Let us consider a value assignment v. Let us also consider a simple language that has predicates and the logical words (called *connectives*), "and", "or" and "it is not the case that". Our value assignment determines the truth or falsity of every sentence that can be constructed in this language. It does so by means of a *recursive* truth definition. This definition tells us how to determine the truth or falsity of simple sentences and then, given this, how to determine whether more complex sentences are true or false. Let "i" be a name and "is F" a predicate. Our recursive truth definition is as follows:

- "$F(i)$" ("i is F") is true according to value assignment v if and only if "i" refers to some object in our domain according to v and this object is in the extension of "is F" according to v.
- "A and B" is true according to v if and only if "A" is true according to v and "B" is true according to v.
- "A or B" is true according to v if and only if "A" is true according to v or "B" is true according to v or both.
- "it is not the case that A" is true according to v if and only if "A" is not true according to v.

The value of a recursive truth definition is that it shows how it is possible for us to understand the truth-conditions for complex sentences once we have mastered the truth-conditions for simple sentences of our language.

5.3.2 The model-theoretic argument

The goal of the model-theoretic argument is, roughly, to show that there are at least two theories that contradict one another that are both true. As we shall see, Putnam thinks that it follows from this that we should stop thinking in terms of true and false theories of the world, and merely think of what is true relative to our own conceptual scheme.

We shall begin with a very simple example to show how the model-theoretic argument works. We start with a model that has a domain of only two things: the dogs, Zermela and Lola. Our language is also very simple. We have two names – "Zermela" and "Lola" – and four predicates – "is a dog", "is a cat", "barks" and "meows". Our value assignment, v, does what one would expect. It makes "Zermela" refer to Zermela, "Lola" refer to Lola, and assigns the extension consisting of both Zermela and Lola to the predicates "is a dog" and "barks" and the empty extension to the predicates "is a cat" and "meows".

Now we take a second domain that consists of the cats, Riboflavin and Salome. We now construct a new value assignment, v'. According to v', the name "Zermela" refers to Riboflavin and the name "Lola" refers to Salome. In addition, v' assigns the extension of both Riboflavin and Salome to the predicates "is a dog" and "barks" and the empty extension to both "is a cat" and "meows". Thus, we have a new model, the domain of which is Riboflavin and Salome, and which has v' as its value assignment. On this new model, exactly the same sentences are true as on the old model. Thus, for example, both models make the sentences "Zermela is a dog" and "Lola barks" true.

The point of this example (and the more technical argument that follows) is to show that *if any collection of sentences can all be made true in a model with a domain D, then for any domain of the same size as D, there is a model that also makes that set of sentences true.*[7] Soon we shall see the importance of this point.

Here is a more technical version of the argument. Suppose that we have a theory, T, that is true on some model M. M contains a domain D and a value assignment v. Now we consider another domain, D', that contains exactly the same number of objects as D does. We pair up objects in D and D' so that everything in D has a unique mate in D' and everything in D' has a unique mate in D. We illustrate this idea with the following table. Suppose that we number all the objects in D and all the objects in D'. Then we can pair up the things in D with the things in D' as follows:

D	is mated with	D'
1	$\leftrightarrow$	1'
2	$\leftrightarrow$	2'
3	$\leftrightarrow$	3'
$\vdots$		$\vdots$

Now we take our value assignment v and create another value assignment v' that assigns objects of D' to names in our language. Suppose that "a" is a name in our language. If "a" refers to an object i in D according to v, then according to v', "a" refers to the mate of i.

What we do with the extension of predicates is very similar. Suppose that "is F" is a predicate in our language. Then, we take the collection of things that v assigns to "is F" and collect together all of their mates from D'. This collection of mates is the extension of "is F" according to v'.

Now we have a new model M' that contains the domain D' and the value assignment v'. This new model makes all the sentences of T true, just as M did. But the only fact about the domain D' that we need to construct this new model is the number of objects that it contains. As long as it has the same number of objects as D, we can construct a model around D' that makes T true.

Suppose, then, that there is another possible world that makes some theory true. This theory contains all sorts of statements that we would take to be false, such as "there are ghosts", "dogs hate to eat meat" and so on. But this other possible world has the same number of things that are in our world. So, there is a way in which our world also makes this theory true.

One might object, however, that the way in which our world makes this odd theory true is by using some weird reference relation, not the *real* reference relation. Putnam claims that there is no unique real reference relation. Rather, all value assignments are as good as one another and have as much right to be called the "real reference relation" as one another.

Here is the model-theoretic argument stated briefly:

(P1) Any collection of sentences that are made true by a model that contains the same number of things as the actual world can be made true in the actual world.

(P2) There are various collections of sentences that are made true by models that have the same number of things as the actual world, and these collections of sentences contradict one another.

(C) There are various collections of sentences, all of which are true of the actual world, but which contradict one another.

This is a very strongly anti-realist conclusion. It says that there are various equally good ways of describing the world that are incompatible with one another. Similarly, (P1) seems to show that any set of sentences that is true of our world is also true of any possible world that contains the same number of objects. This other world might contain all sorts of things that we do not think exist, such as ghosts and unicorns. Now we ask the following question: what if anything makes it the case that our theories (even if they are correct) describe our world rather than some other possible world?

5.3.3 Is there a unique correct reference relation?

If we can say that there is one unique correct reference relation, then we can say which theories are true and which are false, instead of holding with Putnam that they are all true. Moreover, we do think that we know the referents of our words. For example, Ed would like to think that his uses of the word "Zermela" refers to his dog, not to his former flatmate's cat, Riboflavin. But Putnam claims that Ed's belief is just his acceptance of some sentence such as "'Zermela' refers to Zermela". This sentence can be made true even by a value assignment that makes the name "Zermela" refer to Riboflavin. Thus, even Ed's belief that "Zermela" refers to Zermela does little to determine which reference relation is correct.

We call the theory that says that there is a unique correct reference relation "referential realism". Some referential realists have held that the conclusion of the model-theoretic argument can be avoided by the use of the so-called "causal theory of reference". According to the causal theory of reference, names and other nouns refer to things with which they have a causal or historical connection. For example, the second daughter of King Henry VIII was dubbed with the name "Elizabeth". Successive generations have used this name, produced paintings of a likeness of a woman with "Elizabeth I" as a title, and so on. Eventually, we have come to use the name "Elizabeth I". This name when we use it denotes that woman because of the causal chain that links our use with that woman.

Putnam replies to the causal theorist by saying, "Notice that a causal theory of reference is not (would not be) of any help here: for how 'causes' can uniquely refer is as much of a puzzle as how 'cat' can …" (1978: 126). The question that Putnam raises in this passage is about the reference of the word "cause". Just as we can find a value assignment that makes "Zermela" refer to a cat, we can find a value assignment that makes the word "cause" refer to a relation other than the causal relation. We could, for example, find a value assignment that makes true the sentence "a causes b" if and only if a occurs before b. As before, this value assignment would have to alter the referents of many other words but, as we have seen, this can always be done.

We can make Putnam's point in a more general way. Suppose that there are some constraints that we want to place on a semantic theory in order to determine which reference relation should be used. Let us call the collection of these constraints "C". Suppose that T is our original theory. Then, we have a new theory, $T + C$. As the model-theoretic argument shows, as long as there are enough objects in the world, if T is true so is $T + C$ (under some reference relation). But, so is any other theory $T' + C$ such that T' is any theory that is true in a world with the same number of things as exist in the actual world (and does not contain any statements that contradict any of the statements in C).

5.3.4 Not just more theory?

Referential realists realize that merely adding theories will not block the model-theoretic argument. Typically, they claim a special status for their theory of reference. The model-theoretic argument invites us to look at theories or sets of beliefs from two perspectives, internal and external. The internal perspective considers the relationships between various different concepts, words and beliefs in a particular conceptual scheme. From the internal perspective, according to Putnam, it is perfectly right to say that Ed's use of the word "Zermela" refers to Zermela, since Ed believes that it does. This is why Putnam calls his theory "internal realism"; from the internal perspective, it is perfectly realistic. The external perspective, however, looks at the relationship between conceptual schemes and the world. Putnam claims that from this perspective there is no privileged reference relation.

Some philosophers have argued that not all reference relations are created equal. They say that some reference relations are better than others because they help to explain why it is that we have adopted the beliefs that we have. Among the philosophers that have adopted this strategy are G. H. Merrill (1980), Lewis (1984) and Ruth Millikan (1984: 330–33).

Let us look first at Millikan's attempt. According to Millikan, we use words to express mental concepts. Moreover, Millikan holds that at least some concepts are evolutionary adaptations. Our eyes are adaptations. Our ancestors developed binocular vision and this helped them to survive by allowing them to judge the distance to prey. Thus, binocular vision has an *adaptive function*. Similarly, some of our concepts have adaptive functions. For example, people have the concept poison because they have adapted to be able to represent a particular sort of danger. This adaptation is useful to us, for it allows us to avoid this danger and to warn others about it. The key idea here is that the theory of reference not only tells us what words (and concepts) refer to, but also explains why they do so.

Consider two possible extensions for the predicate "is a poison". First there is the extension that includes arsenic, cyanide, strychnine and the other actual poisons. Secondly, there is an extension that includes water, milk, lemonade, cola and other wholesome drinks. We cannot use the latter extension to explain why we use the word "poison" the way that we do. Thus, Millikan holds that any value assignment that attributes the latter extension to the word "poison" is not a real reference relation.

According to the Merrill–Lewis argument, our semantical theory should produce the best fit between the concepts that we use and *natural kinds*. A natural kind is a collection of things that have something important in common. The collection of all dogs is a natural kind because each dog has important things in common with other dogs: the ability to breed with other dogs, genetic structures, behavioural traits and so on. The collection of Ed's toaster, his dog and the moons of Jupiter, on the other hand, do not have anything in common that almost any random collection of things does not have. Thus the collection of dogs is a natural kind and the collection of Ed's toaster, his dog and the moons of Jupiter is not.

One virtue of natural kinds is that they allow us to make projections about the world. If you are told that Fluffy is a dog, even if you have not met Fluffy you can make certain predictions about her. You know with a high degree of reliability that she eats meat, cannot tell the difference between the music of Bach and Mozart, and likes it when her owner scratches her behind her ear.

The fact that our common-sense concepts enable us to make very accurate predictions of these sorts indicates, according to Merrill and Lewis, that there is a good fit between these concepts and natural kinds. Thus, Merrill and Lewis rule out the sort of gerrymandered semantical theories that Putnam uses in his model-theoretic argument.

To reply to Millikan, Merrill and Lewis, Putnam needs to argue that it is somehow illegitimate to impose the criterion on reference relations that they explain how we use words the way we do. We leave it to the reader to decide whether there are good arguments for or against Putnam in this regard.

5.4 Internal realism and relativism

If we accept the model-theoretic argument, we must hold that there is no sense in talking about whether a theory is *really* true of this world. Thus, Putnam abandons the realist's view of truth. Instead, he adopts a view he calls "internal realism".

According to internal realism, it makes sense to ask what exists only relative to a theory or a conceptual scheme (Putnam 1981: 49). Thus, Putnam's view is a form of anti-realism because, although he accepts the existence of a variety of things, he makes their existence depend on a given theory or conceptual scheme. Thus, Putnam is also a relativist. What exists and what is true for a given community of people depend on the theories that are accepted by that community.

This does not mean that Putnam is a complete anarchist when it comes to epistemology. He holds that there are rules for what counts as a justified belief within a community. Putnam claims that these norms of justification are "historical products". They are developed by a community over time. But there are standards for these rules; some sets of rules of justification are better than others (Putnam 1990: 21). For example, if we were to base our beliefs about the future entirely on wishful thinking, we would end up accepting many propositions that would eventually have to be rejected, many more than if we adopted induction on past experience as a guide to future beliefs. Thus we can see that whereas Putnam is a relativist, he does think that there are standards that we can apply to decide whether one set of beliefs and practices is better than another.

5.4.1 Donald Davidson and conceptual schemes

Putnam's view is a form of anti-realism because although he is willing to accept the existence of a variety of items, he makes their existence depend on a given conceptual scheme. Moreover, he thinks that there are various different conceptual schemes. Hence, as we have seen, Putnam is a relativist. According to relativism, which ontology is correct depends on what conceptual scheme we are using.

Donald Davidson (1977) argues against this form of relativism, although he agrees that we cannot use a theory of reference to fix which belief sets are true and which are false. But he also argues that it makes no sense to talk about there being more than one conceptual scheme (Davidson 1974). To understand Davidson's argument against relativism, we will need to know some of his views about language. One thesis that Davidson famously holds is that to understand a sentence is to understand what would make that sentence true. Suppose for example, someone says to you "New Zealand will win the next football World Cup". You might think that this sentence is false, but you can understand it, according to Davidson, because you can conceive what it would be like for that sentence to be true. You conceive something like the New Zealand captain being given the trophy, New Zealand newspapers having "We Won!" on their front pages, and so on. Following this, Davidson holds that to translate what someone else says is to attribute truth-conditions to his or her sentences. Thus, if you were to learn what a German-speaking person says, you would have to be able to attribute truth-conditions to sentences such as "Es regent", which you translate as "It is raining".

Suppose that Ed and Stu appear to have different conceptual schemes when it comes to talking about dogs. Stu points at Irish wolfhounds, briards, Neopolitan mastiffs and so on, and says "There is a collie". Ed, on the other hand, only uses "collie" when he is in the presence of collies. On Putnam's criterion, Ed and Stu have different conceptual schemes about dogs. Ed would deny that a collie is present when Stu asserts that there is one present. But according to Davidson, Ed and Stu do not really have different conceptual schemes. This is because we can translate what Stu says about dogs into Ed's dog-language. When Stu uses the word "collie", Ed can understand that Stu is talking about a dog that is bigger than, say, a chihuahua. Davidson also thinks that we can translate Ed's dog-talk into Stu's language. We might translate the way Ed uses "collie" into Stu's language as "long-nosed, medium sized collie".

Some philosophers, such as Kuhn and Benjamin Lee Whorf, claim that different people have conceptual schemes that cannot be translated into one another. Conceptual schemes that cannot be inter-translated are called "incommensurable". Davidson denies that there are incommensurable conceptual schemes. For Davidson, to have two incommensurable conceptual schemes would be to have two languages A and B such that someone who speaks A could construct sentences in A, the truth-conditions for which could not be expressed in language B. Putnam's example of the mereological language does not meet this criterion, since its statements can be translated into our non-mereological language.

Davidson would not deny that it is logically possible that there be languages that could not be translated into one another. Suppose that we represent the truth-conditions for a sentence by a set of possible worlds (see Chapter 11), that is, those possible worlds in which the sentence is true. Thus, the truth-conditions for the sentence "Dogs bark" is the set of all and only those worlds in which dogs bark. We can easily construct two languages A and B such that there is a sentence in A for which there is no sentence in B that is true at all and only the same worlds.

But Davidson is making an epistemological claim not a logical one. If there are conceptual schemes that are incommensurable with our own scheme they cannot be shown to be so. To do so would be to show that there is a sentence in some other language that cannot be translated into our own language. We would have to say something like "that sentence is true when ... and none of our sentences are true when ...". But to have a way of filling in the "..." is to have a way in our own language of expressing the truth-conditions for the supposedly problematic sentence. If we have no way of filling in a truth-condition for the problematic sentence, then we have no reason to say that this sentence really says anything at all. If we could not translate the sentences from this other language into our own, Davidson says, "we would not be in a position to judge that others had concepts or beliefs radically different from our own" (1974: 197). Thus, if there are conceptual schemes that are incommensurable with our own, we cannot know that there are.

Putnam's view on this is interesting. Putnam agrees with Davidson that others do not hold conceptual schemes that are unintelligible in terms of our own. Putnam agrees with Davidson that we can only think others have a conceptual scheme if we can translate what they say into our own scheme (Putnam 1981: 113–19). But Davidson and Putnam disagree on one important issue. Davidson thinks that because every scheme we can claim to be a scheme can be translated into every other scheme, there are no really distinct conceptual schemes. Putnam thinks that in this Davidson is making a mistake.

To understand the mistake that Davidson is supposed to be making, let us consider the problem from Putnam's two perspectives on conceptual schemes. Let us consider again Putnam's mereology example. Suppose that the mereologist says "The fusion of Lola and Zermela is entirely in Ed's study". The standard logician can interpret this statement as saying "Lola and Zermela are both entirely in Ed's study". For Davidson, what the standard logician has done is attribute a truth-condition to the mereologist's statement. For Putnam, from the point of view of the standard logician's conceptual scheme, Davidson is right. But if we take a perspective external to either conceptual scheme, we will see that all that the standard logician has done is add the following sentence to her own set of beliefs: "The sentence 'The fusion of Lola and Zermela is entirely in Ed's study' for the mereologist means 'Lola and Zermela are both entirely in Ed's study' for me".

To say that, from the external perspective, the mereologist's sentence and the standard logician's sentence *really* have the same truth-conditions would require that we settle the question of which reference relation is the correct one. And Putnam does not think that there is an answer to this question. In other words, the translation itself becomes "just more theory".

Putnam, thus, does not think that the key question is the same as Davidson's. Davidson asks whether we can translate one language into another. For Putnam, a translation is always possible (this follows from the model-theoretic argument), but it proves nothing. What is important for Putnam are what roles various *conceptions* play within a language. The mereologist has a conception of the fusion of two objects. Nothing in the standard logician's language has the same role as "fusion". The role that it plays is the relations that it bears to other conceptions in the scheme. The conception of a fusion impacts on the conception of an object, for example, in terms of the number of objects that mereologists think that there are, and so on. These conceptions make up the ontology of people who speak the language. The relationship between languages, taken by itself, is not very important for Putnam. Other languages, and the world itself, can only be interpreted from the standpoint of some language. Only relative to a given language can we say what is true or false, or even deem one translation between two languages to be correct (Putnam 1981: 113–19). At this point we leave the reader to adjudicate the debate.

Further reading

There are many good books about Kant. Henry Allison, *Kant's Transcendental Idealism* (New Haven, CT: Yale University Press, 1983) is generally acknowledged to be one of the best works on Kant in English. See also his *Kant's Critical Philosophy*, *The Monist* 72(2) (1989). Michael Friedman, *The Dynamics of Reason* (Stanford, CA: Centre for Studies in Language and Information, 2001) is a difficult but extremely interesting defence of a Kantian approach to *a priori* knowledge and to philosophy of science. Paul Guyer (ed.), *The Cambridge Companion to Kant* (Cambridge: Cambridge University Press, 1992) is a very useful collection of articles on a wide range of topics from Kant's philosophy.

The model-theoretic argument is given in Putnam's *Meaning and the Moral Sciences* (London: Routledge & Kegan Paul, 1978) and *Reason,*

Truth and History (Cambridge: Cambridge University Press, 1981). The idea of a conceptual scheme is presented most clearly in *The Many Faces of Realism* (La Salle, IL: Open Court, 1987). On Putnam, see: Peter Clark and Bob Hale (eds), *Reading Putnam* (Oxford: Blackwell, 1994); Mark Q. Gardiner, *Semantic Challenges to Realism: Dummett and Putnam* (Toronto: University of Toronto Press, 2000); and Christopher Norris, *Realism, Reason and the Uses of Uncertainty* (Manchester: Manchester University Press, 2002). Barry Taylor, *Models, Truth, and Realism* (Oxford: Oxford University Press, 2006) is a book-length defence of the model-theoretical argument. It is a difficult but important book.

The "best fit with natural kinds" argument against Putnam is presented in David Lewis, "Putnam's Paradox", *Australasian Journal of Philosophy* 62, 221–36. Reprinted in Lewis's *Papers in Metaphysics and Epistemology*, ch. 2 (Cambridge: Cambridge University Press, 1999) and G. H. Merrill, "The Model-Theoretic Argument Against Realism" *Philosophy of Science* 47 (1980), 69–81.

The teleological reply to Putnam is given in Ruth Millikan, *Language, Thought, and other Biological Categories* (Cambridge, MA: MIT Press, 1984).

Most of Donald Davidson's articles about language are in D. Davidson, *Inquiries into Truth and Interpretation* (Oxford: Oxford University Press, 1984), *Truth, Language, and History* (Oxford: Oxford University Press, 2005), and his Dewey Lectures, "The Structure and Content of Truth" *Journal of Philosophy* 87 (1990), 279–328. These articles are all very interesting but extremely difficult.

Some good books about Davidson's philosophy are: Simon Evnine, *Donald Davidson* (Cambridge: Polity, 1991); Marc A. Joseph, *Donald Davidson* (Chesham: Acumen, 2004); Ernest Lepore and Kirk Ludwig, *Donald Davidson: Meaning, Truth, Language, and Reality* (Oxford: Oxford University Press, 2005); and Bjorn T. Ramberg, *Donald Davidson's Philosophy of Language: An Introduction* (Oxford: Blackwell, 1989).

6 Verificationism

6.1 What is a theory of meaning?

Verificationism is primarily a theory of *meaning*. A theory of meaning is supposed to tell us how we understand what we hear when someone speaks, what we read, what is signed when someone uses sign language, or what we understand when any other utterance of a sentence in language occurs. Philosophers have been studying the meaning of words and sentences since antiquity, but the modern debate about meaning begins in 1892 with the publication of Gottlob Frege's article "On Sense and Reference" (1984). In that paper Frege distinguished between the meaning (or "sense") of a word or sentence and its referent. The referent of a name, say, is the thing that it names. So the referent of the name "Zermela" is Ed's dog. According to Frege, the meaning of that name is the way in which a person comprehends the thing when he or she uses the name. When Ed uses the name "Zermela", he has a complex meaning in mind that captures the fact that she is his dog, that she is a rough-haired collie, that she is sweet natured and so on. When Stuart uses the name "Zermela", he has a much simpler meaning in mind, because he does not know her as well as Ed does.

Frege distinguished between the meaning and reference of expressions in order to solve an interesting philosophical puzzle. Suppose for a minute that the meaning of an expression is the same as its referent, that is, the thing to which the expression refers. Then we have a puzzle about *informative identity statements*. Suppose I tell you that there is a mountain in New Zealand called "Mount Egmont". Then you will know that Mount Egmont is identical with itself, since everything is identical with itself. But you might not know that Mount Egmont is identical with Taranaki, even if I also tell you that there is a mountain in New Zealand called "Taranaki". The statement "Mount Egmont is identical with Taranaki" is called an "informative identity statement", because it gives us substantive information that uninformative identity statements such as "Mount Egmont is identical with itself" and "Taranaki is identical with itself" do not give us.

On Frege's view, meanings are abstract objects. We shall meet many different types of abstract objects in this book, such as (Platonic) moral properties, mathematical objects, ersatz possible worlds and abstract fictional objects. An abstract object is roughly something that does not exist at any place in space. Frege postulated the existence of these abstract objects because although people typically associate different senses with words, he did not want to make senses *essentially private*; that is, he wanted it to be possible for different people to grasp the same sense. So, he made them public objects in this sense.

Most philosophers would argue, however, that Frege's meanings are not public enough. Frege's senses are not things that anyone can see, hear, taste, touch or smell. Thus the question arises as to how we are supposed to know anything about them and what they could have to do with our uses and understanding of language. Although there are defenders of Frege,[1] we shall leave this topic at this juncture, since one of the motivations for verificationism is to come up with a more accessible theory of meaning.

The sort of meanings that interest us here are the meanings not of individual words, but of declarative sentences. Frege called the meanings of sentences "thoughts" (or *Gedanken*, in German). Although their name makes them sound like things in people minds, thoughts too were supposed to be abstract entities. Sentence meanings are philosophically useful entities. Consider for example the sentence "I am in New Zealand". This sentence, by itself, has no meaning. It must be said in a particular context. If Helen Clark (the Prime Minister of New Zealand) were to say that as this sentence were being written, it would be true, but if George W. Bush were to say it at the same time, it would be false. Philosophers of language say that in these two cases the sentence uttered would express something different. According to Frege, what it expresses on these different occasions are different thoughts.

6.2 Verificationism

Verificationism is a theory of meaning. To understand verificationism, we first have to understand what a verification is. Consider, for example, the following sentence: "Zermela has 42 teeth". We can easily imagine a situation in which we can confirm this statement: we simply need to coax Zermela into opening her mouth and count her teeth and find 42 of them. If we do this, we have verified the statement that Zermela has 42 teeth. Verificationism equates truth with verification. For verificationists, it makes no sense to talk of a sentence being true even though no one can tell that it is true. To say that a sentence is true is to say that it is verified.

We shall discuss two sorts of verificationism: (Logical) Positivist verificationism and Michael Dummett's verificationism. These two theories have slightly different theories of meaning:

- *Positivist verificationism*: A sentence is meaningful if and only if there are some conditions under which it can be verified.
- *Dummett's verificationism*: The meaning of a sentence is the class of its canonical verification conditions.

A verification condition is a condition under which a sentence is verified. We shall discuss canonical verification conditions below. A sentence need not be true to have verification conditions. Consider, for example, the sentence "Zermela has 41 teeth". We can just as easily imagine opening Zermela's mouth and counting 41 teeth in it. That a statement be true is not required. For a statement to be verifiable, what is needed is that it be *possible* to verify the statement. A verification condition is a possible situation in which a statement is proved. To return to our example of Zermela's teeth, the imagined situation in which she is found to have 41 teeth is a verification condition for the sentence "Zermela has 41 teeth".

One difference between Positivist verificationism and Dummett's verificationism can be seen by considering an example. The sentence "it is both raining and not raining in the same sense right now" cannot be verified under any circumstances. It is a contradiction. Thus, for the Positivists, it is meaningless. But for Dummett it has a meaning. Its meaning is the empty class of verification conditions. This might seem like a minor difference, but it does have an interesting consequence. According to most contemporary theories of meanings, meaning is compositional. That is, the meaning of a sentence is determined by the meaning of the parts of that sentence. Thus, for example, the meaning of a statement "not S" is determined by the meaning of negation and the meaning of S. The negation of a contradiction is a valid sentence, or a *law of logic*. Thus, according to the Positivists, some (in fact all) laws of logic are negations of meaningless statements. This entails, according to the Positivists, that the laws of logic are also meaningless. This seems rather odd to say the least. For Dummett, the laws of logic are verified under all conditions, and hence they are meaningful.

Now we turn to the subject of why one would want to be a verificationist. In §6.3, we shall look at the Logical Positivist movement. The Logical Positivists had a particular reason for wanting to be verificationists, but we shall begin with a different sort of motivation, which comes from the writings of Dummett.

For Dummett, a collection of verification conditions is a *sentence meaning*, that is, it is what we understand when we comprehend a sentence, according to verificationists. Frege's sentence meanings – Frege's "thoughts" – are abstract objects. It is difficult to see how we are supposed to grasp Fregean thoughts, since we never experience them. A verification condition, on the other hand, is something we do experience. Suppose I tell you that Zermela has 42 teeth. If you ask me for evidence, I can open her mouth and we can count her teeth together. On the verificationist theory of meaning, one can be said to understand a statement at least in part if he or she can imagine or recognize at least some verification conditions for that statement. Clearly, there can be degrees of the understanding of a statement; if one can imagine or recognize more verification conditions for the statement one understands its meaning better.

Moreover, the verificationist theory of meaning allows meanings to be public. We can put in place the requirement that verification conditions must be publicly accessible. The counting of Zermela's teeth is something that several people can witness. It is not a private or subjective procedure. An act of verification is something that can be communicated or learned. Thus, it seems that the verificationist theory of meaning meets Frege's requirement that meanings must be public and does not have the problem of making the understanding of meanings difficult to explain.

Verificationists classify themselves as anti-realists. But they are anti-realists in an unusual way. As Alex Miller (2003) points out, verificationists do not deny the existence or mind-independence of individual objects. Nor do they deny that things can have properties independently of those that we attribute to them. But they do deny that facts can hold independently of the abilities of minds to tell that they hold. They claim that nothing can be true that we cannot discover to be true and that nothing is true until it has been verified. Thus, facts are, to a certain extent, mind-dependent according to verificationists.

6.3 Logical Positivism

Verificationism was the central tenet of the philosophical school known as Logical Positivism. Logical Positivism began in the 1920s in Vienna and spread to Germany, the United Kingdom and America in the 1930s. The Logical Positivists adopted verificationism in part because it deemed many traditional philosophical questions to be pseudo-questions. The philosophy of positivism – at least under that name – was first developed by Auguste Comte. Comte held that philosophers should reject all theses that could not be supported by observation. The Logical Positivists thought that the philosophy of the nineteenth and early twentieth centuries had, by and large, become far too speculative.[2] They wanted philosophy to become more "scientific", and so they did not want to countenance any claims that went beyond the realm of empirical verifiability. So, as we have seen, they adopted a principle that ruled any unverifiable sentence to be meaningless.

6.3.1 Conventions

The Logical Positivists, however, realized that many of the apparent claims that scientists made and that the Logical Positivists themselves made were not verifiable. One straightforward example of such a "statement" is the principle of verifiability itself, that is, only verifiable statements are meaningful. This principle cannot itself be proved. The Logical Positivists thus claimed that there are certain utterances that we make that are not verifiable but are somehow legitimate nonetheless. These are statements of convention. We adopt a convention and then treat as true the statements that we derive from it. For example, all the "truths" of mathematics and logic are statements of conventions. This is why they adopted the name "Logical" Positivism. Unlike nineteenth-century positivism, Logical Positivism treated logical and mathematical statements as legitimate in addition to verifiable statements about empirical matters.

Another sort of convention is a *linguistic framework*. For example, we might adopt a convention according to which we describe the world in terms of atomic physics. On this view, it is part of the linguistic framework that there are atoms (and other things that we cannot directly perceive). We could have instead adopted a framework in which we talk about the world in terms of sensations (as Berkeley would have us do), or in terms of ghosts and spirits. Our choice of one linguistic framework over another is a pragmatic one, that is, one linguistic framework is chosen over another if it is simpler, easier to use and so on. There is no one true linguistic framework.[3]

According to the linguistic framework of atomic physics, if there are any physical objects they are made of atoms. Thus, the statement "There are atoms" has the same verification conditions as the statement "There are physical objects". Moreover, this latter statement is verified just in case we have experiences that we deem to be of physical objects.

With regard to purely conventional utterances, such as "2 + 2 = 4" and "only verifiable statements are meaningful", the Logical Positivists claimed that they were legitimate but "devoid of content" (Carnap 1959: 143). This means that they are meaningless. In the case of mathematical statements, their legitimacy is due to the fact that they are useful in helping us derive verifiable scientific statements, count our change at the supermarket and so on. The situation with regard to the principle of verifiability is somewhat more difficult. Some of the original Logical Positivists got into a tangle over this problem (see Passmore 1968: 37ff.). We shall follow A. J. Ayer's tidier interpretation of the principle. The principle is a normative principle, rather than a descriptive one (Ayer 1959: 15). According to the Logical Positivists, norms are never descriptions of facts, but instead express attitudes of the people who adopt them. Thus, the Logical Positivists were non-factualists with regard to norms of all kinds (including ethics). Since the principle of verifiability is normative, it just expresses the attitude that the Logical Positivists will only accept verifiable statements as meaningful.

6.3.2 Positivist verificationism and metaphysics

One effect of adopting the Positivist verificationist principle is that it deems many traditional philosophical theories to be meaningless. Consider the following claim: "There is a world outside our minds". If the world is only a construct of our minds out of sensations, as Berkeley maintains, then things would appear to us in exactly the same way as they would if the physical world did exist. So there is no verifiable difference. Thus, the first claim is meaningless. In addition, Positivist verificationists claim that the question of whether the external world exists is a *pseudo-question*. We cannot verify either a positive or negative answer to this question, so the question itself is deemed to be improper.

According to the Positivists, the following are all pseudo-questions:

- Are there possible worlds other than the actual world?
- Is there a super-sensible realm of mathematical objects?
- Is there a super-sensible realm of moral truths?
- Are there non-existent objects?

We think that this is an untoward consequence of Positivism. If we did not think that these were interesting and meaningful questions, we would not have written a book about them.

6.3.3 Problems with Logical Positivism

There are various objections to Logical Positivism. Some philosophers – most famously W. V. Quine – have objected to Logical Positivism's conventionalism. But we shall concentrate only on objections to the use of verificationism by the Logical Positivists. The first objection is perhaps the most famous. Consider the statement "All storks have red legs". To verify this statement, we would have to check every stork that has ever lived or will ever live to see whether it has red legs. It is at least imaginable that the world will never end and there never will be a final stork. For an even more striking example, consider: "Every piece of matter in the universe attracts every other piece of matter". This is a statement that is easily derivable from Newton's theory of gravity. According to Newton's theory, there never will be any end to the universe nor to the existence of matter. So, this sentence too is unverifiable.

We call statements that begin with "all" or "every" universal statements. Universal statements are found in scientific theories, in particular in stating scientific laws. The Logical Positivists were interested in justifying scientific method and they wanted philosophy to follow science. The thought that philosophers should tell scientists that their claims are illegitimate would have been a complete anathema to the Logical Positivists.

The Logical Positivists realized rather early that universal statements of natural laws were a problem for them. Moritz Schlick's response is to claim that universal statements do not contribute directly to the meaningful content of a scientific theory. Rather, a universal law is just a means for deriving many individual verifiable statements (Carnap 1963: 57). The idea here is that we do not consider general statements such as "All matter attracts all other matter" as part of a scientific theory. Rather we only consider individual statements, such as "The earth attracts the moon at 9:16pm NZDST on 3 March 2004". Each of these statements could be verified, at least in principle. Thus, each is verifiable and hence meaningful.

Carl Hempel (1950) argued that there is a serious problem with the Logical Positivists' position. Recall the principle of the compositionality of meaning. According to this principle, the meaning of a sentence is determined by the meaning of its component parts. Thus, for example, the meaning of the sentence "Zermela woke up and asked to go outside" is determined by the meanings of the component sentences "Zermela woke up" and "Zermela asked to go outside", as well as the meaning of the word "and". According to the Positivists' theory of meaning, what we do in understanding the sentence "Zermela woke up and asked to go outside" is take the verification conditions for the first component sentence and the verification conditions for the second component sentence. The word "and" indicates that at least one verification condition for "Zermela woke up" obtains and at least one verification condition for "Zermela asked to go outside" obtains.

Now consider the sentence "Not all storks have red legs". Clearly, this sentence is verifiable. If we found a stork with blue legs, for example, the sentence would be verified. But there is a problem with it. The only component sentence that is a proper part of this sentence is "all storks have red legs". The Logical Positivists have claimed that this sentence has no meaning. So, if we stick with the principle of compositionality, can we obtain a sentence with genuine meaning merely by prefixing the word "not"? It looks as though we can get a meaningful sentence by negating a meaningless one.

6.4 Dummett's verificationism

The most prominent contemporary verificationist is Michael Dummett. His verificationism is motivated by different concerns than that of the Logical Positivists. Dummett begins, not with the philosophy of science, or the desire to make philosophy more scientific, but with the philosophy of language and the concern of creating a theory that explains how we use language in our ordinary everyday lives. Dummett thinks that verificationism rather than realism about semantics better describes the way in which human languages work. As we have seen, Dummett thinks that the meaning of a sentence is the set of conditions under which we can verify it. Now we need to be a bit more rigorous in our presentation of Dummett's views.

For Dummett, there are two sorts of verification: canonical (or direct) and non-canonical (or indirect) verification. Consider the following example. Stu has just returned from the shop with some apricots and he puts them in a bowl on his countertop. He notices that he was charged £3 for them and he knows that they charge £4 per kilogram. Thus, he works out that he has bought 0.75 kg of apricots. Now if you were to ask anyone (who had not heard this story) to tell you how to work out the truth of the statement "There are 0.75 kg of apricots in this bowl", the first thing that they would suggest would be to weigh them. Weighing the apricots is the canonical method of verifying this statement. It is the method that we most closely associate with determining the truth of the statement. Using the price paid for the apricots and dividing through by the price per kilogram is a non-canonical method of verification. The meaning of a statement is just the set of its canonical means of verification.

When we learn language, according to Dummett (2004: 54), we learn to associate canonical methods of verification with sentences and to distinguish between canonical and non-canonical methods of verification for particular statements. Consider the following sentence: "There are four apricots in the bowl". Suppose that Stu says this sentence to his son, Julian, when Julian was learning to talk. To show Julian what this means Stu counts the apricots for Julian. Thus, Julian is taught a canonical means of verifying that there are four apricots in the bowl and he learns to associate the sentence with it. Taking the meaning of a sentence to be the set of its canonical means of verification facilitates the language-learning process. The set of canonical means is finite (and usually quite small), as opposed to the set of non-canonical means of verification, which for a given sentence may be infinite. Thus, to understand a sentence, we only have to learn a small number of methods of verifying that sentence.

This theory of meaning gives rise to a theory of truth. Consider again the statement "There are four apricots in the bowl". The meaning of the statement is that if we count the apricots, we will find that there are four of them.[4] Thus, the statement is correct if this verification procedure can be carried out successfully. In other words, the statement is true if and only if there is some canonical procedure to verify it.[5]

6.4.1 Verificationism and semantic realism

Here we contrast Dummett's view to a position that we call "semantic realism". According to semantic realism, there can be meaningful and true statements without there being any means to verify them. The verificationist would thus ask the semantic realist how the realist connects statements with their meanings.

On one version of semantic realism, sentences represent external facts because of causal connections that the words and phrases of sentences have to external objects and properties, like those described in §5.3.3. Suppose that Stu says to Julian, "This apricot is rotten". The phrase "this apricot" is causally connected to the apricot that Stu is indicating and the predicate "is rotten" is connected causally to the property of being rotten. Thus, the meaning of "This apricot is rotten" is the structure $<t$, the property of being rotten$>$, where t is the apricot.[6]

Verificationists have replied that external theories of meaning such as this version of semantic realism are illegitimate. According to Dummett, a theory of meaning is a theory of how we understand language. Causal connections between words and external objects do not explain how we understand anything (see Wright 1993: 34). Dummett thinks that to understand language is to gain "the mastery of a practice" (Dummett 1993: 219). Thus, in learning the meaning of statements, we learn to behave in certain ways (e.g. to perform certain sorts of verifications, to challenge others in their claims by showing that those verifications cannot be performed and so on). Externalist theories of meaning do not explain our linguistic behaviour, and so they are not real theories of meaning for Dummett.

6.5 Davidson's realism

Davidson's view is also interesting in this context. On Dummett's view, Davidson is a realist, because he accepts the principle of excluded middle (see §6.6). But Davidson is not a semantic realist in the sense of §6.4.1. As we saw in §5.3.3 and §5.4.1, he rejects the view that words have unique referents.

As we have seen, the meaning of a sentence for Davidson is the set of conditions under which it is true. To understand a sentence is to be able to give a *T*-sentence for it (in terms that one does understand). Dummett thinks that Davidson's theory of meaning is incomplete. Dummett thinks that Davidson's theory of meaning only explains how we understand sentences in terms of concepts expressed in our own language, but does not explain what these concepts themselves are (Dummett 1993: 6). For example, on Davidson's view, a competent speaker of English knows that the sentence "The earth moves" is true if and only if the earth moves. But what is it to know that a thing moves? This Davidson's theory of meaning does not explain. But Dummett's theory does explain this. To know that something moves is to know what canonical tests can be made to show that it moves. Thus, Dummett says that Davidson's theory is inadequate as it stands (*ibid*.: 5).

6.6 The law of excluded middle

Consider the following sentence (taken from Davidson 2005b: 47): "There will never be a city built on this spot". Suppose that it is said by Ed as he stands in the middle of a farmer's field in a rural place in New Zealand. Also suppose that Ed believes this statement. According to Dummett, Ed understands what he has said if and only if he knows the canonical means to verify it. For a universal statement about the future, such as the one given above, the canonical means of verification is a method of proof such that, given any future time t, a canonical verification will show (now) that at t no city will be built on that spot (see Dummett 1977: 14f.). It might be that there are such canonical means of verifying that there will never be a city built on that spot – for example, seeing the earth destroyed from space by the Vogon constructor fleet – but we do not have any such means available to us now. Thus, Ed and the rest of us can understand this statement, but we do not know now (and cannot know now) whether it is true.

Dummett points out that there is a problem here. According to a venerable principle of logic, every statement is either true or false. This is called the "principle of bivalence". The principle of bivalence is a semantic principle: it is a principle about the structure of the models that we accept for our language (see §5.3.1). If we believe in bivalence, we hold that every sentence in a model is given the value true or the value false. Dummett, however, thinks that we should reject bivalence. For him, a statement is true only if it can be shown to be true and it is false only if it can be shown to be false. But some sentences can neither be shown to be true nor shown to be false. Hence, bivalence fails.

As we have seen, on standard model theory the sentence "not-A" is true if and only if "A" is false. And the sentence "A or B" is true if and only if at least one of the sentences "A" and "B" are true. Thus, if we have a standard model theory that accepts bivalence, we also are committed to the *principle of excluded middle*: for every sentence A, the sentence "either A or not-A" is valid (i.e. true in every model): it is a law of logic (see §6.2). Dummett rejects the law of excluded middle as well (1991: 9).[7] The law of excluded middle is a principle of classical logic. Dummett thinks that we should adopt an alternative form of logic: intuitionist logic (described in §9.7).

Dummett characterizes the debate between realists and anti-realists in a different way from us. He claims that a philosopher is an anti-realist about a subject X if he or she thinks that the true statements concerning X are not closed under the law of excluded middle. That is, if there is at least one sentence *A* about *X* such that neither *A* nor not-*A* is true about *X*, in the verificationist sense. Dummett adopts this rather idiosyncratic view about the realism debate because of his own verificationism. One problem on which Dummett has written a great deal is the problem of realism in mathematics. As we shall see in Chapter 9, Platonists about mathematics think that there are mathematical objects that exist outside space and time. For a verificationist, what could this mean? There are no conditions under which we could verify Platonism. According to Dummett (1978b: xxv), Platonism about mathematics is merely a metaphor. As a metaphor, it is not by itself a claim to be debated (as opposed to what it is a metaphor for). The aspect of Platonism that Dummett treats literally is the claim that the truths of mathematics are closed under the law of excluded middle.

6.7 Verification and belief

Let us return to the sentence "There will never be a city built on this spot". As we have seen, Dummett holds that we can understand what it means without being able to verify that it is true or that it is false. And surely we can also believe that it is true. Thus, Davidson writes:

> On Dummett's view, we can understand a sentence like "A city will never be built on this spot" without having any idea what it would be like for this sentence to be true (since the sentence, or any utterance of it, has no truth value according to Dummett). It would seem that, for Dummett, having a belief that one expresses by a sentence one understands is not necessarily to believe that the sentence is true.   (2005b: 47)

This is strange. Usually we think that to believe a proposition *p* is to believe that *p* is true. Suppose that someone said to you "I believe that Canberra is the capital of Australia". If you ask him or her "Do you believe that the sentence 'Canberra is the capital of Australia' is true?", what are you asking? Most of us would say that you are asking whether the person really believes that Canberra is the capital of Australia. It seems that we take believing and believing to be true to be very closely connected. Dummett writes: "We recognise as legitimate grounds for assertion what does not guarantee the correctness of the assertion, being willing to believe, and to assert, much more than we have *conclusively* established" (1991: 278, original emphasis).

Belief does not require that one have conclusive verification. Note that Dummett does not say that we can believe something without thinking that we can find conclusive proof that it is true. But we agree with Davidson that Dummett should admit to this. In the case of beliefs about the future, we almost never have or have available to us conclusive grounds for our beliefs. Moreover, we realize that we cannot now find conclusive grounds for these beliefs.

Thus it seems that Dummett has a choice to make. He must choose between taking a belief in something and believing it to be true as distinct states of mind or abandoning the notion that truth of a statement consists in its being able to be conclusively verified. Suppose that Dummett were to choose to relax his view of truth and allow that statements that cannot now be conclusively verified still count as true if there are strong grounds for asserting them. This choice would create another problem. Consider, for example, a current historical debate: the debate about the place of origin of the Maori people. The Maori were the first people to settle in what is now New Zealand about 700 years ago. One school of thought claims that they came from what is now Taiwan and another school says that they originally came from present-day Indonesia. Suppose that five years ago there was better evidence that they came from Taiwan and now there is better evidence that they came from Indonesia. Should we say that five years ago the Maori came from Taiwan and now they came from Indonesia? This seems very odd. As Davidson writes (2005b: 46), what we have good grounds to assert can change over time, but what is true remains true: truth cannot be "lost".

It seems that the less uncomfortable horn of this dilemma is to accept that for someone to believe something need not entail that she also believe that it is true. Moreover, we think that Dummett would also choose this horn of the dilemma. One reason why Davidson holds that to believe p is to believe that p is true, say, is his belief in the disquotational principle, that is, that sentences of the form "'p' is true if and only if p" are always true. Recall that Davidson thinks that to know the meaning of a sentence is to know its truth-conditions. Thus, if "p" is a meaningful sentence in one's own language, it has truth-conditions and those truth-conditions are expressed by "p" itself (perhaps among other sentences). For Davidson, the disquotational principle has the status of a necessary *a priori* truth. Thus, suppose that a person believes that p and knows that the content of her belief is expressed by the sentence "p". Moreover, suppose that she knows the disquotational principle. Thus, she also believes that "p" is true.

But Dummett does not accept the disquotational principle. He points out that the disquotational principle leads to paradoxes, such as the liar paradox ("this sentence is false" on the disquotational principle is true if and only if it is false) and he thinks that we can apply the disquotational principle only in certain cases (Dummett 2004: ch. 1).[8] At any rate, Dummett does not hold that the disquotational principle is a necessary or *a priori* truth. Thus, it would seem that Dummett does not have to hold that believing and believing to be true are logically related, as Davidson does. Still, we may admit that it is counterintuitive to drive this wedge between believing and believing to be true. We leave it to the reader to decide how much of a difficulty this is for Dummett's view.

6.7.1 The reality of the past

Let us return to one of the examples used in the previous section. Suppose that the evidence about the place of origin of the Maori people remains inconclusive forever, either because of a lack of compelling evidence, or because new evidence keeps being found that supports new hypotheses. Dummett ([1969] 1978a) claims that in such cases there is no fact of the matter about the past. Thus, it would seem that there is no fact of the matter about the place of origin of the Maori. This seems very counterintuitive.

More recently, Dummett has changed his view. He thinks that this sort of radical anti-realism about the past is "implausible or repugnant" (2004: 70). In accepting facts about the past that we cannot verify, Dummett has modified his position in interesting ways. He says that "the truth of a proposition consists of its being the case that someone suitably placed *could have* verified it" (*ibid.*: 44).

Dummett has always maintained that certain sentences can be true without our being able immediately to verify them. Statements about the future may cause us to wait until the appropriate time to verify them (Dummett 1978a). And Dummett has always held that just because someone asserts a sentence does not mean that she can verify the statement; it might be someone else who can verify it (*ibid.*: 78). We do not need to gather knowledge alone; we have help to do so. We depend on other people – scientists, journalists, our friends and family, philosophy lecturers and so on – to tell us about the world. This collection of people is our "epistemic community". But here Dummett is saying something quite strong. He is claiming that it is not a necessary condition to belong to this epistemic community that someone be alive: "dying does not deprive anyone of the status either of an observer or an informant" (*ibid.*: 68).

Dead people are part of our knowledge-gathering community in the sense that a lot of what we know is transmitted to us from them, in their writing, art and so on. The point, however, is not merely that we now have evidence of the past because of what they left behind, but rather that what they themselves experienced still counts as an act of verification, regardless of whether they have left any evidence of this experience or not.

Thus Dummett holds the view that a statement is true if and only if it could have been verified by someone at some time. So, we can now treat the case of the origin of the Maori people in a more satisfactory manner. There is a matter of fact about where the Maori came from, because someone (namely the ancient Maori themselves) observed where they were before coming to New Zealand. That insufficient evidence remains now to decide this issue conclusively in no way shows that there is no such fact.

6.8 Summarizing Dummett

We realize that Dummett's views are difficult for those first exposed to them, and even for those exposed for the second or third time. So we summarize them here. Dummett holds that to understand a sentence is to know a certain way of determining whether it is true: its canonical means of verification. These processes of verification can be carried out in public, and so meanings are publicly accessible entities. In addition, this verificationism explains how we learn language. We are taught these processes of verification.

In addition, Dummett holds that truth is just verification. A sentence is true at a given time if people have the ability then to verify the sentence. This identification of truth with verification leads Dummett to deny bivalence. Some sentences at a time can be proved neither true nor false, thus at that time they are neither true nor false.

Dummett's original verificationism led him to hold that many statements about the past are neither true nor false, since we no longer have the means to verify or refute them. He has more recently come to reject that view by including past people among "us". Dummett now holds that a statement about the past is true now if and only if someone in the present or in the past could have verified it. Thus, our epistemic community includes people who are now dead.

Further reading

On verificationism in general see Cheryl J. Misak, *Verificationism: Its History and Prospects* (London: Routledge, 1995). Also, James O. Young, *Global Antirealism* (Aldershot: Ashgate, 1995) sets out an interesting version of global anti-realism that combines verificationism with the coherence theory of truth.

On Logical Positivism, A. J. Ayer (ed.), *Logical Positivism* (London: Macmillan, 1959) is a classic collection of work by the Logical Positivists. See also J. Alberto Coffa, *The Semantic Tradition from Kant to Carnap: To the Vienna Station* (Cambridge: Cambridge University Press, 1991) and John Passmore, *A Hundred Years of Philosophy* (Harmondsworth: Penguin, 1968).

On Dummett, see: Mark Q. Gardiner, *Semantic Challenges to Realism: Dummett and Putnam* (Toronto: University of Toronto Press, 2000); Karen Green, *Dummett: Philosophy of Language* (Cambridge: Polity, 2001); Darryl Gunson, *Michael Dummett and the Theory of Meaning* (Aldershot: Ashgate, 1998); Barry Taylor (ed.), *Michael Dummett: Contributions to Philosophy* (The Hague: Nijhoff, 1987); and Bernhard Weiss, *Michael Dummett* (Chesham: Acumen, 2001).

Two clear papers explaining Dummett's anti-realism are Alex Miller, "The Significance of Semantic Realism", *Synthese* **136** (2003), 191–217, and "Realism and Anti-Realism", in *Handbook of the Philosophy of Language*, Ernest Lepore and Barry Smith (eds), 983–1005 (Oxford: Oxford University Press, 2006).

7 Colour

In Part I we discussed whether there is a mind-independent world. Let us assume from here on that there is one. There is still room to debate whether or not *everything* we (apparently) talk about is real. Certainly, there is much controversy, at least in philosophical circles, about the reality of all sorts of things. And in Part II we shall take a close look at a selection of philosophical debates about the reality of a variety of contentious domains. We dedicate a chapter to each debate. While this is not really enough space to do full justice to any of these topics, it will serve as an introduction to each topic. More importantly, though, we hope to illustrate how the very general themes and rhetorical moves talked about in Part I are applied over and over again in each case. As with Part I, further reading is suggested at the end of each chapter for those who want to delve more deeply into a given topic.

With this in mind, there is no better place to start than with a discussion of the philosophy of colour. We have evolved to perceive the colours of objects, and no wonder. Without this ability, we could not see anything at all. It is by virtue of seeing the colours of objects that we can see their contours, edges and shapes. Even visibly transparent objects can be seen only in virtue of seeing and contrasting the colours of other objects in the immediate environment. And so, given that so much of our knowledge of the external world comes via the modality of sight, colour perception must be one of the most important human adaptations, or so it might be thought.

Philosophers and scientists who work in this area are in general agreement that objects appear coloured, and that we base many of our beliefs about the world on those appearances. But they are also in general agreement that it is extremely difficult to fit colours – at least when conceived of as intrinsic properties of objects – into any reasonable metaphysical picture of the world. There is a sharp division on the question as to whether physical objects are really coloured and, if they are, what the nature of these colour properties is. Among the options canvassed in recent years, the most prominent are that the colours of objects are microphysical properties,[1] reflectance properties,[2] the extensions of response-dependent concepts,[3] non-physical properties[4] or nonexistent properties.[5] In order to appreciate the merits of each alternative, though, we must first draw attention to a number of assumptions that will play an important role in what follows.

First, we shall concentrate only on one dimension of colour: hue. We shall all but ignore the other dimensions along which colours may vary, such as saturation and brightness. Moreover, we shall only focus on the colours of surface properties of objects. We shall pay no attention to the colours of after-images, light sources, diffuse objects such as the sky, and volumes such as jelly and wine. These restrictions are meant to simplify our topic, thereby making it a little more tractable. They are not intended to give the misleading impression that the subject matter is simpler than it really is. Indeed, part of our aim is to illustrate how complex these issues really are even after such simplifying assumptions have been made.[6]

Secondly, we assume that visual experiences have propositional contents, that is, these experiences *represent* objects as being a certain way.[7] It is in virtue of this fact that our visual experiences can be said to be either veridical or illusory. We say a visual experience is veridical to the extent that it represents the world accurately. And we say that an appearance is illusory to the extent that it does not. So, for example, when we see a pencil in normal conditions it appears straight. Such experiences are (usually) veridical. When we place it in a glass of water, however, it appears bent. Such experiences are (usually) illusory. And in such circumstances, the content of our experiences comes apart from the content of our beliefs. We see the pencil as bent but do not believe that it is. Likewise, when we see objects in normal daylight, they appear coloured: our visual experience represents the objects as being coloured. This is all relatively uncontroversial. What is controversial is whether or not this experience is veridical, and the extent to which it is.

Finally, we want to re-emphasize that realism about a domain of colours – like any other domain – is a view about colour *properties* and colour *facts*. It is not directly a view about colour concepts. This is important to keep in mind when evaluating the lively philosophical debate about whether colour concepts and categories are universal. C. L. Hardin (1993), for example, believes there are basic colour concepts universal to all societies. J. van Brakel (1993), on the other hand, disagrees. While these philosophical hypotheses – and the cross-cultural studies that support them – are interesting and informative in their own right, we must guard against drawing the wrong conclusions from them. Barry Maund (2002), for example, claims that van Brakel's theory implies that "colors are socially or culturally constructed properties". But to our minds, this is a mistake. At best, van Brakel's views lend support to the idea that our *concepts*, but *not* the properties picked out by them, are socially constructed. We are sympathetic to the view that colour concepts are socially constructed (whether or not they are universal). If we have a choice about how we conceptualize the world, then perhaps *every* concept is socially constructed. But such a view is tangential to the realism debate. It is one thing to construct our concepts; it is quite another to construct the properties that fall under them.

7.1 Error theory

Error theories claim that all except the *cognoscenti* are guilty of making a systematic and widespread mistake about the nature of colour properties, and about whether material objects have such properties. And the reason we make this mistake, it is maintained, is because we are falling victim to a perceptual illusion, like the one we experience when we place a straight pencil in water and it looks bent to us. In both the colour case and the pencil case, our perceptual experience *misrepresents* the world. Unlike the pencil in water, though, it is not so easy to uncover the illusory nature of our colour experience. So we continue to believe that objects are coloured when in reality they are not.

Error theories of this kind extend back as far as the ancient Greeks. Democritus, for example, claimed that there are no colours and we are all mistaken for thinking there are. He famously stated his position thus: "by convention colour, but in reality only atoms and void".[8] And his argument can be reconstructed as follows:

(P1) All physical objects are composed of nothing but atoms.
(P2) No atoms are coloured.
(C) Therefore, no physical objects have colours.

Arguments of this kind are seductive. Both of the premises seem true. All material objects are composed of atoms (albeit not as Democritus conceived of them). Atoms are invisible to the naked eye, and so (it is commonly thought) they are not coloured. Nonetheless, the argument is fallacious. In order to make the argument valid, a tacit premise must be added. Let us call this premise "Compositionality". It might be stated thus:

> *Compositionality*: No object has a property that none of its proper parts have (for some way of carving the object into parts).

But Compositionality is clearly false. It is not hard to think of counter-examples to it. You might be six feet tall and weigh 70 kilograms. But if we think of you as composed of two legs, two arms, a torso, a neck and a head, then none of your parts have any of these properties; they are properties of the whole and not the parts.

Nonetheless, it might be thought that Compositionality can be modified to capture a truth that, when added to the Democritean argument, will make it valid. One natural development of this thought involves distinguishing between *determinate* and *determinable* properties. Having a determinable property is roughly to have a property that can be exemplified in many different determinate ways. Thus, having a weight and having a height are determinable properties. Having the height six feet and the weight 70 kilograms are determinate properties. Likewise, having a colour is a determinable property, while being the colour blue is a determinate property. The modified principle, then, might read:

> *Compositionality**: No object has a *determinable* property that none of its proper parts have (for some way of carving the object into parts).

This modified principle is more plausible than the original. The counter-examples to our original principle are *not* counter-examples to Compositionality*. Moreover, when we include it as a premise in the Democritean argument, the argument becomes valid.

Nonetheless, Compositionality* too is a controversial thesis. And Zeno of Elea, another ancient Greek philosopher, illustrates strikingly where its acceptance leads: no object could make a sound when dropped, because atoms do not make a sound when dropped (cf. Zeno's paradox of the grain of millet); nothing could be in motion throughout a period, because nothing is in motion during any instant of the period (cf. Zeno's paradox of the arrow); and nothing could be extended, because mathematical points are extensionless (cf. Zeno's paradoxes of plurality). We would do better to reject Compositionality* than to accept consequences such as these.

There is, however, a more impressive argument for embracing an error theory. The argument gained popularity during the Enlightenment with great thinkers such as Descartes, Galileo, Newton, Locke and Boyle, and is still influential to this day. The argument might be stated thus.

(P1) Colours are superfluous to our explanatory needs.
(P2) If colours are superfluous to our explanatory needs, then there are no colours.
(C) Therefore, there are no colours

The argument is an application of the argument from parsimony introduced in Chapter 2.[9] (P2) is an instance of Ockham's razor, and (P1) is plausible in its own right. Our best scientific theories do not talk about colour properties. Physics, along with the biological and psychological sciences, give a very satisfying causal explanation of everything colours might reasonably be thought to help explain. In particular, science gives us an explanation of colour experience without invoking the colours of objects in the causal story. Very roughly, the idea is as follows. In the retina of our eyes, there are two different kinds of photoreceptors: rods and cones. The cones are responsible for our experience of colour. There are three different kinds of cones, each primarily responsive to lights of different wavelengths: long, medium and short wavelengths. As light is reflected off objects and into our eyes, the cones convert this light into a neural signal. Colour vision is based on the neural outputs of the cones. Light with a short wavelength will be experienced as blue, light with a medium wavelength will be experienced as green and light with a long wavelength will be experienced as red. The story is, of course, much more complicated than we make it out to be here.[10] But the point emphasized by error theorists is that even when the theory is filled out with all its bells and whistles, there is simply no reference to the colours of objects. And so, given that we all believe that the physical world is coloured, to that extent we are guilty of making a widespread and systematic mistake.

This justification for (P2) will not, however, do as it stands, for it is still an open question as to whether it is possible to give some sort of reductive analysis of colours in terms of properties physicists do countenance. If it is possible to pull this off, colour realism will be vindicated, for reduced properties are not superfluous properties. In the next section, we consider and evaluate two different kinds of physicalist reductions that have been proposed in the philosophical literature. Before embarking on this project, though, it is important to point out that contemporary error theorists recognize that reductive realism is an option to be reckoned with on the philosophical landscape. It is just that they think the reductive project simply cannot work in this domain, for our concept of colour (and its cognates), it is thought, is inconsistent with this kind of analysis. We shall consider why in §7.2.

If error theorists are right, and most of us are mistaken about the nature of colour properties, what should our response be in light of this discovery? Some philosophers advocate that we become revisionary realists. Even if nothing fits our current colour concepts perfectly, we can look for intrinsic properties of objects that imperfectly match them. And, so long as those properties fit our theoretical needs well enough, we should keep our colour categories but revise our way of conceptualizing them (cf. Lewis 1997). Alternatively, we might be better served by identifying colour concepts with dispositional concepts: concepts of looking a certain way to perceivers in certain contexts. Such a proposal would be anti-realist in so far as it suggests that colours are the extensions of response-dependent concepts (cf. Johnston 1992). Or one might become a fictionalist (of either stripe) about colour talk, suggesting that it might well be useful to continue thinking and talking about colours "for the purposes of describing objects in public discourse" (Boghossian & Velleman 1989: 84), even after realizing that in reality there are no such properties. Or, finally, one might be a colour eliminativist, suggesting that our mistake is so pernicious that we would be better off ridding the vernacular of colour terms altogether. This final proposal, though, is a position of absolute last resort. It would require that we not only uncover a mistake in the various realist alternatives, but that we also reveal a problem associated with all other revisionist proposals. Could our error be that deep? Let us see.

7.2 Physicalism

Recall that physicalism is the view that all properties can be reduced to physical properties, where a physical property is simply a property investigated by those in the physical sciences. All physicalists suggest that there is a correlation between the colours of objects and our experience of them as coloured. But the connection between the two is not conceptual. The connection is instead nomic. According to the physicalist, colours are to be identified with the physical properties that *cause* our colour experience.[11]

What might these physical properties be? Many physicalists have suggested, in response to this question, that colours are microphysical properties of objects: the ones that cause our colour experiences (cf. Smart 1975; Jackson & Pargetter 1987). Let us call this view "microphysicalism" about colours. Many philosophers have had qualms about the prospects of this variety of physicalism, for the microphysical properties responsible for our colour experiences are many and varied. For any hue we choose to consider, there is an extraordinary variety of very different microphysical properties associated with it, each with the potential to cause the same kind of (colour) experience in human observers. And so, as Smart observes, it is a consequence of this variety of physicalism that colours are "highly disjunctive and idiosyncratic properties of the surfaces of objects" (1975: 60).

An alternative version of physicalism identifies the colours with special kinds of dispositional properties: the dispositions to reflect proportions of light at a range of wavelengths. Spectral reflectance dispositions are physical properties of surfaces just as the micro-physical properties are. And two surfaces that share a disposition of this kind will look the same to normal observers if observed in the same lighting conditions. Let us call this view "reflectance physicalism".

Because many different kinds of microphysical properties will have the same spectral reflectance disposition, many are initially tempted to think that reflectance physicalism can dodge the multiple realizability problem. But can it really? The short answer is "No". Physical science has taught us about the existence of metamers. Metamers are pairs of objects that differ in their spectral reflectance dispositions but that cause the same colour experience (in at least one set of viewing conditions). Because metamers are not uncommon, reflectance physicalism faces the same multiple realizability problem as microphysicalism. How might the physicalist respond to the multiple realizability problem? Two responses are possible.

- *Response 1.* The physicalist might suggest that colour properties are disjunctive properties. Disjunctive properties might not be natural properties (in so far as they do not "carve nature at its joints"), but they are physical properties. To illustrate, consider the property of being composed of *jade*. Jade, once thought to be a natural property, turns out to be a disjunctive property: the property of being composed of either jadeite or nephrite. Likewise, the physicalist might suggest that with the help of science we have discovered that colours, once thought to be natural properties, are in fact disjunctions of different microphysical or reflectance properties (cf. e.g. Smart 1975).
- *Response 2.* Alternatively, the physicalist might suggest that the fact that there are different kinds of physical property that cause the same appearance in normal observers is the discovery that there are indistinguishable colours. We know already that there can be two different colours that are indistinguishable *to the colour blind*. Maybe the lesson to be drawn from the discovery of metamers is that all of us are colour blind in a different way (cf. e.g. Lewis 1997).

Neither reply is unreasonable, so we leave it up to the reader to decide which response is to be preferred. There is, however, a much more serious cluster of related problems for the physicalist.[12] The first might be expressed as follows.

(P1) Normal perceivers can (in normal daylight) see the colours of objects.
(P2) Normal perceivers cannot (in normal daylight) see the microphysical or reflectance properties of objects.
(C) Therefore, physicalism is false.

Boghosian and Velleman (1991) call this the "naive objection" to physicalism, because it is the first objection that is likely to come to mind when presented with either version of colour physicalism. But despite its naivety, the argument is a stumbling block for all colour physicalists. Any realist about the colours should accept (P1). And (P2) should be uncontroversial. Microphysical properties are invisible to the naked eye in normal conditions. They can only be observed with the aid of a microscope, or some other scientific instrument. And dispositional properties cannot be observed at all. They are merely inferred.

It seems to us that the physicalist can respond in one of two ways. The first response points out that the argument presupposes that microphysicalism and reflectance physicalism exhaust the possibilities for a physical reduction of colour properties. And that has yet to be established. The physicalist, however, is unlikely to press this objection, because the onus will be on her to come up with an alternative. And as far as we are aware, there are no physicalist alternatives that are in a better position to dodge this kind of objection than microphysicalism or reflectance physicalism.

The second response is more impressive. It might be pointed out that the argument has the classic form of an attitude problem. And, like all attitude problems, it is vulnerable to the same kind of objection. In this case, a physicalist may respond that (P2) of the argument is false.[13] If the colours just are microphysical or reflectance properties of surfaces, then by seeing the colours of objects you are *thereby* seeing the microphysical or reflectance properties of those objects. After all, when Lois sees Clark, she also sees Superman – even if she does not see him under the guise of Superman – because Clark is identical to Superman. And when you see the water in the glass, you see the H_2O in the glass, even if you are not aware of the fact that water is H_2O. If you can substitute synonyms in these cases, and preserve the truth of what is said, you should also be able to do the same in the colour case.

Problem solved? Not quite. The success of this response rests on the idea that "seeing" contexts are transparent contexts. But we can give this attitude problem a new twist simply by recasting it in terms of the knowledge we gain on the basis of this experience. Consider the following.

(P1) Normal perceivers can know the colour of an object on the basis of their visual experience of that object (in normal daylight).

(P2) Normal perceivers cannot know the microphysical or reflectance properties of an object on the basis of their visual experience of that object (in normal daylight).

(C) Therefore, physicalism is false.

Let us call this new argument the "sophisticated argument". The physicalist is unlikely to want to object to (P2) of the sophisticated argument, for knowledge contexts, unlike perceptual contexts, are opaque contexts. Lois sees Superman in front of her, but she does not know that he is there because he is in disguise. You might see the H_2O in front of you but not know that there is H_2O in front of you, because you have not learnt the relevant chemistry yet. Likewise, you might see the colour of an object, and thereby see its microphysical and reflectance qualities, but not know that there is an object with those microphysical and reflectance properties before you. Such observations, though, suggest a different response open to the physicalist. Rather than deny (P2), perhaps she can embrace it along with (P1), and suggest that the two premises are consistent with physicalism; if that is right, the argument is invalid.

Strictly speaking, of course, the physicalist is right: the argument is invalid. But there is still a problem in the offing that must be grappled with. In order for the physicalist's response to succeed, she must commit herself to the hypothesis that the essential nature of colour properties cannot be known merely on the basis of experience. According to the physicalist, unearthing the essential nature of the colours is a matter of scientific *a posteriori* discovery. And while such a supposition is plausible in the case of water and H_2O, it leads to trouble in the colour case. Following Johnston (1992), let us call the thesis about colours denied by physicalism "perceptual availability". This thesis has been articulated by philosophers as follows:

> So far as concerns knowledge of the colour itself, as opposed to knowledge of [inessential] truths about it, I know the colour perfectly and completely when I see it and no further knowledge of it is even theoretically possible.   (Russell 1912: 47)

> Justified belief about the canary yellowness of external things is available simply on the basis of visual perception. That is, if external things are canary yellow we are justified in believing this just on the basis of visual perception.
> (Johnston 1992: 222)

Perceptual availability is a thesis about what we can know on the basis of our visual experience of the colours. For those sympathetic to the view that not all cases of knowledge and justified belief involve inferences from other beliefs, beliefs about the colours will provide a paradigm to illustrate the idea. According to this view, merely by *seeing* the colours, we can *know* about the essential nature of them. No inference is required; our knowledge is direct. But perceptual availability need not be wedded to such an epistemological position. Perhaps knowledge and justified belief about the colours requires that we be in possession of – and make inferences from – some background beliefs about the colours and their relations to our perceptions. Perceptual availability tells us that if such beliefs are required, then they will be trivial beliefs that no one could reasonably lack.

Perceptual availability tells us only that we can have knowledge about the *essential nature* of the colours on the basis of our perceptual experiences. It does not imply that we can know everything about the colour on the basis of that experience. We cannot know merely by seeing a red tomato, for example, that red is also the colour of a tamarillo, that red capes provoke anger in bulls,[14] or that red is the colour Stu and Ed are thinking about most often as they write this book. So what exactly is the essential nature of the colours that we know on the basis of experience? That is a very tricky question to answer. But whatever the right answer is, if a physical-ist reduction of colour properties is possible, this fact will be part of the colours essential nature. And so, it follows that perceptual availability would make the sophisticated argument valid if it were added as a premise.

How central is perceptual availability to our beliefs about the colours? Clearly, Johnston and Russell take the thesis to be at the core of our beliefs about the colours, approaching the status of an analytic truth. Certainly to deny it, as the physicalist does, must count as a cost to the theory. And the cost, to our minds, is a con-siderable one indeed. To see why, consider the following platitudes about the colours:[15]

1. Orange is more similar to red than it is to blue.
2. Orange is not one of the unique hues; it is a blend of red and yellow.
3. Orange and blue are the same kind of property – they are dif-ferent determinants of the same determinable.

Perceptual availability implies that we can know propositions 1–3 on the basis of our visual acquaintance with orange, red, blue and yellow. And that seems right. But the physicalist must deny it. At best these three "hypotheses" will be confirmed by further empiri-cal investigation. At worst we might discover – by *a posteriori* means – that they are false. To the extent that you find this physicalist commitment implausible, you will be motivated to look elsewhere for an account of the colours.

7.3 Response-dependence

Advocates of a response-dependent theory[16] urge that colours are dispositional properties. But they are not dispositions to reflect light. Instead they are *dispositions to cause colour sensations in normal human perceivers in standard conditions*. According to this view, then, colours are the properties picked out by a special class of response-dependent concepts. And so a tight conceptual connection – not merely a causal connection – is postulated to hold between the colours of objects and our experiences of them. The response-dependent theorist thus hopes to capture the grain of truth in more radical subjective theories. But unlike extreme subjectivists, she claims that the colours of objects do not depend metaphysically on us; they would continue to exist even if human beings did not.

More importantly, though, the response-dependent theorist about colours hopes to gain all of the advantages of colour physicalism, without succumbing to the problems associated with that view. Those who embrace a response-dependent account emphasize the fact that perceptual availability is consistent with it. Normal perceivers can have knowledge about the essential nature of the colours on the basis of their perceptual experiences, because colours are essentially dispositions, and perceptual experiences are the manifestations of these dispositions. Furthermore, one can know, for example, that orange is more similar to red than it is to blue on the basis of the similarity relations that hold between our experiences of blue, red and orange things. Finally, response-dependent theorists do not face the multiple realizability problem, for there is a single and readily identifiable dispositional property that unifies everything of the same colour.

The prospects of a response-dependent theory of the colours, then, look good, at least at first. But a full evaluation of the view must be postponed until the details of the theory are fleshed out, and different philosophers will flesh them out differently. To see how important a more complete characterization of the theory is, consider how the response-dependent theorist might analyse the concept of redness. She will say that something like the following biconditional is *a priori*:

> *Redness*: x is red if and only if x has the disposition to look red to normal human beings in standard conditions.

The response-dependent theorist must now answer the following questions. What is a *normal* human being? And what are *standard* conditions? Many different answers are possible. But an adequate answer must specify a class of perceivers and a set of environmental conditions that gets the extension of the concept right. And as Hardin (1993) demonstrates, this is not easy to do in a substantive non-trivial way (cf. Hardin 1988: 67ff.). It will not do, for example, to specify that the object in question be viewed under the mid-day sun, for what colour is the moon or the stars on this account?

Next, the response-dependent theorist must specify what it is for something to "look red". Such a specification is not necessary simply because of the threat of circularity in the analysis. Certainly, the analysis does seem circular – the term "red" appears on both sides of the biconditional – but circularity can in some circumstances be virtuous (or at least harmless) if the analysis contributes to our understanding of the term. The worry is that in this case the analysis does not obviously make such a contribution, for we do not have an independent grip on what it is for an object to have a second-order disposition to look as though it has a disposition to look red. Presumably this is not what is meant by the phrase "looks red", but the onus is now on the response-dependent theorist to tell us something more about what is meant.[17]

Finally, the response-dependent theorist must explain what it is for something to have a disposition of the relevant kind. Here it is important to see that a simple counterfactual account of dispositions will not work. The reason can be illustrated vividly with the following example. Imagine a chameleon. The chameleon is green, and so, suitably construed, has the disposition to look green in standard conditions. But suppose also that (i) the chameleon's beliefs about whether or not it is in standard viewing conditions are extremely reliable, and (ii) the chameleon is so shy that it blushes bright red whenever it believes it is in standard viewing conditions. The chameleon, therefore, would not look green if it were put in standard viewing conditions.[18] None of these considerations are meant to be serious objections to response-dependent views of colour. But they are meant to put pressure on the response-dependent theorist to fill in the missing details.

However the account is developed, though, it will face two problems. First, it is inconsistent with the truism that colours *cause* perceivers to have colour experiences, for dispositions are not causes of their manifestations. To say that something has a disposition is to say that *something else* – its causal basis – will cause its manifestation. Fragile objects are disposed to shatter when dropped. But the fragility does not cause the shattering when such an object does shatter. Instead, it is the dropping, in conjunction with facts about the object's categorical nature, that cause the shattering. To say that the object was fragile is just to say that these *other things* – the dropping and the categorical base – would cause the shattering.

And if that is right, colours could not be dispositional properties of objects. They must instead be intrinsic properties of objects that can play a role in causing our sensations of them.[19]

Secondly, the response-dependent theory is inconsistent with another central intuition about the colours. The intuition Johnston calls "revelation" is rather difficult to articulate, but here is how some philosophers have attempted to express it.

> Colour words are words for properties which are of such a kind that their whole and essential nature as properties can be and is fully revealed in sensory-quality experience given only the qualitative character that that experience has.
> (Strawson 1989: 224)

> The intrinsic nature of canary yellow [and by analogy with any other colour shade] is fully revealed by a standard visual experience of a canary yellow thing.   (Johnston 1992: 223)

> To understand ascriptions of colour, one [need only have an] … experience of colour … The character of the property is … transparent to this way of grasping it.   (Campbell 1993: 258–9)

Revelation is a thesis about how much is represented in visual experience. It is not a claim to the effect that our perceptions of colour are veridical. Nor is it a claim about what we are justified in believing on the basis of such experiences. It says simply that our visual experiences of colour are complete in so far as they represent everything essential in the nature of the colours. How central is revelation to our beliefs about the colours? Each of the philosophers quoted above take revelation to be at the core of our beliefs about the colours, approaching the status of an analytic truth. But at the same time, it should be fairly obvious that response-dependent theories cannot accommodate the truth of revelation. Dispositions are not the sorts of things one can see directly, for dispositions are modal properties, and modal properties can at best be inferred from their manifestations (cf. Chapter 11).

This last objection, then, spells real trouble for the response-dependent theorist. We shall not presume to respond directly to the objection on behalf of the response-dependent theorist, but it is worth noting that she does have an indirect *tu quoque* response available to her. For if dispositional properties are not uncovered in experience, reflectance properties are not either, for they are equally dispositional properties (albeit not dispositions to produce psychological manifestations). Moreover, presumably the microphysical properties of objects are not revealed in experience either, and this is why microphysicalism has such trouble accommodating perceptual availability. And so, if the physicalist and the response-dependent theorist can join forces to stave off the threat of eliminativism, they can fight among themselves over which theory better accounts for our intuitions about the colours, so long as there is no other theory on the horizon that promises a better account of our revelatory intuitions.

7.4 Non-reductive realism

A natural response, in light of the difficulties that confront the other theories of the colours, is to propose that colour is a *sui generis* property, not reducible to other physical properties and not reducible to a disposition to appear a certain way. According to this view, colours are simple, real and intrinsic properties of objects. Let us call such a view "non-reductive realism".[20] Such a view is a natural one; perhaps it is the common-sense notion.

Non-reductive colour realism is plausibly matched with the thesis that the colours of objects are fully revealed to us in experience. That is, revelation is consistent with non-reductive realism. Likewise, the view is naturally coupled with perceptual availability. Because the colours really are the way they appear to us, our experiences of them can act as the foundation for our knowledge about them. And because the colours really are the way they appear to be, the apparent similarities between the colours are genuine similarities. Such advantages make the view seem so attractive that it is surprising that it does not have more proponents. (Despite its increasing popularity, it is still a minority view.) What could explain this fact?

One explanation is this. Non-reductive realists are forced to say that the colours are not physical properties, for those in the sciences are not explicitly committed to the colours, and the position denies that any sort of reduction is possible. Many philosophers, of a naturalistic bent, are disinclined to admit such "weird, bizarre and spooky" kinds of properties into their ontology. But this is not the only reason non-reductivism is unpopular. There is a more substantial objection often mounted against the view.

Recall that one objection against response-dependent theories was that such theories could not account for the obvious truism that colours are the causes of our colour experience. Physicalism could account for this fact; indeed, it is the main virtue of the account. But can the non-reductive realist account for it any better than the response-dependent theorist? It is often contended that she cannot; in fact, she does much worse. Consider Hardin's indictment of Cornman's theory. After suggesting that Cornman is a non-reductive realist, Hardin writes:

> Either the colors that Cornman supposes to attach to physical objects (call them *Cornman colors*, or *C-colors* for short) are causally connected to other physical properties of those objects or they are not so connected. Suppose that they are, and that C-colors have physical effects. Then one ought to be able to test for their presense or absence by physical means, and a physical theory that made no reference to them would be incomplete. But Cornman makes no claim to be remedying a deficiency in existing physical theories. So it seems that we must take C-colors either to be free of causal relations to an object's physical properties or else to be epiphenomena of some of them. In neither case will C-colors play a role in determining what wavelengths of light are emitted or reflected from or transmitted throughout the surface of a physical object.
>
> (Hardin 1993: 61)

Hardin is impressed by the current science of colour vision. As was noted in §7.2, physics, psychology and biology give a very rich and complete explanation of our experience of colour in terms of an object's microphysical and reflectance properties. But the non-reductive realist tells us that the colours are not reducible to such physical properties of objects. So the colours cannot be the causes of our colour experiences. The adherent of this view, therefore, cannot accept the causal truism.

If Hardin is right here, the case against the non-reductive realist is very strong indeed. Colours, it seems, really are superfluous

112 REALISM AND ANTI-REALISM

entities; they do no explaining at all. According to Ockham's razor, superfluous entities are nonexistent entities, so there are no colours. This, of course, is the argument from parsimony, and so we have come full circle. Recall that error theorists posed the argument, and we attempted to dodge it by looking for a reduction of the colours to properties that science is prepared to countenance. All such reductions led to trouble, so we were led to non-reductive realism. But this position is really the main target of the original objection.

Can the non-reductive realist avoid Hardin's charge? Many different adherents of the view – in their own distinctive way – have struggled to do just that. But here we leave it to the reader to investigate further, and evaluate the alternative proposals for him or herself.

Further reading
For those interested in books or collections devoted to the issue of colour realism, we recommend: Justin Broakes, *What is Colour?* (London: Routledge, forthcoming); Alex Byrne and David Hilbert, *Readings on Color, volume I: The Philosophy of Color* (Cambridge, MA: MIT Press, 1997); Alex Byrne and David Hilbert, *Readings on Color, volume II: The Science of Color* (Cambridge, MA: MIT Press, 1997); Alex Byrne and David Hilbert, "Color Realism and Color Science", *Behavioral and Brain Sciences* 26 (2003), 3–21 (commentaries and responses appear in the same issue, 22–64, 785–94); C. L. Hardin, *Color for Philosophers: Unweaving the Rainbow* (Indianapolis, IN: Hackett, 1993); Barry Maund, *Colors: Their Nature and Representation* (Cambridge: Cambridge University Press, 1995); and Joseph Tolliver (ed.), *Papers on Colour*, special issue of *Philosophical Studies* 68(3) (1992).

8 Morality

8.1 The problem of moral facts and moral properties

A moral fact is a fact such as *Don is bad*, *Helen is good* or *Stu ought to buy Ed a new house*. These facts do not just describe the world, they are normative: they tell us what someone should do. Telling us that Don is (morally) bad tells us that we should not act like Don. We characterize as moral realists those who believe (i) that there are moral facts, (ii) that the same facts are moral facts for everyone, and (iii) that what determines which facts are moral facts is *opinion-independent*. Moral facts themselves may not be mind-independent. Many moral facts may be about human minds, for example, about whether individuals have good intentions. But what makes them moral facts, according to realists, is independent of what anyone thinks is morally good or bad, that is, they are moral facts independently of anyone's moral opinions.

Before we go on to discuss particular positions in the debate over moral realism, we need to distinguish carefully between the debate over the *objectivity* of moral claims and moral realism. Moral objectivists claim that the same set of moral rules hold for everyone. Moral realists are moral objectivists, and some use moral realism as a way of defending moral objectivity. But, as we shall see, some moral anti-realists also support moral objectivity. Thus realism about morality is a sufficient condition for being a moral objectivist, but it is not a necessary condition.

8.2 Non-reductive realism

The usual distinction that metaethicists make when discussing varieties of realism is between ethical naturalism and non-naturalism. Naturalists hold that ethical properties are natural properties. But how to distinguish between natural and non-natural properties is itself controversial. G. E. Moore's version of the distinction is to hold that natural properties are those that are the "subject of the natural sciences and also of psychology" (1903: 40).[1] For example, if we define what is good as what promotes happiness, then we have (at least in part) a naturalistic ethics, for happiness is a psychological property and what promotes it can be explained by psychologists in terms of natural facts.

Other philosophers, such as Charles Pigden, hold that non-naturalism is the view that moral properties cannot be reduced to other sorts of properties (1993: 421f.). As Michael Ridge (2003) points out, this version of the distinction is problematic, since there may be what we would normally call natural properties that cannot be reduced to other sorts of properties.

But we can see what Pigden is getting at, and the difference between his version of the distinction and Moore's is important. Consider, for example, divine command theory, which holds that good actions are those that God tells us to do. On Moore's view, this is a form of non-naturalism, for *being an action commanded by God* is not a property that we find in any natural science or psychology. On Pigden's view, divine command theory is a form of naturalism. Here, Pigden is attempting to represent a line of reasoning originally given by Hume. Hume famously claimed that divine command theory is guilty of a fallacy: that it attempts to derive what ought to be the case from what merely is the case. Hume claimed inferences from what is the case to what ought to be the case are always problematic (*Treatise*: bk III, pt I, §I). On Pigden's view, naturalism is just the view that we can derive what ought to be the case from what is the case, because what ought to be case can be reduced to what is the case.

These ways of making the distinction between naturalism and non-naturalism have polemical agendas built into them. As we just said, Pigden's version of the distinction is meant to capture the distinction between those who think that we can derive ought from is and those who think that we cannot. Moore's distinction captures the difference between those who think that ethics is a natural or social science and those who think that it is not. For our purposes, Pigden's version of the distinction is more interesting. We want to examine the view that there is a class of properties and facts that have their normative properties built into them and these properties and facts cannot be reduced to other sorts of properties and facts. We do not, however, think that Moore's distinction (or any other version of the distinction) is illegitimate. Thus, to avoid confusion, instead of distinguishing between naturalism and non-naturalism, we call the two sides of the debate "reductivism" and "non-reductivism". Also, to have a more neutral term than "natural property", we shall use "descriptive property".

The most extreme form of non-reductivism is Platonism. According to Platonism, there are concepts or forms that exist outside space and time. Some of these concepts, such as the form of the Good and the form of Justice are moral concepts. Giving concepts this status makes them opinion independent in a very strong sense. One problem for Platonism is metaphysical: it seems rather extravagant to postulate a realm of entities outside space and time. Thus, there is pressure from Ockham's razor (see §2.2.1) to eliminate this realm of objects if possible. Another problem is epistemological. We have no sense organs to detect things outside the spatiotemporal world. Thus, it is difficult to understand how we can know what good is, what justice is and so on.[2]

Less extravagant forms of non-reductivism are put forward by Moore and W. D. Ross. They hold that we do not have sensory experience of moral properties, but we have an *intuitive grasp* of the moral properties that actual or hypothetical events have or will have. This power of moral intuition is rather like the power to intuit truths about mathematical objects postulated by Kurt Gödel (see §10.2). The need to postulate a moral sense in addition to our normal senses is a serious difficulty for the non-reductivist.[3] In addition, those philosophers who postulate moral intuition also need to show that this intuition is reliable: that it usually tells the truth about moral properties. Otherwise we have no reason to rely on it as a moral guide. The rather mysterious nature of this intuition makes this further explanation rather difficult.

There is another influential argument against non-reductivism: the argument from supervenience.[4] The following principle is called a supervenience principle: "If two possible worlds have the same descriptive properties they have exactly the same moral properties". Because moral properties have this relationship to descriptive properties, moral properties are said to *supervene* on descriptive properties.[5]

Reductivists clearly support the principle of supervenience, but so do most non-reductivists. The supervenience principle can be motivated by performing the following thought experiment. Choose an action you think is bad. Now describe the action, the situation in which it occurs, the people who did it (and their beliefs, desires and so on), its consequences and so on, as much as you like without using any moral language (so leave out your evaluation of the action – include only your description of it). Now consider an action that takes place in another possible world but satisfies all these descriptions. Is this action bad? Most people (everyone we have asked) answer that the action in the other possible world is to be evaluated in exactly the same way as the action in this world. The supervenience principle just generalizes this thought experiment.

The non-reductivist holds that no moral property is identical to any descriptive property or any conglomeration of descriptive properties. If we accept the supervenience principle, we have good reason to ask the non-reductivist the following question: if moral properties are distinct from descriptive properties, why do the same moral properties occur in cases in worlds in which the conglomeration of descriptive properties is the same? It would seem that, for the non-naturalist, moral properties are independent of descriptive properties. Thus, it would seem that a given moral property could occur in conjunction with any possible collection of descriptive properties. This is not to say that this problem is insurmountable for the non-reductivist; we only think that the plausibility of the supervenience principle puts the onus on the non-reductivist to provide us with more theory.

Thus we have three arguments against non-reductivism:

- Non-reductivism is ontologically extravagant. It postulates an odd sort of property that seems unconnected with the natural world.
- Non-reductivism is epistemologically difficult. It postulates the existence of some sort of mysterious means by which we know about these moral properties.

- Non-reductivists have difficulty explaining why moral properties supervene on descriptive properties.

8.3 Reductive realism

There are various sorts of reductive realisms about ethics. We have already mentioned two. First, J. S. Mill defines a good action as one that tends to bring about the most happiness. Secondly, divine command theory defines an action as good as one that God tells us to do.[6] Moore's famous "open question argument" is an attitude problem (in the sense of §2.2) directed against every sort of reductive realism. Consider the question "Are all bachelors unmarried?". If you understand the meaning of the word "bachelor" you will know the answer to this question. This question contrasts with "Are all bachelors happy?". This second question is substantive: knowledge of our language alone will not answer it. Now consider any attempted definition of the word "good", for example, "what is good is what tends to produce the most happiness", "what is good is what God tells us to do" and so on. Now we ask "Is X good?", where X is any one of the supposed definitions of "good". If this question seems to be substantive – a mere knowledge of our language cannot answer it – then X cannot be used to define "good". Thus, Moore claims, no reductive "definition" of "good" is a real definition.

Some reductive realists concede that there is no *a priori* definition of "good" in terms of the properties to which they want to reduce goodness. But they maintain that this does not prevent goodness from being identical to some descriptive property. Consider the fact that water is H_2O. The question "Is water made up of hydrogen and oxygen?" is a substantive question (or at least it was until this became part of elementary chemistry). Yet this does not alter the fact that water is identical to H_2O. Richard Boyd calls the statement "water is H_2O" a "natural definition". He thinks that the word "good" can also be given a natural definition (Boyd 1988).

Boyd's idea is to use the causal theory of reference (see Chapters 5 and 6) to explain how "good" gets its natural definition. We use "good" to denote specific actions and from this the word comes to refer to a kind of action, just as our pointing at samples of water in cups, lakes, rivers and so on, makes water define H_2O. There is a causal link between our use of the word "good" and certain actions, that is, the actions that we consider to be good. This causal link is not something internal to our own minds, and so we do not know *a priori* which natural kind is denoted by "good". Rather, determining the nature of goodness is an empirical matter.[7]

8.4 Arguments against realism

8.4.1 The argument from relativity

This argument (also an attitude problem of sorts) has been put forward by John Mackie (1977: 36–8). The argument is quite simple:

(P1) If moral facts were determined independently of individuals' opinions, then we would expect convergence in the moral facts accepted by people from different societies and cultures.

(P2) There are many important differences between people of different societies and cultures in terms of their moral principles. (empirical fact)

(C1) Therefore, realism supports an expectation that is not borne out by the empirical facts.

(C2) Therefore, we should reject moral realism.

The first premise is clearly the most controversial. At first glance it may seem quite false. There may be objective scientific facts, but we would not expect different societies to have the same access to these facts. Some may be more technologically advanced than others and have better testing equipment, and so on. But there may not be a close analogy between scientific facts and moral facts. Scientific facts may concern things that happened long ago or happen at very large or very small scales. It is less clear how moral facts can be hidden from ordinary view in this way.

8.4.2 The parsimony argument

Here we shall look at Gilbert Harman's argument against the existence of moral facts. This is an argument from parsimony in the sense of §2.2.1. Harman argues first that there is no good reason to postulate moral facts and that the fact that there is no good reason to postulate them is a good reason to reject moral facts. On Harman's view, we are only justified in inferring entities and facts that are not observable if our best available theories used to explain observable phenomena appeal to such facts or entities (Harman 1977). In other words, Harman thinks that the only reason we should believe in what is beyond our experience is that we have an abductive argument for doing so.

Are there any observed phenomena that are best explained by an appeal to moral facts? Harman considers an example of a person feeling revulsion at the sight of some children burning a cat. In explaining the phenomena it would seem that we could appeal to the moral fact that the children's act is wrong or we could appeal to social facts about the observer's background that make no use of moral facts. If we take the latter course, we could appeal to facts about how the observer was raised, what her parents taught her as a child about harming animals, her own attachment to her pets and so on. According to Harman, the latter explanation is better. It postulates a clear casual connection between the observer's upbringing and her attitudes and between those attitudes and her reaction to the burning of the cat. The use of moral facts, according to Harman, is superfluous. Saying that the burning of the cat was wrong plays no essential causal role in the explanation of the reaction of the observer. Thus Harman thinks that we should not appeal to moral facts in this case, nor does he think that there are any other observable phenomena that require moral facts in their explanation (*ibid.*: ch. 1).

Here is Harman's argument generalized:

(P1) All observed phenomena for which we have explanations, can be given explanations by theories that do not appeal to moral facts.   (empirical fact)

(P2) Any theory that does not make use of moral facts provides, all other things being equal, a better explanation than a theory that appeal to a special class of moral facts.

(P3) We should accept only theories that explain observed phenomena.

(P4) We should accept only the best available theories.

(C) Therefore, all other things being equal, we should not accept a theory that appeals to moral facts.

Clearly the realist can take issue with (P3). One might hold that there are intuitive criteria that our metaethics should satisfy. For example, one might hold that our metaethics should do as little violence as possible to our pre-theoretic intuitions about morality. Similarly, the realist may also reject the second premise, which says that theories that do not postulate moral facts are thereby better than theories that do postulate moral facts. We talk, and perhaps think, as if there are moral facts. Thus, one might argue that theories that admit moral facts, in some cases, are better than those that eschew moral facts. It may be that theories that reject moral facts are simpler than theories that postulate them, but simplicity is only one theoretical virtue. Intuitiveness is another. If a theory that postulates moral facts fits better with our intuitions, then it may be for that reason better than one that does not.[8]

8.5 Error theory

At the other end of the spectrum from realism is error theory about morality. The most influential error theorist is Mackie. Here we give a brief reconstruction of Mackie's argument for error theory. Mackie thinks that realists are correct about the nature of moral discourse. When we use moral language, we talk as though there are facts about what is good and bad, right and wrong, and about what people ought to do, and that these facts are so not because of what we think is right and what is wrong and so on. The question for Mackie is whether there are any properties like goodness that are moral properties in some opinion-independent sense.

We have already seen the other elements of Mackie's argument. He rejects the view that there are any non-natural properties for the epistemological and metaphysical reasons given in §8.2. Moreover, he thinks that no class of natural properties has any distinctive opinion-independent feature that makes them worthy of being called "moral properties". Thus there are no moral properties.

If there are no moral properties, then moral terms such as "good", "right" and so on do not refer to anything. Thus, statements such as "Don is evil", "Stu should buy Ed a giant flat-screen television" and so on are all false. The predicates of these statements, on Mackie's view, all fail to refer and this means that atomic sentences[9] that contain them are all false. Thus Mackie puts forward an error theory.

8.6 Relativism

One reaction to the difficulties of realism is to adopt social relativism. Social relativists hold that there are moral facts but that they are opinion-dependent, hence social relativism is a form of anti-realism. The moral opinions of the people of a society determine what is morally right for the people in that society. In its crudest form, social relativism says that whatever the authorities in a society deem to be right is right, and whatever they deem to be wrong is wrong. Thus, moral facts are reduced very cleanly to facts about what certain people say.

There are several advantages to social relativism. First, it is not metaphysically suspect. It does not postulate anything other than social facts. Secondly, social relativism accounts for the problem of the relativity of moral opinions in a very straightforward way. Thirdly, it explains the apparent normative force of moral facts. According to social relativists, we are conditioned to react to certain states of affairs in particular ways. This conditioning is so thorough that it seems as though the facts to which we are reacting are universally motivating.

Despite its having the virtue of simplicity, crude social relativism is intuitively unattractive. Most people think that something can be right despite opposition from the authorities; otherwise, we would never feel that a revolution or even a protest were right.

Luckily there are more subtle versions of relativism than this crude version. A more subtle version is given by Hume and Harman (1977; Harman & Thomson 1996). On the Hume–Harman view, our moral principles are in fact societal conventions. These conventions are often not explicit, but rather are tacit. For example, it is a convention in our culture that people keep promises. It is also a convention that people do not eat other people, even if they die of natural causes. We think of the principle that one should keep his or her promises and the principle that people should not eat other people as moral principles.

How relativistic is the Hume–Harman view? Consider a case of a society in which there are slaves and slave-holders. Can we say (from our moral perspective) that the slave holders are wrong for having slaves? According to Harman, this depends on the details of the case. Suppose that the slave-holders believe that it is wrong to treat other human beings with disrespect, but do not consider their slaves really to be human beings. In this case, the slave-holders are wrong, because they are making a factual mistake: the slaves are as human as the slave-holders. They are misapplying their own conventions.

Suppose, however, that the slave-holders only have a convention that it is wrong to treat others of their own race with disrespect. In this case, the content of the principle itself is supposed merely to be to treat people of a particular race with respect. We cannot accuse the slave-holders in this society of misapplying their rule by having slaves. As we shall see in §8.10, there are ways of dealing with this sort of case by appealing to ideal moral systems.

8.7 Non-cognitivism

A central argument for moral non-cognitivism appeals to the distinction between *moral internalism* and *moral externalism*. Moral internalists believe that moral judgements are *intrinsically motivating*. This means, for example, that if someone judges an action to be good, he or she is, all other things being equal, motivated to do or emulate that action. Of course this does not mean that everyone always does what he or she judges to be right; other motivations may override one's moral judgements. Moral externalists, on the other hand, think that something other than the judgement itself – such as a desire – is needed to motivate someone to act.

The usual argument for internalism is a conceptual one. We can use moral judgements as reasons and justifications for actions. Suppose that someone does a particular action and someone else asks him why he did it. It would seem a reasonable response to say "because I thought the action was right": the judgement of the rightness of the action explains why someone did that action. The explanatory power arises, according to internalists, from the fact that the judgement of rightness itself is motivating. Externalists need another element in their explanations, such as a pre-existing desire on the part of the individual to do what is right.[10]

Some philosophers have argued that internalism is incompatible with cognitivism. Their argument is as follows:

(P1) Cognitivism holds that a moral judgement (a judgement about what is right or wrong, what ought to be the case, etc.) is merely a belief that a fact of a certain sort obtains.

(by the definition of "cognitivism")

(P2) Beliefs are not intrinsically motivating; only desires
     motivate us to act.

(P3) Internalism holds that moral judgements are
     intrinsically motivating.   (by the definition of "internalism")

(C) Therefore, it cannot be that both cognitivism and
     internalism are true.

The only controversial premise is (P2). The view dates back to Hume (*Treatise*: bk III), who thought that the "passions" (i.e. desires) motivate and that reason is motivationally inert. He thought that beliefs cannot act alone to cause actions; they need to be combined with desires. This view about psychology is still popular among philosophers.

One way to accommodate internalism is to adopt a form of non-cognitivism called "emotivism". According to emotivism, a moral statement expresses an emotional attitude towards something. If Stu says that Julian is a good person, then Stu is expressing the fact that he likes Julian. Note that Stu is not *saying* that he likes Julian. What Stu is doing is more like saying "Yay Julian!". So Stu is not expressing a proposition at all: he is not saying something that could either be true or false. Thus, emotivism is a form of both non-cognitivism and non-factualism.

Emotivism connects motivation and moral judgement in a very straightforward way. Emotions motivate us to act; emotions incorporate desires. Thus, emotivism has a very clear explanation of why moral motiviation seems intrinsic to moral judgement.

According to emotivists, in a serious moral debate someone tries merely to get her opponents to adopt the same emotional attitudes towards things as she has. It is not the case that one side can be wrong and the other side right, because no moral judgements can be true or false. If neither side can be moved, then the debate is a failure for both sides. Thus, emotivism leaves open the possibility of rather extreme relativism.

We also sometimes think that our past moral judgements were mistaken. This cannot be the case if moral judgements have no truth-value (Harman 1977: 39). But an emotivist can deal with this by saying that our past judgements were not really mistaken at the time, but rather do not accord with our current emotional attitudes.

Expressivism is an attempt to deal with the shortcomings of emotivism while accepting its advantages. The view we present here is not exactly one that is in the literature but is a reconstruction based on the views of Allan Gibbard (1990). According to expressivism, our moral statements are not expressions of the emotional attitudes that we actually have; rather, they express an ideal moral system based on these attitudes. In §8.10, we shall look in detail at how to construct ideal moral systems, but the rough idea is that we take our actual emotional attitudes, resolve any contradictory attitudes, remove any attitudes based on factual errors and resolve any other tensions. This ideal moral system need not be actually constructed by anyone.

Clearly, we can be in error about the idealized form of our own value systems, so the problem in emotivism of the impossibility of moral mistakes is removed. On the other hand, we can judge with some reliability what the idealization of our value system would be like. Thus, moral judgement is, according to expressivism, fallible but reasonably reliable.

Moreover, for expressivists it is not contradictory to say "I want to do it, but I know that it is not right". One can say this truthfully, according to expressivism, when one is expressing a desire that would be eliminated from the idealization of his value system.

Both emotivism and expressivism reject the existence of opinion-independent moral properties and facts, and so they are forms of anti-realism.

8.7.1 Quasi-realism

Peter Geach's (1964) argument, called the "Frege–Geach problem", against emotivism and expressivism is that they cannot handle logically complex judgements. Consider the sentences "One ought to be nice to dogs" and "One ought to be nice to cats". According to emotivists and expressivists, the first sentence expresses a positive attitude towards dogs and the second expresses a positive attitude towards cats. Now consider the statement "If one ought to be nice to dogs, one ought also to be nice to cats". What sort of attitude does this complex statement express? According to the emotivist, say, "one ought to be nice to dogs" really means the same as "Hoorah dogs!" and similarly for "one ought to be nice to cats". But "If hoorah dogs, then hoorah cats" makes no sense.

Simon Blackburn has put forward a theory that incorporates expressivism but avoids this problem. According to quasi-realism, expressivism is correct in holding that when we make moral judgements we are expressing our attitudes and not reporting moral facts. Thus, quasi-realism is a form of non-factualism. But quasi-realism differs from expressivism in the way that it treats the logical nature of moral claims.

Quasi-realism avoids the Frege–Geach problem by saying that our thought and talk about morality has a dual nature. When someone says "One ought to be nice to dogs", she is (i) expressing her values concerning dogs but also (ii) *acting as if* there is an objective moral fact about our treatment of dogs. This theory is called quasi-realism because it claims that the expressivist is right about the meaning of moral utterances (that they express values) but that we act as though realism is right that there are opinion independent moral facts. Originally Blackburn called his view "projectivism" because according to it we project our values on to the external world.

What is most important for our purposes is that, according to quasi-realism, when we make moral judgements and claims we attribute truth-values to those claims. Thus, if we have positive values regarding cats and dogs, we attribute the values true to both "One ought to be nice to dogs" and "One ought to be nice to cats". Then, using the usual truth-tables that philosophy undergraduates learn, we can attribute truth also to the sentence "If one ought to be nice to dogs, then one ought also to be nice to cats".

Quasi-realism, however, does not merely claim that we attribute truth or falsity to moral judgements. Rather, it claims that moral judgements can really be true or false. What gives these judgements their truth-value are our moral values. Thus, "One ought to be nice to dogs" is true because we value dogs.

Lewis (2005) claims that quasi-realism is a form of fictionalism. Blackburn's claim that it is legitimate to talk "as if" there were moral facts makes his view rather similar to fictionalism (see §8.8). According to moral fictionalism, when we make moral judgements we enter a game of make-believe, that is, we act as if moral realism were true.

But Blackburn (2005) replies that there is a very important difference between quasi-realism and fictionalism. According to fictionalism, the realist's picture of morality makes up a fictional story. What is true in this story is not only what is explicitly stated by realists, but what follows from their views. According to Lewis's own theory of fiction, what follows in a story is determined in the following way. We find a particular set of possible worlds in which the stated parts of the story is true. It does not matter for our discussion exactly which set of worlds this is. What matters is that if some sentence is true in all of these worlds, then it is true according to that story.

If a fictionalist accepts Lewis's theory of fiction, then he must postulate a possible world exactly like our world but that also accords with realism, that is, that contains moral properties and moral facts. Realism says that this world contains moral properties and moral facts, and so if there is a world that is exactly as the realist says it is, then it is descriptively the same as our world but different in its moral properties. Thus, it would seem that the fictionalist is committed to denying the supervenience principle (see Blackburn 2005: 325).

The fictionalist can avoid this problem by rejecting the possible world account of truth in fiction. But fictionalism is committed to factualism, that is, that moral sentences do represent what the realist thinks that they represent: a world with moral properties and moral facts (Kalderon 2005a). Thus, the fictionalist needs some account of the content of moral statements, and hopefully one that does not violate the supervenience principle.

Blackburn, on the other hand, is a non-factualist about morality. He holds that realist claims about morality do not represent propositions, even thought they do have truth-values. We cannot understand what it would be like for a world to make realism true, because we cannot understand the claim that there are moral properties or moral facts. Thus, realism cannot be taken to be a story: it tells us nothing. Rather, we act as though realism were true. For example, when we point at someone saving a child and say "That is a good action", the apparent subject matter of the sentence is the action and there is an apparent attempt to attribute a property ("goodness") to that action. But there is no property of goodness, nor can we understand what such a property would be like. Likewise, there are no moral facts that make this statement or others like it true. The only truth behind these moral assertions lies in our holding the values that they express. Thus, by our lights, despite the fact that quasi-realism holds that moral statements have truth-values, it is a form of anti-realism, for it denies the existence of opinion-independent moral properties and facts.

8.8 Fictionalism

Michael Ruse (1995), Richard Joyce (2001), Nolan *et al.* (2005) and Kalderon (2005b) advance a non-cognitivist fictionalism about morality. According to this view, when we talk morally about the world we engage in a form of make-believe or pretence. There are no moral facts according to this form of fictionalism.

Like quasi-realists, fictionalists recognize that moral discourse appears to be realistic. The literal truth of moral claims presupposes that there is an opinion-independent selection of moral facts. But fictionalists also hold that there are no such facts. Fictionalism is an attempt to accommodate both these theses. When we seem to make moral claims, according to fictionalism, we make-believe or pretend that there is an opinion-independent selection of moral facts.

Fictionalism yields a straightforward treatment of moral debate. What we debate is the content of the moral fiction. We can debate the content of a fictional story, in the simplest cases by looking at a presentation of the story such as a book, or by talking about what we can reasonably infer from what is said in that book. Likewise, we can examine the principles of the moral fiction and discuss what they entail.

Suppose that fictionalism is correct. What is it about the moral fiction that gives it normative force? This question can be read as two very different questions: (i) why do we feel the normative force of the moral fiction, and (ii) when we realize that morality is a fiction, should it still have any normative force?

Let us begin with question (i). Ruse and Joyce suggest that the process of evolution produced in us a moral sense. Morality is useful to people, both as individuals and to people as a group. Acting morally gives us the trust of others and often convinces others to become our friends. Human life and human societies require the sort of trust that moral action brings about. Ruse and Joyce suggest that our feeling that we must do what is right (and punish those who do wrong) evolved to help people bond into groups.

The evolutionary explanation of ethics has certain virtues. In particular it can explain the apparent objectivity of ethics. The evolutionary theory also explains why almost everyone feels the motivating pull of the same facts. Everyone has the same evolutionary background and we all (or almost all) have evolved the same moral sensibility. This does not mean that we find the exact same actions, people and so on, to be morally good. Rather, as Ruse says, a basic moral structure is the same in almost all of us.[11]

Let us now turn to question (ii): when we acknowledge that morality is a fiction, can it still have any normative force? This is a much more difficult problem for fictionalism than that expressed by question (i). Ruse (1995: 238) says that even after we realize that morality is a fiction, we can still appreciate its usefulness and we will still have the desire to act morally that evolution has instilled in us. But consider the following case: a person is wondering whether he should do something he does not want to do but thinks is the right thing to do. Moreover, he knows that if he does what he wants to do, there will be no repercussions against him. If he realizes that morality is a fiction, what reason does he have to do what is moral rather than what he wants to do? It would seem that this evolutionary theory can give him no reason why the urge to do what is moral should override his other desires.

Before we leave moral fictionalism, we should discuss one last topic. As we have seen, fictionalists hold that we talk as though moral facts exist. Moreover, few people believe that this talk is fictional. Thus, it would seem rather strange to say that when we talk about morality we mean something that is fictional. Contrast the case of a person talking about Sherlock Holmes, knowing that he is the creation of Arthur Conan Doyle, and the case of someone talking about ghosts who thinks (mistakenly) that ghosts really exist. The first person's discourse is clearly fictional, whereas the second person's talking about ghosts is talk about the world, but in error. Thus, we would want to describe the second person's discourse using an error theory rather than a form of fictionalism. Joyce (2001) and Nolan et al. (2005) have a response to this problem. They recognize that it is implausible to claim that fictionalism is an accurate description of moral discourse. Rather, they think that we should reform our thinking to recognize that our moral statements, if taken literally, are in error and we should come to see moral talk as fictional. Thus, they have a revolutionary conception of their fictionalism (see §2.3).

8.9 Response-dependence

Michael Smith has developed a response-dependent theory of morality in an attempt to give a factualism that (i) provides an account of the motivational force of moral judgements and (ii) makes moral facts epistemologically accessible. According to Smith, a person X ought to do an action Y in a particular circumstance if and only if an ideally rational version of X would judge that X should do Y in that circumstance. The picture is this: when we are deliberating about what we morally should do, we are supposed to imagine what an ideally rational version of ourselves would tell us to do in our current situation.

An ideally rational version of oneself has the following four characteristics (Smith 1994: 156–61):

1. he or she must have no false beliefs;
2. he or she must have all the relevant true beliefs;
3. he or she must deliberate correctly;
4. he or she must have *systematised desires*.

The first three characteristics are reasonably straightforward; the last has become a staple of modern moral theory. The idea is that the ideal version of one has made one's desires coherent by subjecting them to the process of reaching reflective equilibrium. This process is described in §8.10.

Response-dependence implies a view that is very close to moral internalism. What you ought to do is determined by facts about the idealized form of you. If someone judges that her "better self" would want her to do a particular action, she would seem to have a motivation to do it. Thus Smith's view avoids the argument of §8.7 by having moral judgements be beliefs about desires: the desires of a better version of oneself.

This theory gives us an answer to the question "Why be moral?". It tells us that moral action is merely rational action; an action is moral if it is what we would judge from an ideal standpoint is the rational action in the given situation. In effect Smith collapses morality into rationality.[12]

The theory also gives us a coherent view about moral reasoning. In giving reasons for past or future actions, on this view, one is attempting to approximate one's better self. Others may challenge the reasoning by disputing the facts used in such justifications or by different analyses of the logical relationships between facts, desires and the actions under consideration.

Response-dependence is an interesting sort of anti-realism. It says that what is moral is independent of the opinions of any actual people. But moral facts and properties still depend on the opinions of certain hypothetical people.

8.10 Ideal moral systems

In the previous section, we briefly introduced the idea of a systematization of one's desires. In this section, we shall explore the idea that one route towards an objective ethics is to take an existing moral code and systematize it in much the same way. This idea has been put forward both by factualists, such as Smith and Jackson, and non-factualists, such as Blackburn.[13] Roughly, the position is that we take a system of moral principles and imagine what would happen if it were subjected to certain sorts of reasoning processes. What would result from the application of these reasoning processes to the set of moral principles is an ideal moral system. Here we present a compilation from the literature of various methods used to make a moral code ideal.

The first of these processes is one that we have seen Harman and Smith describe: we must remove any factual errors from the principles themselves, from their justifications and from the way in which they are applied. Suppose, for example, that some people believe that women are not as intelligent as men and accordingly have a principle that women should always defer to the judgements of men. Given the fact that men and women are on average of the same intelligence, this principle is unmotivated and should be removed.

The second process is a test for consistency. Suppose that a group of people think that they should treat everyone alike but that some people in the group also believe that people of a certain race should be treated worse than everyone else. Then at least one of these principles must be rejected.

The third method is the process of reaching *reflective equilibrium*. The people who are supposed to accept the moral system consider proposed principles of this moral system in light of particular cases. Sometimes these cases will conflict. Perhaps you remember from your first course in ethics a case used as a counter-example against act utilitarianism. A lonely stranger comes to a town in which a horrible murder occurs. The police cannot find the actual murderer but in order to make the people of the town feel happier and secure they hang the stranger, even though he is innocent. It would seem that this act is wrong even if it obeys the principle that we should maximize overall happiness. In trying to reach reflective equilibrium, one must decide whether to accept the principle of utility, reject it, modify it or change one's evaluation of the particular case. If the person chooses to modify the principle, then as wide a variety of cases as possible should be used to test it. After all possible cases are used to test every principle, and no more changes are needed to the moral principles or to people's evaluations of particular cases, the moral system is said to be in reflective equilibrium.

The fourth process is not as widely discussed in the philosophical literature, but appears in Blackburn (1984: 200). The group of people in question should examine other moral systems and the motivations for them. They should take into account the values that are expressed in these other moral systems. We do make adjustments to our own moral views when we come into contact for reasonable lengths of time with people of other cultures. At first we may find their moral outlooks quite foreign, but after seeing the conditions under which they live, we often come to understand and appreciate their moral values. In some cases, we even integrate these values into our own.

There may be other processes that should be used to produce an ideal moral system, but we can see that just by the application of these processes we can achieve some measure of moral objectivity. It produces objectivity in the sense that if everyone were to produce ideal moral systems from their own moral codes there would be a good measure of overlap between these ideal moral systems. In addition, the view that our real moral codes are idealizations of the codes that we know, allows a good deal of room for serious moral debate (about what sorts of principles will be left after idealization). There is nothing in the processes of constructing an ideal moral system that presupposes realism. Thus there may be a way to have an objective morality without realism.

8.10.1 From an ideal moral system to realism?

This section is more technical than the others. Nothing else in the book relies on it and it can be skipped, but it may be of interest to readers interested in the more technical end of metaethics. According to Frank Jackson, once we have an ideal moral system, we can show that there exist moral properties and moral facts. To do so, Jackson applies a technique called "Ramsification", after the philosopher Frank Ramsey, who invented the technique for use in the philosophy of science.[14]

For Jackson, the meaning of a moral term is its *role* in the system, that is, where it fits into the network of concepts and how it enters into the opinions and principles that make up the system. Jackson gives us a means for determining what roles are played by each moral concept and, using these roles, how to figure out which property is expressed by each moral concept. We describe Jackson's method for determining the role of a moral concept as a two-step process:

- *Step 1.* Remove every moral term in the theory and replace each with a different variable (such as "x", "y", "z" and so on). Thus, for example, we remove every occurrence of the word "good" and replace it with "x" and replace every occurrence of the word "bad" with "y" and so on.
- *Step 2.* Let us call the system with variables replacing the moral terms M (for "morality"). We now add a bunch of quantifier phrases – "there is a unique x such that", "there is a unique y such that" and so on – on the front of M for each of the variables that we have replaced for moral terms.

The final system (the one with all the "there is a unique x such that ...", etc., phrases on the front) is a "Ramsified system". The variables mark out the roles of each of the moral terms. Now all we need to do is find out which properties actually fit these roles. An entity fits a role exactly if and only if we can assign the relevant variable to that entity and it makes every sentence about that thing true.

Let us look at an example. Suppose the following sentences are in our ideal moral system:

- Actions that harm dogs are forbidden.

- Actions that harm cats are forbidden.
- Actions that harm children are forbidden.

In our Ramsified system, we remove the word "forbidden" from each of these sentences and replace them with a variable, to get "Actions that harm dogs are X", "Actions that harm cats are X" and "Actions that harm children are X". Any property of actions that fits the role of X will have to be one that is shared by actions that harm dogs, cats and children. What sort of property is this? Can we assume that there is such a property?

Jackson thinks not only that there is such a property, but also that it is a natural property. He argues for this claim using the assumption that there are *disjunctive properties*. Suppose that we have three properties, P, Q and R. Then the property of being P, being Q or being R is a disjunctive property. In the case of our moral system, the variable X can refer to the disjunctive *property of harming dogs, harming cats, or harming children*.[15] Thus, a Ramsified moral system will determine for each role a descriptive property that fits that role. Thus Jackson has argued for a reductivist realism.

One criticism of Jackson's view has been made by Michael Smith (1994: §2.11). According to Smith, it could well turn out that the Ramsified theory cannot determine what property fits what role. Consider our everyday theory of colour, which philosophers call the "folk theory of colour". On the folk theory of colour, each colour concept bears certain relations to other colour concepts. And no colour is defined in the folk theory (as opposed to scientific theories of colour) using non-colour terms. Smith supposes, for the sake of his argument, that all we can say about a colour is that things look that colour to people when seen in normal light. Thus, in our folk theory we get statements such as "the property of being red is the property of looking red to people in normal light" and "the property of being yellow is the property of looking yellow to people in normal light". Ramsifying these we get "the property of being x is the property of looking x to people in normal light" and "the property of being y is the property of looking y to people in normal light". Thus, what is said about red in the Ramsified theory is the same (changing x for y) as what is said about yellow. Thus "we have lost any distinction between the properties of being red, being orange, being yellow, and the rest" (Smith 1994: 50).

Therefore, we cannot say that there is exactly one property *x* that fits the *x* role; there are many such properties. Smith asks how we know that our ideal moral theory will be different: that a single property fits each role.

What Smith needs to bolster his argument is another argument to show that moral terms are like colour terms, that is, that they cannot be defined except by circular means. Smith's argument (if correct) does show that Ramsifying theories does not always give us a way of determining which properties fit which roles. But his argument does not show that moral theory is not a fit candidate for Ramsification. Thus, Smith gives us a concern about the efficacy of Ramsification in the case of morality, but it does not provide us with a knock-down argument against Jackson's position.

Further reading

We recommend the following resources on metaethics and the realist debate in ethics: Stephen Darwall, Allan Gibbard, and Peter Railton, "Toward *Fin de siècle* Ethics: Some Trends", *Philosophical Review* 101 (1992), 115–89; David Copp and David Zimmerman (eds), *Morality, Reason, and Truth: New Essays on the Foundations of Ethics* (Totowa, NJ: Rowman and Allanheld, 1985); Gilbert Harman and Judith Jarvis Thomson, *Moral Relativism and Moral Objectivity* (Oxford: Blackwell, 1996); Alexander Miller, *Introduction to Contemporary Metaethics* (Cambridge: Polity, 2003); James Rachels (ed.), *Ethical Theory I: The Question of Objectivity* (Oxford: Oxford University Press, 1998); Geoffrey Sayre-McCord (ed.), *Essays on Moral Realism* (Ithaca, NY: Cornell University Press, 1988); Walter Sinnott-Armstrong and Mark Timmons (eds), *Moral Knowledge? New Readings in Moral Epistemology* (Oxford: Oxford University Press, 1996); and Michael Ridge, "Moral Non-Naturalism", in *Stanford Encyclopaedia of Philosophy*, Ed Zalta (ed.) (2003), http://plato.stanford.edu/entries/moral-non-naturalism/

9 Science

9.1 Introduction

Standard scientific realism concerns the truth of scientific theories and the existence of theoretical entities. A theoretical entity is an entity that is postulated by a scientific theory but cannot be perceived directly. A theoretical entity can be a type of thing, such protons or quarks, or events such as the Big Bang. Scientists also postulate laws of nature, such as the law that everything in the universe exerts a gravitational force on everything else in the universe. The problem about realism about science is the question of whether we should believe that these entities exist or that the laws of science are true.

In the literature, there are two sorts of realists about science. First, there are the standard realists, who believe that the purpose of science is to provide us with true postulates of laws and entities. These philosophers argue also that science has largely been successful in this regard and that our best scientific theories are true or at least are approximately true. Secondly, there are philosophers who reject the idea that there are laws of nature, or that the laws that scientists postulate are largely true, but hold that the entities that they postulate often do exist.

Anti-realists about science also come in several types. We do not have room to examine them all, so we shall look at the two most influential forms of anti-realism. We shall look at the fictionalism of Bas van Fraassen and the relativism of Thomas Kuhn. We begin by looking at standard realism about science.

9.2 What is scientific realism?

Scientific realists take scientific theories seriously. If a scientific theory is to be considered true it to be taken as literally true. Similarly, if a scientific theory postulates a theoretical entity, and that theory is true, then that entity really exists. Very few scientific realists believe that all of our current scientific theories are completely true or that all of the entities that they postulate actually exist. Rather, *standard scientific realism* is characterized by three attitudes:

- Confidence in scientific method. As time progresses, the theories that scientists accept are progressively closer to being true.
- Confidence in contemporary science. The most successful of our current theories are approximately true.
- Belief that our current scientific ontology – the list of the entities that scientists currently accept – is approximately right.

Philosophers of science do not think of science as a completed body of knowledge. Rather, it is developing and changing. To believe in science is to accept not that it has given us all the truths there are to find, but rather that its method yields better and better theories all the time and that current theories are pretty much true.

One problem with standard scientific realism is that there are no generally agreed on theories of approximate truth and of how to measure whether one theory is closer to the truth than another. A theory of closeness to the truth is called a theory of *verisimilitude*. The debate over the nature of verisimilitude and approximate truth is extremely interesting, but rather technical and we do not have space to discuss it properly here. For the purposes of this chapter, we shall assume that the notions of verisimilitude and approximate truth are coherent and that some reasonable theory of them can be given.

The central problem for realism is the problem of the *empirical underdetermination of theories by evidence*. For every set of observable phenomena, we can come up with many theories that explain that data.[1] For example, there are fossils that most of us think come from dinosaurs that died many thousands of years ago. But one could postulate that a mischievous spirit placed them there to fool us. Thus, the challenge for the realist is to come up with an argument to show that science is on the right track, rather than coming up with incorrect theories that make the approximately right empirical predictions.

9.2.1 The abductive argument for realism

One such argument is an *abductive* argument (in the sense of §2.2.1) put forward by J. J. C. Smart and others. This argument is based on one given in Smart (1989: ch. 3).

(P1) The theories of contemporary science provide very accurate predictions about observable events. (empirical fact)

(P2) The theories of contemporary science postulate theoretical entities and laws. (empirical fact)

(C1) Observable phenomena behave *as if* the theoretical entities of science exist and the laws postulated by science are true (or are at least approximately true). (from P1 and P2)

(P3) The best available explanation of why observable phenomena behave as if the theoretical entities of science exist and the laws postulated by science are true (or are approximately true) is that these theoretical entities do exist and that the postulated laws are true (or are approximately true).

(P4) We should believe the best available explanation. (abductive premise)

(C2) We should believe that the theoretical entities of physics exist and that the laws postulated by physics are correct (or at least approximately correct). (from C1, P3, and P4)

There are many replies to this argument. We shall not survey all of them here; instead we look at two of the more interesting replies.

9.2.2 Fine's argument

Arthur Fine (1986) argues that it is inappropriate to use abduction to bolster scientific realism. Here is a reconstruction and simplification of Fine's argument.[2] Part of what one is arguing for when one defends scientific realism, according to Fine, is the use of abduction by science. Abduction is a central method of science. The antirealist questions the reliability of abduction, for if abduction is reliable, then, by definition, it leads us reliably to accept true (or at least approximately true) theories. Once the reliability of abduction is questioned, it must be set aside as a method for convincing the anti-realist of the realist's case.

In reply, the realist may agree that the abductive argument is not sufficient to refute scepticism about science, but it is a means whereby a non-sceptic can *justify* her acceptance of scientific realism. According to certain epistemologies, it is not required of a means of justification that we be justified in using it, only that it have certain properties that make it a legitimate means of justification, for example, that it be reliable. Now, suppose that abduction actually is reliable (or has whatever other properties are necessary for it to count as a means of justification). Then, the realist can justify his or her own beliefs using abduction (see Lipton 1991).

9.2.3 The argument from predictive similarity

In this section we look at Kyle Stanford's (2000) argument against the abductive argument. In what follows, we both simplify and elaborate on Stanford's argument.[3] First, we need a definition. We say that a theory T is *predictively similar* to a theory S if and only if T makes the same empirical predictions as S. (Note that every theory is predicatively similar to itself.) Here is the argument. Suppose that we have a theory T that makes very accurate empirical predictions about some range of phenomena. We can believe either:

(i) T is approximately true; or
(ii) T is predictively similar to a theory that is approximately true.

Stanford puts the problem in terms of probability. According to him, we have to see whether it is more probable (from our point of view) that T is approximately true than that it is predictively similar to a theory that is approximately true.

Putting the problem in terms of probability is particularly illuminating. Consider what we have said about the problem of empirical underdetermination. For any theory, we can construct many other theories that are predictively similar, many of which are not approximately true. So, what is the probability that we have chosen a theory that is approximately true given that for any such theory here are many other theories that are predictively similar to it? We cannot tell from the empirical evidence alone which of (i) or (ii) is right. Moreover, it would seem that, given that there are at least as many predictively similar theories as there are approximately true theories, the probability of choosing an approximately true theory are not particularly high. Therefore, it would seem that the approximate truth of T provides no better explanation of T's empirical success than does the predictive similarity of T to an approximately true theory.

Stanford's argument places the burden on the realist to tell us why we should think that, instead of all the very false but predictively successful theories, we have chosen one that is approximately true. The problem of the number of theories indicates that there is no immediately apparent reason to think that it is more likely that we have chosen a theory that is approximately true. Thus, there is no reason to hold that the approximate truth of our best scientific theories is the best explanation of their success. Hence Stanford rejects the third premise of Smart's argument.

Stanford's argument is not just an attempt to undermine an argument for realism, but rather it is an argument for anti-realism. It attempts to show that it is more probable that we choose false theories than true ones.

9.3 The pessimistic meta-induction

Another argument for anti-realism, that of Larry Laudan (1981), is the "pessimistic meta-induction". It has the following structure:

(P1) There have been many theories in the past that were highly empirically successful but not approximately true.

(empirical fact)

(P2) If there have been many highly empirically successful but not approximately true theories in the past, we cannot infer that it is highly probable that any given present theory is approximately true just because it is empirically highly successful.

(inductive premise)

(C1) We cannot infer that it is highly probable that any given theory is approximately true just because it is highly empirically successful.

(from P1 and P2)

(P3) If we cannot infer that it is highly probable that a theory is approximately true just because it is highly empirically successful, then without further evidence we should not adopt the approximate truth of a theory as an explanation of its success.

(C2) We should not adopt the approximate truth of a theory as an explanation of its empirical success without further evidence.

(from C1 and P3)

Laudan lists twelve theories that were successful but that we now do not think are approximately true. We shall look at two of these.

The first of these theories is the late-nineteenth-century view that there is an "electromagnetic ether". Late in the nineteenth century, physicists such as Heinrich Hertz showed that electricity acts as if it is made up of waves. Through some remarkable experiments, Hertz showed that electricity can be reflected, refracted and diffracted like waves of water or, more importantly, like waves of light. Physicists concluded that electricity is in fact made up of waves. But waves need a medium in which to move and it was thought that electricity could move through space that was supposedly empty. So, physicists postulated a medium that fills all of space called the *electromagnetic ether*.

The existence of this ether was dealt a blow by an experiment performed by A. A. Michelson and E. W. Morley and another when Einstein's theory of relativity became generally accepted. Michelson and Morley's experiment was inconsistent with the only coherent version of the ether theory and the theory of relativity is inconsistent with the existence of ether. The idea here is that whereas the wave theory of electricity combined with the ether theory was extremely empirically successful, we now consider it to be false.

Similarly, the Greek theory of planetary movement was very empirically successful, but is now known to be false. On this theory, the planets, the moon and the sun each moved around the earth on a series of "crystalline spheres". This theory was able to accommodate all known data on the movement of the heavenly bodies for many years. But the theory was abandoned for the view that the planets move around the sun and are held in the orbits by a "force": the gravitational force. Moreover, we have found that we can fly spacecraft to other planets. This would be impossible if each planet were suspended on a crystalline sphere.

Given enough examples of theories that were empirically successful but very false, we are supposed to come to believe that there is no connection between empirical success and approximate truth for a scientific theory or at least we are supposed to doubt whether there is such a connection.

The pessimistic meta-induction can be attacked along several lines. First, one can argue with Laudan's use of historical examples. He sometimes picks the very false aspects of theories that are still regarded to be approximately correct. One example of this is his use of the theory of the electromagnetic ether. One could instead point out that this is just a part of the wave theory of electricity. This theory is currently considered to be approximately true. According to current theories, electricity does act as a wave and can be considered in certain respects to be carried by waves. But, according to current views, these waves can considered to be particles as well, so there is no need for a medium (i.e. for the ether).

Secondly, one might argue that the use of theories from the past is an unreliable basis for the induction, for the empirical evidence that supported them was quite limited. Consider, for example, the crystalline sphere theory of planetary motion. This accorded with the empirical evidence available in the ancient and medieval worlds, but not with our current evidence. We have flown spacecraft to other planets and so passed solid objects through the positions that were supposed to have been occupied by crystalline spheres. Our wider range of empirical evidence and our more reliable testing methods make our current theories much more believable than past theories.

9.4 Van Fraassen's fictionalism

The first anti-realism about science that we shall examine is Bas van Fraassen's (1980) non-cognitivist fictionalism. Van Fraassen is agnostic about the existence of theoretical objects: he is committed to neither their existence nor their non-existence. But he does not think that scientific statements about theoretic entities are false, even if these theoretical entities do not exist. Rather, he holds that it is not the function of scientific statements about theoretical objects to state the truth.

Van Fraassen holds that for a scientist to accept a theory is for him or her to be committed to working with that theory *as if* it were true. That scientist should use the concepts and laws of the theory to predict observable phenomena if he or she accepts a theory. That scientist should also use the concepts and laws of the theory in order to produce further theories, to help confirm or reject other theories and so on. Thus, van Fraassen is a non-cognitivist fictionalist.[4]

Accepting a scientific theory, according to van Fraassen, entails the belief that the theory is empirically adequate. One who accepts a theory must believe that all the empirical predictions made by the theory are true. In other words, he or she must believe that the observable phenomena that the theory predicts are true. But one need not believe anything that the theory says about theoretical entities.

Thus, van Fraassen requires a distinction between observable phenomena and theoretical phenomena. His view is that only those phenomena that can be perceived with the naked senses are observable. He gives us the following "rough guide" to the distinction between observable and theoretical phenomena: "X is observable if there are circumstances which are such that, if X is present to us under those circumstances, then we observe it" (1980: 16). The moons of Jupiter, van Fraassen claims, are observable even if we cannot see them from earth with the naked eye. An astronaut could see them if she were close enough (*ibid.*). But there are no circumstances under which we can see (or feel, hear, etc.) things such as individual bacteria or electrons. So phenomena that involve individual bacteria or individual electrons do not count as observable.

Van Fraassen thinks that this line between what is observable and what is theoretical is vague. There are phenomena to which it is not clear whether the term "observable" applies. But we can use vague terms meaningfully. The predicate "bald" is vague, but we can say meaningfully and truthfully that certain men are bald.

Some have pointed out to van Fraassen that the limits of our own sensory apparatus are contingent. Why should science be limited by these limits? Van Fraassen claims that the limits of science are also contingent. If we were to meet beings with different sensory apparatus who also do science (and we trust what they say), then our understanding of what is observable would and should change (*ibid.*: 18). Van Fraassen's view is that we have an *epistemic com-*

munity, that is, we are in a community of beings who trust one another for information: we trust news reporters to tell us the truth about distant events; we trust scientists to tell us the results of their experiments. Others trust us to tell them about what we can see, hear, smell and so on. This community of people who trust each other to give them information sets the bounds to what counts as observable. It is what they can perceive with their naked senses that determines what is observable.[5]

9.4.1 Hacking on van Fraassen and microscopes

If we are to accept van Fraassen's anti-realism, we must hold that there is something epistemologically important about the distinction between observable and theoretical entities. That is, we must agree with van Fraassen that what we know about observable entities is more certain that what we claim to know about theoretical entities. Here we present Hacking's argument against this claim (1985: 146f.).

When using a microscope, scientists often use a tiny grid that they can see though the microscope. The grid is marked by numbers and letters and is used to identify things by their positions. These grids are drawn by a draughtsperson and photographically reduced. The photographic negative is then placed on a tiny plate, which is exposed to light (charging the plate along the lines of the grid). Metal is then deposited along those charged lines. Should we believe that this tiny grid exists and that it is as it appears through the microscope? One might think so. For we can do the exact same process without reducing the image quite so far, so that it is still visible to the naked eye. This would seem to show that the process is reliable.

Not according to van Fraassen. He thinks that we are merely drawing an analogy between the case when we have produced an observable grid and the case when we have produced one that we cannot see. This sort of argument from analogy is exactly what he rejects. He thinks that it is always unwarranted to make claims about what happens at the sub-perceptible level based on what happens in perceptible phenomena. Thus, he thinks that Hacking's argument begs the question against his view (van Fraassen 1985).

9.5 The experimental philosophy

Hacking's argument of the grid nicely introduces a position that he shares with Nancy Cartwright and Ronald Giere. This is the view that has become known as the "experimental philosophy", so called because it removes the emphasis on observation and places it instead on experimentation and on the manipulation of nature. The experimental philosophy is a mixture of realism and anti-realism. On one hand, it is realistic about the existence of some theoretical entities; on the other hand, it is anti-realistic about the existence of laws of nature.

The experimental philosophers have put forward a battery of arguments against the view that science yields true laws of nature. The most famous of these are in Cartwright (1983). We shall not look at all of her arguments, but rather discuss an illustrative example and then examine one of her arguments.

The experimental philosophers hold that laws of science are not literal truths, but are instead approximations or idealizations. Here is an example of an idealization: the Hardy–Weinberg law of population genetics. Let us assume a simple case in which a particular location on a strand of DNA can have either a dominant gene or a recessive gene. If both strands in the DNA have the recessive gene it is expressed. If one strand has the dominant gene it is expressed. Let us say that the proportion of the population that has the dominant gene is some fraction d and the proportion of the population that has the recessive gene is some fraction r. *Assuming that mating in this population is random, that is, the creatures involved do not prefer mates in which the dominant or recessive gene are expressed,* the probabilities of gene distribution in the population after mating takes place are determined by the following equations: the proportion of the population that has two copies of the dominant gene is d^2; the proportion of the population that has two copies of the recessive gene is r^2; the proportion of the population that has one copy of the dominant gene and one of the recessive gene is $2dr$.

The italicized clauses above state the assumption of the Hardy–Weinberg law. This assumption is that mating in the population is random. This makes this scientific law an idealization. It is rarely the case in nature that mating really is random. So, the Hardy–Weinberg law is not a description of a universal regularity, and hence not a law of nature in the sense that we discussed at the start of this chapter.

instead, this law of science is an idealization and an approximation of the way in which genes are distributed in real populations.

What is interesting is that the experimental philosophers claim that many (perhaps most) laws of science are like this. That is, they claim that laws in fact only describe what happens in rather special conditions, such as within a particular experimental set-up.

Other scientific laws, Cartwright claims, are outright fictions. For example, consider Newton's law that a force on an object is equal to the mass of that object multiplied by its acceleration (symbolically, $F = ma$). Hold your arm still in front of you. According to Newton's theory of gravity, there is a gravitational force on your hand. Moreover, your hand has mass. Thus, your hand should be accelerating towards the ground. But it is not moving, so it would seem that the acceleration is zero. Do we have a contradiction here? Newton avoids the contradiction by saying that the *net* acceleration of your hand is zero, but it has a positive acceleration component in the direction of the ground. Your muscles are also making the hand accelerate towards the sky and the two accelerations cancel each other out. On Cartwright's view, Newton's components of acceleration are fictions. They are added to the theory to make it coherent, but they are merely mathematical constructs to work around the obvious fact that your hand is not accelerating at all.

In contrast to their views on laws, the experimental philosophers are realists with regard to some theoretical objects. According to the experimental philosophers, scientists develop experiments and engineers develop technology using models of the sorts of entities that they believe to exist. For example, physicists believe in the existence of particles of light, called "photons". They may use the wave or particle model of the photon in order to help them build things like lasers (see Cartwright 1983). The laws that they use are approximations, but they have confidence in these approximations because they believe that the entities that underlie the models exist. Moreover, when scientists find that they can employ these models in very predictable ways, it is reasonable for them (and for us) to think that these things really do exist.

Here is a more straightforward example from human biology. The human egg can only be seen through a microscope. Thus, van Fraassen is agnostic about its existence. But the experimental philosophers believe in its existence. This is because we can not only observe human eggs, we can *manipulate* them. Scientists use human eggs in performing various fertility treatments including *in vitro* fertilization. They may already somewhere be experimenting on them towards producing the first human clones. And women for some time have been manipulating their own eggs by taking birth control pills, fertility pills and the morning-after pill. We believe in the existence of human eggs to such an extent that we are willing often to trust our futures and our fortunes on what can be done to them, either to ensure that they are fertilized or to ensure that they are not. The human egg has become part of our worldview to the extent that anyone who questioned its existence would be treated as very ignorant or eccentric.

In this case it is obvious that laws play at best a very minor role. There are few mathematical scientific laws that predict the behaviour of the human egg. Rather, scientists have a more informal picture of how eggs behave and interact with other things such as sperm. Yet this informal picture is sufficient for the predictable manipulation of eggs in the many ways currently undertaken by medical science. This predictability warrants our belief in the existence of the human egg.[6] Moreover, it would be irrational to continue to try to manipulate theoretical objects if we did not believe in their existence. This is especially true when there is a lot at stake, as in the case of our manipulations of human eggs.

Consider for comparison the following example. During the next few years NASA plans to launch a probe called SIM Planet Quest, which will detect slight "wobbles" in the motion of stars, and on that basis scientists will postulate the existence and location of planets.[7] We (Stu and Ed) accept the theories on which these postulations are based. On van Fraassen's view, we are thereby committed to believing that the planets found in this way exist. But he claims that we should withhold belief in the existence of human eggs. It seems, however, that we have much better justification for the belief in human eggs than we do for the belief in the existence of these planets.

9.6 Kuhn's relativism

Here we examine the philosophy of science set out by Kuhn in his famous book *The Structure of Scientific Revolutions* (1970). In this book, Kuhn argues for a very strong form of relativism and social constructivism[8] (see §3.2). According to this relativism, even what empirical evidence is depends on the social structure from which it is perceived. These social structures are called "paradigms". Kuhn uses the word "paradigm" with various different meanings, but the one that we shall use here is a group of scientists who have certain views, concepts and methods in common. An example of a paradigm is the astronomers who during the eighteenth and nineteenth centuries worked using Newton's theory of gravity.

Sometimes there is a shift in paradigms. Sometimes a new paradigm comes along and becomes dominant. An example of this is when Einstein's theory of gravity replaced Newton's and became the dominant tool for astronomers in the twentieth century. When there is a paradigm shift, there is a scientific revolution.

Kuhn thinks that the paradigm in which a scientist works helps to determine how she perceives the world. Thus, we cannot say, in a paradigm-neutral way, that one paradigm deals better with the empirical data. What the empirical data itself is (at least in part) is determined by the paradigm of the scientists who collect it and report it. This dependency of empirical data on the background of the scientists who collect it is called the "theory-ladenness" of data. Most philosophers agree that theory-ladenness is a real phenomenon, but they differ as to whether it creates a serious problem for scientific realism. Some think that with careful observation by a wide variety of individuals the effects of theory-ladenness can be overcome. Others, like Kuhn, think that theory-ladenness is more resilient than that.

As we have seen in Chapter 5, Kuhn is a Kantian. He distinguishes between the world as we perceive it and the world as it is in itself. There is no way of getting beyond how we perceive the world to how the world is in itself. All we have are the ways the world is construed through various paradigms. Thus, Kuhn is an anti-realist and a relativist.

Kuhn's relativism is extremely strong. He claims that different paradigms are *incommensurable* with one another. This means that we cannot even compare what different paradigms say about the same things. For example, according to Kuhn, we cannot really compare Ptolemaic astronomy and Copernican astronomy, because they mean different things by the words "earth" and "motion".

Kuhn writes: "Copernicus' innovation was not simply to move the earth. Rather, it was a whole new way of regarding the problems of physics and astronomy, one that necessarily changed the meaning of both 'earth' and 'motion'" (1970: 149f.).

Kuhn's central argument for his incommensurability thesis assumes a *holistic* theory of meaning. On the holistic theory of meaning, what a word means is determined by every belief that one holds that is connected to that word. According to Ptolemaic astronomy, the earth is the motionless centre of the universe. In the sixteenth century Copernicus postulated that the earth moves around the sun. Thus, part of the meaning of the word "earth" for the Ptolemaic is "the motionless centre of the universe" and, for the Copernican, part of its meaning is "planet that circles the sun".

There are many counter-arguments to Kuhn in the literature. We have already seen one in Chapter 5. As we saw there, Davidson argues that translation between apparently different conceptual schemes is always possible. Another tactic in use against Kuhn is to reject the holistic theory of meaning. This tactic has been employed in two different ways. First, there are those who maintain a *localist* theory of meaning. They maintain that the meanings of words are determined (at least in part) by our beliefs concerning them, but not all our beliefs determine their meanings. Thus, the meaning of "gravity" might be "a force that draws objects together over great distances". This meaning can be accepted by both Newtonians and Einsteinians. Localism, however, has the difficulty that it seems to owe us a theory of how we distinguish between meaning-determining beliefs and other beliefs. Such a theory has been difficult to produce, but there are many attempts in the philosophical literature and we shall leave it to the reader to decide which, if any, are successful.

A second way of rejecting the holistic theory of meaning has been through the use of the theory of direct reference (see §6.4.1). The theory of direct reference says that the meaning of some terms (including many theoretical terms in science) is just the referents of those terms. Thus, for example, the meaning of "gravity" is just the actual force of gravity. On the version of this theory that we have discussed, a term gets its meaning from the causal relationships that uses of the term have to things in the external world. Suppose that when the word "gravity" was first used a person said that he would call the force that is pulling things towards the earth "gravity". This dubbing fixed the reference (and hence the meaning) of the word and afterwards people with different theories of gravity can talk about one and the same force.

But, as Kuhn (1990) points out, there is a problem with this use of the theory of direct reference. In the eighteenth century there was a debate about the nature of combustion. Priestly claimed that it was caused by a substance that he called "phlogiston" that exists in all things, and that combustion was phlogiston escaping from the thing that was burning. Lavoisier opposed this view, claiming instead that combustion is a form of oxidation. Suppose that Priestly originally coined the word "phlogiston" by saying that the substance responsible for that (pointing at a burning object) is called "phlogiston". Does "phlogiston" refer to oxygen? If so, every historian of science who has said that phlogiston does not exist is wrong.

Further reading

There are many good textbooks and books of readings on philosophy of science and on the realism debate in particular. Here are some that we especially like: Barry Barnes and David Edge (eds), *Science in Context: Readings in the Sociology of Science* (Milton Keynes: Open University Press, 1982); Richard Boyd, Philip Gasper, and J. D. Trout (eds), *The Philosophy of Science* (Cambridge, MA: MIT Press, 1991); Paul M. Churchland and Clifford A. Hooker (eds), *Images of Science: Essays on Realism and Empiricism with Replies by Bas C. van Fraassen* (Chicago, IL: University of Chicago Press, 1985); Paul Horwich (ed.), *World Changes: Thomas Kuhn and the Nature of Science* (Cambridge, MA: MIT Press, 1993); and David Papineau (ed.), *Philosophy of Science* (Oxford: Oxford University Press, 1996).

10 Mathematics

10.1 Introduction

This chapter is slightly more technical than the others. This is required by the subject matter. We try as much as possible either to avoid technical notions or to restrict discussion of them to footnotes. The material presented here is appropriate for readers who have studied a little logic or even those who remember at least some of the mathematics that they learnt in school.

A mathematical statement is a statement such as "2 + 2 = 4" or "the square root of two is not a fraction". What makes these statements true? And what makes other mathematical statements false, such as "2 + 2 = 5" and "the square root of two is a fraction"? Realism about mathematics claims that there are mathematical objects, such as numbers, that have mind-independent properties that make these statements true or false. Thus, for example, realists claim that there is something that is the number two that has the property that it is half of the number four. One might think that it is obvious that there are numbers: that we produce numbers by writing them. But realists think that in addition to numerals that we write there are numbers that are not created by human beings.

A mathematical theory is a set of statements about a putative class of mathematical objects. Thus, for example, arithmetic is a theory about the natural numbers, 0, 1, 2, 3, ... One way of viewing the realist debate in mathematics is to think in terms of mathematical theories. Two central problems in the philosophy of mathematics, when looked at from the point of view of theories, are the following:

- *The truth problem*: What is it that makes some mathematical theories true and others false?
- *The necessity problem*: Mathematical theories, if they are true, are not just contingently true but necessarily true. What makes them necessarily true?

As we have seen, realists have a straightforward answer to the truth problem: a mathematical theory is true if and only if what it says about a class of mathematical objects is really true of them.

The necessity problem, however, is more difficult. A statement is necessarily true if and only if it is true in every possible world (see Chapter 11). In order to make mathematical theories necessarily true, it would seem that realists are committed to holding that mathematical objects necessarily exist, that is, that they exist in every possible world. Platonism about mathematical objects was constructed in part to deal with the necessity problem. Platonism holds that there is a realm of mathematical objects that is distinct from the physical world and that this realm exists in every possible world.

As we shall see, Platonism has epistemological problems. As alternatives, we shall look at naturalist realism and hybrid realism. Naturalists hold that mathematical objects are parts of the natural world. Naturalists have difficulty dealing with the necessity problem (but, as we shall see, some naturalists have tried to overcome it). There are also hybrid realists who believe that some mathematical objects are natural objects, but that others are Platonic objects.

10.2 Platonism

Most Platonists hold that either all or some mathematical objects are *sets*.[1] To understand mathematical Platonism we need to understand what sets are and their role in modern mathematics. We shall begin not by talking about sets *per se*, but about numbers. There are different sorts of numbers. The natural numbers are the numbers 0, 1, 2, 3 and so on. The rational numbers are the fractions, $\frac{1}{2}$, $\frac{1}{4}$, $\frac{3}{4}$, $\frac{1}{3}$, $\frac{1}{8}$ and so on. The real numbers are the decimal numbers 0.5, 0.3333..., 3.1415... and so on. For each natural number there is a unique next natural number: the natural numbers are discretely ordered. The rational and real numbers, in contrast, are densely ordered: between any two rational numbers there is another rational number and between any two real numbers there is another real number. There are other sorts of numbers, such as negative numbers and complex numbers, but we will not deal with them in this chapter.

In the late-nineteenth century, mathematicians found a way of reducing all these sorts of numbers to a single sort of thing: sets. A set is a collection of things.[2] The set of x, y and z, for example, is written $\{x, y, z\}$. Some sets have other sets as members. One of the fundamental notions used in this reduction is that of a sequence. A sequence might seem to be unlike a set in that the same thing can occur more than once in a sequence and the order in which things occur matters in a sequence. A sequence with n members is written $<x_1, ..., x_n>$. A sequence, however, is just a set. The two-member sequence $<x, y>$ is really the set $\{x, \{x, y\}\}$, the three-membered sequence $<x, y, z>$ is the same as $<x, <y, z>>$, which is $\{x, \{x, \{y, \{y, z\}\}\}\}$. Four-membered sequences, five-membered sequences and so on are constructed in the same way. We can even construct infinitely long sequences in this way.

Let us turn to the construction of the natural numbers. The number 0 is the empty set, $\emptyset$. The other natural numbers are just sequences. The number 1 is the sequence $<0>$ or $\{\emptyset\}$. The number two is the sequence $<0, 1>$. The number three is the sequence $<0, 1, 2>$. In general, for each number n, we define the number $n + 1$ as the sequence of all the natural numbers up to and including n.

Rational numbers are taken to be sets of sequences of natural numbers with two members. For example, ½ is a set that includes the pair $<1, 2>$, the pair $<2, 4>$ and so on. We use infinite sequences of rational numbers to construct real numbers. For example, the square root of 2 is the sequence of all rational numbers such that squaring them yields a number less than or equal to 2.

Note that the construction of the real numbers requires the existence of infinite sets. In order to accomplish such a construction, set theorists need to assume that there are infinite sets. But this is not all. The mathematician Georg Cantor showed that, given some reasonable assumptions, the existence of an infinite set implies that there are sets that are bigger than this infinite set. In fact, he showed that there is a hierarchy of infinities: there are infinitely many infinities, each larger than those that came before. These infinite sets are sometimes called "transfinite sets".

Other sorts of mathematical objects, such as functions, spaces and so on, are also reducible to sets. For example, consider the function x^2. This function can be taken to be a set of pairs of numbers. The first member of each ordered pair is a number and the second member of that ordered pair is the square of that number, for example, $<2, 4>$ is in this set. Thus, out of the late-nineteenth century came a unified ontology of mathematics: the universe of sets.

If we are to be realists about the existence of sets, Platonism would seem to be the obvious theory. Sets do not seem to be the sort of things that exist in the natural world. It would seem that we cannot see them, hear them, taste them or have sense experience of them in any way. Of course, there may be things in the natural world that we cannot sense, such as subatomic particles. But subatomic particles (according to physical theory) act causally on things to bring about phenomena. Subatomic particles are *causally efficacious*. Sets, however, do not seem to be causally efficacious. Thus, if they exist, sets seem to stand apart from the natural world.

As we shall see, Penelope Maddy denies that sets are nowhere. She claims that they are located in space and are constituents of the natural world. She holds, for example, that not only are there some books in Stu's office, but also that the set of those books is in his office. This may do for sets of physical things, but the Platonist postulates that there are pure sets in addition to sets of things. Pure sets are the sets that can be built up from the empty set, as in the construction of natural numbers given above. Nothing that is not a set can enter into the construction of a pure set (nothing else can be members, or members of members, etc., of pure sets). It would seem that pure sets cannot be located in the same place as their members. (As we shall see in §10.3, however, Maddy has a reply to this objection.)

Platonism about mathematical entities is not without its own problems. It has two of the problems that we saw with regard to non-reductive realism in ethics (see §8.2):[3]

- Platonism is ontologically extravagant. It postulates an odd sort of entity that seems unconnected with the natural world.
- Platonism is epistemologically difficult. It postulates the existence of some sort of mysterious means by which we know about mathematical entities.

Platonism is ontologically extravagant also in the sense that it is not quantitatively parsimonious; it postulates that there is a very large number of these strange objects (or, more correctly, it postulates these entities in "quantities" beyond number).

Some Platonists, for example the mathematician Kurt Gödel (1947), try to solve the epistemological problem by holding that we have a special faculty of intuition that allows us to know about these objects. As we saw, some non-reductive realists about morality adopt the very same move. Paul Benacerraf (1973), however, points out that the mere postulation of a type of intuition is not enough by itself. One way of putting Benacerraf's complaint[4] is to say that it is not clear how this intuition can be reliable. We can justify a belief that, say, it is raining outside by citing a causal mechanism that connects the raindrops falling outside with our belief that it is raining. Why should we believe an intuition about mathematics? The Platonist tells us that there can be no causal connection between our minds and mathematical objects, since we understand causation to be a natural relation between physical events. In the case of our belief that it is raining, we can cite the process of perception that leads us to believe that it is raining: light rays reflect off surfaces and enter our eyes, our optic nerves are excited and so on. This mechanism is reliable; it is not perfectly reliable, but it is reliable enough to justify trusting it in this case. But there is no such causal mechanism connecting us with the Platonic realm that justifies accepting our intuitions about sets. Thus, Benacerraf's complaint gives us a reason for believing that we could not possibly have any knowledge of a Platonic realm of sets. And this in turn can be used as a premise in an argument against the realist. The argument has the form of an attitude problem: we have abundant knowledge of the mathematical facts; we could not have any knowledge of a Platonic realm of sets; therefore, mathematical facts are not reducible to facts about a Platonic realm of sets.

10.2.1 Platonism, logic, and knowledge

Postulating a special faculty of knowing for mathematics should be a last resort. It is preferable to say that our knowledge about mathematics comes about in similar ways to other sorts of knowledge. Traditionally philosophers divide what is known into what is known *a posteriori* (or empirically) and what is known *a priori*. Since we cannot know about Platonic objects empirically, Platonists are forced to claim that mathematical knowledge is *a priori*.

In Chapter 5, we saw that Kant claims that we know the truths about geometry by reflecting on an innate sense of space. In addition, Kant claims that we know the truths about arithmetic by reflecting on an innate sense of time. We understand the series of numbers, for example, through our understanding of what it is for things to be placed one after another in time. Kant's view explains our understanding of at least two branches of mathematics in completely *a priori* terms; moreover, he appeals to faculties of thought that he uses for a wide range of other purposes in his epistemology.

But Kant's view has two rather important problems. First, as we saw in Chapter 5, Kant's view had a serious problem with incorporating non-Euclidean geometry. Moreover, Kant's view is psychologistic: it turns mathematics in effect into a branch of psychology and treats mathematics merely as a way in which we organize the world, not as a way in which the world is organized independently of us. Hence psychologism is very clearly an anathema to Platonism and a form of anti-realism about mathematics. Thus, if we are to find an epistemology for Platonism, we have to look at views other than Kant's.

One of the historically most important epistemologies of mathematics is *logicism*.[5] According to logicism, mathematical knowledge is a type of logical knowledge. That is, we know the truths of mathematics (or at least of some branches of mathematics) in the same way that we know the logical truths. A logical truth, for example, that every object is identical with itself (formally, "$\forall x\ x = x$"), is supposed to be self-evident or at least to follow from self-evident truths by means of self-evident principles of reasoning. When applied to a branch of mathematics, for example arithmetic, a set of axioms that are supposed to be self-evident is laid down. Then all the other truths of arithmetic can be derived from that set of axioms and the rules of logic.

Of course, one might object that it is not clear what makes logical truths self-evident, and so we have not cleared up a mystery by saying that we know mathematical truths in the same way. It does seem, however, that we know (at least some of) the logical truths. We know that everything is identical to itself, that every proposition implies itself and so on. So whatever epistemology we accept had better allow us to know these facts. Thus, we are making an advance by reducing mathematical knowledge to logical knowledge.

Perhaps the most widely cited problem with logicism is that it can be shown that given any computable set of axioms sufficient to prove a given fragment of the truths of arithmetic there is a formula that intuitively is true but that cannot be proved to be true by those axioms. This is the famous first incompleteness theorem of Kurt Gödel.[6] A logical system is computable if it is of the sort that can be programmed into a computer, that is, if there is some finite representation that will generate it.[7]

Modern defenders of logicism have avoided Gödel's problem by adopting logical systems that are not computable. These systems cannot be represented in a finite way.[8] This makes the epistemology more complicated. We cannot merely survey a finite set of axioms to see whether they are all self-evident. It might be, on this view, that we cannot be said to know all of arithmetic. Whether this is really a difficulty for logicism, we shall leave to the reader.

Another objection is that mathematical truths cannot be logical truths since they postulate the existence of things. Logicism tells us that the statements of our mathematical theories are literally true. Some of these statements postulate the existence of objects. For example, the standard axioms for arithmetic (the so-called Peano axioms) have as their first axiom "0 is a number". From this axiom and the principles of standard logic, we derive "There exists at least one number". Thus, realism about numbers is logically true if logicism is correct.

Many philosophers have held that we cannot derive things into existence, that the existence of a thing cannot be a logical truth. Consider again the sentence "There exists at least one number" and compare it to the sentence "Everything is identical to itself". The latter seems more certain: if someone denies it, we would think him or her crazy. But if someone were to deny the existence of numbers, we would not think him or her crazy. (In this chapter we discuss several such people.) To make matters worse, the Peano axioms imply not only that there are numbers, but that there are infinitely many of them. Does this seem like a logical truth?

A logicist may reply, however, that there are grades of self-evidence. Not all of the axioms of standard logical systems are as obvious as the principle that everything is self-identical. For example, classical logic (the standard logical system) is often axiomatized with the double negation axiom ("not not A, implies A", for any proposition A). There are people, such as intuitionist logicians (see §10.8) who doubt this principle. In fact, there are very few supposed logical axioms that have not been doubted by someone at one time or another.

Another form of Platonism, due to Mark Balaguer (1998), provides us with a different epistemology for Platonism. Balaguer claims that every consistent mathematical system exists. This means that if we have a set of mathematical statements from which we cannot derive a contradiction, they represent a group of mathematical objects. Balaguer calls this view "full-blown Platonism". It avoids the epistemological problem with standard Platonism by claiming that in order to know that certain objects exist all we need is to know whether the set of statements about that class of objects is consistent.

A consistency proof does not require any connection with the entities themselves. It only requires that we know whether a contradiction follows logically from a set of postulates. Now, consistency proofs in mathematics are often extremely complicated and they often require even more mathematics than are in the theories to be proved consistent. Often they are "relative consistency" proofs: they prove only that one theory is consistent if another one is consistent. These sorts of consistency proofs have limited epistemological value.[9] Balaguer, however, does not appeal to such proofs. He claims instead that there is an intuitive notion of consistency and that we can come to know whether a theory is consistent in this sense (1998: 69–75). He does not, however, give us details of how we can come to know whether a theory is consistent, but merely claims that we can (*ibid.*: 73).

10.2.2 Reference to mathematical objects

Closely connected with Bennaceraf's epistemological problem is an issue from the philosophy of language. Recall our discussions in Chapters 5 and 6 of the causal theory of reference. According to the causal theory of reference, words refer to things because they are connected to those things through a causal chain. For example, the name "Stu" is connected to Stuart Brock because as a child he was dubbed with this nickname (perhaps someone pointed at him and said "Thi is Stu") and then this use of the name was transmitted to others. One problem with Platonic objects is that it is difficult to describe a causal process, in particular the start of a causal process, whereby a word, such as "0", or "set", comes to designate these objects.

According to Balaguer, this worry about Platonism is misplaced. He distinguishes between a word referring to an object in a *thick* sense and its referring to an object in a *thin* sense (1998: 49f.). When Stu says "Ed is in his office", this sentence is about Ed in a thick sense. There is a causal chain that leads from Stu's use of the name "Ed" to the person Ed. On the other hand, suppose Stu tells his son Julian a story about a village and describes certain events that happen in that village. Also suppose that, unknown to Stu, there is a village that exactly matches Stu's description. Stu's story is about this village in the thin sense: it just happens to match Stu's description.

On Balaguer's view, mathematical theories are about mathematical objects only in this thin sense. He says that every consistent theory describes some mathematical reality, but it does not do so because of any causal connection between mathematical entities and the theory.

10.3 Naturalism

Let us now move on to naturalism about mathematics. Naturalists construct mathematical objects from physical objects or other natural objects. On this view, we can have causal links between mathematical objects and our thought and talk, and so causal explanations of mathematical knowledge and of reference to mathematical objects are possible.

We have already been introduced to Maddy's naturalism. She holds[10] that sets are natural objects. Sets exist in time and space: they occupy the same space as their members. Thus, for example, the set of the three eggs in Stu's refrigerator is also in Stu's refrigerator. Moreover, Maddy says that when you see some things, you also perceive the set of those things. So when Stu looks in his refrigerator and sees the three eggs, he also sees the set of those three eggs. Thus, Maddy has a straightforward reply to the epistemological problem regarding Platonism. She thinks that our knowledge of mathematical objects has its origin in perceptual knowledge. We abstract from our perceptual experience of sets the general properties of sets. And, on the basis of this, we develop our mathematics.

Maddy does not explicitly give a reply to the necessity problem, but we think one can be given on her behalf. According to Maddy, not only is the set of, say, the three eggs in one's refrigerator also in the refrigerator, but the set of that set is in the refrigerator and so on. If Maddy were to hold that a set of things necessarily exists wherever and whenever those things exist, then she can hold that in every possible world in which one object exists, a whole hierarchy of sets exists in that world. As long as there are no empty worlds, this will be enough to secure the truths of standard mathematics.

Maddy appeals to the fact that we have numerical knowledge about the world (e.g. Stu's knowing that there are three eggs in his refrigerator) to argue that we perceive sets (1990: 58–63). According to Maddy, numbers are properties of sets. Thus, for example, the number three is a property of all sets with three members (such as the set of eggs in Stu's fridge). Maddy claims that when we perceive a numerical fact, such as that there are three eggs in the refrigerator, we perceive that a set has a particular property, hence we perceive a set. The following is her argument:

(P1) We perceive numerical facts about the world. For example, that there are three eggs in the refrigerator.   (empirical fact)

(P2) It is part of our best theory of the world that numbers are properties of sets, not of ordinary physical objects.

(C1) The fact that there are three eggs in the refrigerator is more perspicuously stated as "the size of the set of the eggs in the refrigerator is three".   (from P2)

(C2) Therefore, we perceive facts about sets. For example, when we see that there are three eggs in the refrigerator, we in fact are seeing that the size of the set of eggs in the refrigerator is three.   (from P1 and C1)

Perceiving facts about sets is, for Maddy, tantamount to perceiving sets.

Perhaps the most controversial premise in this argument is (P2). Maddy argues for (P2) by examining and discarding the alternatives. In particular, she argues that it is implausible to suggest that numbers are properties of physical objects. In the example above, it would seem odd to claim that the number three is the property of the three eggs put together. It is implausible to suggest this because these physical objects would have to have all sorts of numerical properties, depending on how they are construed. The number of atoms in the eggs, for example, is much larger than three, as is the number of molecules, and so on.[11] In sum, Maddy thinks that there is no plausible alternative to holding that numbers are properties of sets (1990: 60–62).

A Platonist might complain to Maddy that even if we do perceive sets, we never perceive the empty set or the pure sets: the sets constructed from the empty set. On Maddy's naturalism, the pure sets do not exist (1990: 156f.).[12] But this objection can be met. We can reconstruct mathematics without the pure sets. Instead of having a special empty set, we can nominate anything that is not a set to be our "empty set". The defining characterization is that the empty set has no members. Let us choose a particular egg to be the empty set. The egg has no members, so we call it the "empty set". Then the set of the empty set is just the set that has this egg as its only member and so on. Maddy thinks that we also perceive the set of the set of the egg when we perceive the egg. So we perceive the number one as well. And so on.

Balaguer has another criticism of Maddy. Balaguer points out that stimulations of our sensory organs only contain patterns that are created by the structure of the matter perceived. For example, the pattern on someone's retina when she looks at three eggs is determined merely by the light reflecting from the three eggs. There is no information in this retinal image about anything "over and above the aggregate" of material objects that are perceived (Balaguer 1998: 33). Thus, he thinks that Maddy's view is empirically false. If we accept Balaguer's criticism of Maddy, and accept the second premise of her argument, we must reject the first premise. It would seem that we do not perceive numerical facts about the world. Thus, Maddy could ask in reply: how do we know numerical facts about the world?

Another sort of naturalism appeals to mereology (which we met in §5.3). Mereologists think that instead of talking about sets and their members, we should talk about objects and their parts. Lewis (1991), together with John Burgess and Allen Hazen, has developed a theory of how to construct things that have all the formal properties of sets from natural objects and mereology.

One worry about mereology is that it takes the fusion of two things to be a thing. So, the fusion of Ed's left elbow and Zermela's nose is itself a thing. But this does not seem like a natural object in the normal sense.

With regard to the necessity problem, Lewis claims that we should not look just at the objects in a single possible world. Rather, we should take the objects that exist in any possible worlds.[13] If a mathematical statement is taken to be about the totality of possible objects, then it will get the same truth-value in every possible world. Thus, the truths of mathematics are necessarily true and the mathematical falsities are necessarily false.

The epistemological problem is supposed to be solved by having our mathematical knowledge develop through our understanding of aggregates of normal objects. The metaphysical problem is supposed to be solved by rejecting the view that there are any special mathematical objects.

10.4 Hybrid realism

Hybrid realism is the view that some mathematical objects are natural and others are Platonic. This view is quite popular, although it is often categorized by its proponents as a form of naturalism. The motivation for hybrid theories is epistemological. We have causal relationships with some mathematical objects and from these we abstract their structure. We then make generalizations to justify beliefs about mathematical objects to which we have no direct access.

Some *structuralists* are hybrid realists.[14] Structuralists hold that mathematics is not about a particular class of objects, but about the structure of all objects. Let us consider the example of arithmetic. Traditional Platonists think that arithmetic is about a particular sequence of objects: the natural numbers. Structuralists hold that arithmetic is not about any particular sequence of objects, but about anything that has the same structure as this sequence. Arithmetic is no more about a sequence of abstract objects then it is about any such sequence of concrete objects.

For structuralists, we gain mathematical knowledge through a process of abstraction and generalization. For example, consider the following series of marks: | || ||| ||||. We abstract from our experience of structures like this the idea of a series of four objects.

According to structuralists, we generalize from these sorts of experiences to get the idea of series with any number of members. From this process of abstraction and generalization we get the idea of infinite series, such as the series of natural numbers.[15] The appeal to abstraction and generalization is how the structuralists attempt to avoid the epistemological problem with traditional Platonism.

Structuralists worry that there are not enough concrete objects to provide all the structures that we need to do all of mathematics. Moreover, they agree with Platonists that mathematics is necessarily true. So, they postulate abstract objects as well. Some structuralists, such as Michael Resnik (1997) and Stuart Shapiro (1997) postulate a supersensible realm of sets, like traditional Platonists. John Bigelow (1988), on the other hand, claims that mathematical structures are *universals*. A universal is a property. According to Bigelow, a mathematical universal is a property that may be instantiated by a group of objects. Some universals – those that are instantiated by groups of objects – exist in space and time. Others, however, are uninstantiated: they are Platonic abstract objects (see Bigelow & Pargetter 1990).

Thus, hybrid realism still has the metaphysical problem. Hybrid realists postulate a great many objects and some of them are Platonic objects.

10.5 Formalism

Let us now turn to anti-realism. Our first form of anti-realism is also the most extreme. According to formalism, mathematics is just a game played with symbols, or rather a collection of games. Each of these games has very strict rules. These rules tell us what we can assume (as axioms) and what we derive from what. But on this view there are no objects that these symbols are about. The symbols refer to nothing and they have no meaning outside their use in the game.

One objection to formalism comes again from Gödel's first incompleteness theorem. Recall that, according to this theorem, no computable theory can entail all of the truths of arithmetic. Thus, no game with a finite set of rules will allow the derivation of all the truths of arithmetic. This may be a useful argument against a particular sort of formalism[16] but it is not an argument against formalism in general, for we can set up a further game – a "metagame" – that llows us to make mathematical claims about the first game. In this metagame it can be asserted that the particular "unprovable but true" statement is true of the first game. Similarly, we can invent metametagames and so on, to do the similar work with regard to the metagame, the metametagame and so on.

A more important objection against formalism is that it divorces mathematics from its uses. For example, if mathematics merely consists of games, then there would seem to be nothing to ensure that they can be used to produce scientific theories that give accurate predictions about the world. Particular formalist philosophies of mathematics do give us ways of dealing with this problem,[17] but we shall not deal with these. For the most part, they are of purely historical interest or are more complicated than can be treated in this sort of book. Instead we turn to the contemporary successor of formalism: fictionalism. Fictionalism differs from formalism in that formalism is a form of non-factualism (it holds that mathematical statements do not represent propositions). Fictionalism, on the other hand, does hold that mathematical statements mean propositions, and that these propositions are the contents of a story rather than true of the real world. Before we discuss fictionalism, we look at an argument that makes more precise the objection that we have just been discussing.

10.6 The indispensability argument

A key argument for realism is Quine's (1953) and Putnam's (1971) so-called indispensability argument. Our version owes a good deal to Mark Colyvan (2001).

(P1) Some mathematical theories are indispensable to our best scientific theories.
(P2) We should accept whatever is indispensable to our best scientific theories. (scientific realism)
(P3) We should accept these mathematical theories. (from P1 and P2)

(P4) These mathematical theories are committed to the existence of mathematical entities.
(P5) We should accept the entities to which our theories are committed. (principle of ontological commitment – see §2.1)

(C) Therefore, we should accept the existence of mathematical entities.

(from P3, P4 and P5)

Premise 1 needs to be explained. There are two senses in which mathematical theories are indispensable to scientific theories. First, scientific theories themselves sometimes explicitly use the concepts of and quantify over the objects of particular mathematical theories. For example, the following passage is taken from a popular textbook in quantum mechanics:

> *Postulate 4.1* For every dynamical system there exists a wave function that is a continuous, integratable, single-valued function of the parameters of the system and of time, and from which all possible predictions of the physical properties of the system can be obtained.
>
> (Rae 1992: 63)

This is the first postulate of quantum mechanics. It postulates the existence of a certain sort of function – a Schrödinger wave function – for each physical system (an electron, an atom, etc.). This function has certain features, such as being continuous and integratable, that are defined in a particular mathematical theory: calculus. The point is that this statement is in a standard formulation of one of our best scientific theories and it uses concepts from and quantifies over entities of a mathematical theory.

Secondly, science also uses mathematical theories. And these mathematical theories quantify over mathematical objects. Mathematics is used a great deal in science to derive various principles, laws and other sorts of scientific facts. These facts often cannot be deduced from the basic principles of scientific theories without the use of mathematical theories.

Recall the example of the Hardy–Weinberg law in §8.5. The derivation of this law uses the binomial theorem, that is, for any two numbers x and y, $(x + y)^2 = x^2 + 2xy + y^2$. This simple law of mathematics is used to justify a law of genetics. And this law quantifies over numbers. There are a great many examples of this sort.

Thus, if the anti-realist about mathematics wants to be a scientific realist, she needs to accomplish two tasks: (i) she must show that our best scientific theories can be formulated without quantification over entities that are not accepted in her form of anti-realism; (ii) she must show that her anti-realist reconstruction of mathematics is adequate to allow for the derivation of what is considered to be scientific fact.

10.7 Fictionalism

The indispensability argument attempts to show that mathematics is necessary for the way in which we understand the world. But as Balaguer points out, there is something rather superfluous about mathematics in our descriptions of the world. Consider the statement, "The water in the bath is 30°C". The number 30 here is used to describe the average motion of the particles in the water, for that is what temperature is. The number itself is not really part of the physical system being described. Rather, it is part of the description of the system (Balaguer 1998: 133). Fictionalism is one sort of anti-realism that attempts to capture the idea that although mathematics can be used to describe the world, its entities are not really part of the world and can be eliminated.

The doctrine of mathematical fictionalism is the view that mathematical theories are fictions that we use to describe the world. We can use sentences that seem to refer to mathematical entities in our descriptions, but these entities do not exist and the phenomena that they are used to describe exist independently of mathematics.

The most famous fictionalist is Hartry Field. Field's programme has two parts. The first step is to reformulate our descriptions of the world, in particular our scientific descriptions of the world, to eliminate reference to mathematical objects. In this way, it can be shown what it means for physical phenomena to be independent of mathematical objects. The second part of the programme is to show how we can understand mathematical theories and their applications in a fictionalist way.

Let us begin with the removal of mathematical entities from science. This is called the "nominalization" of science. We start with an easy example. Consider the statement "The set of aardvarks in Stu's house is of size two". In this statement, we seem to refer to two mathematical entities: a set of aardvarks and the number two. We can eliminate the purported reference to the set quite easily, for the content of this sentence can be rewritten as "There are exactly two aardvarks in Stu's house". We still seem, however, to be referring to a number. But this too can be eliminated, for we can say "There is an aardvark x and an aardvark y such that x and y are not identical, x and y are both in Stu's house, and x and y are the only aardvarks in Stu's house".[18] Here we have a sentence that does not seem to make reference to any mathematical object. This sentence is, however, much more complicated than the first two sentences. Thus the fictionalist says that purported reference to mathematical objects can be removed from our descriptions of the world but allowing such reference in certain cases makes our descriptions much simpler. Hence, mathematics is a useful fiction.

Nominalizing real scientific theories is a very complicated business. In his book *Science without Numbers*, Field gives a nominalization of classical gravitation theory (essentially the theory that Newton developed, but that was tidied up in the eighteenth and nineteenth centuries). In order to nominalize the theory of gravity, he must get rid of purported reference to mathematical objects in statements such as "The force of gravity between two objects m_1 and m_2 is the gravitational constant times the masses of m_1 and m_2 divided by the square of the distance between them". Here we have several cases of purported reference to mathematical objects. The masses of the two objects are given in numbers, and so is the distance between them. In addition, the gravitational constant is the number 6.67×10^{-11}. It is a tall order to eliminate all of these, and Field does so in terms of points, lines and regions in space, and relative motions of objects.[19]

Consider the distance between two objects. Suppose we want to say that it is 5 metres. Then what we do is take two objects that are one metre apart. We can then say that the distance between these latter two objects is congruent to five non-overlapping segments of the line between the first two objects. Moreover, we can say that these five segments add together to make the whole line between the objects. We can get rid of the reference to the number five in the same way that we got rid of the reference to two in the aardvark example above. Thus, we have a description of the distance between two things that only makes use of lines in space. A line moreover is a one dimensional region in space, and Field thinks that regions in space exist. Similar reductions must be done to remove reference to numbers measuring mass, the gravitational constant and so on, in order to provide a nominalized theory of gravity.

Clearly, when all of these nominalizations have been done, the theory becomes very complicated. Colyvan uses the complexity of nominalized scientific theories to argue against Field's programme. Colyvan asks us to contrast a theory that refers to mathematical objects and its nominalized counterpart. If the original theory is simpler and more elegant (as is the case with the theory of gravity), then we have grounds to prefer to believe the original theory over the nominalized theory (Colyvan 2001: ch. 4).

The second part of Field's project is his fictionalism. Field is not entirely clear whether he is a prefix or non-cognitivist fictionalist, but this will not matter for our discussion. One worry about taking mathematics to be a fiction is that it would seem foolhardy for scientists to trust a mere fiction when deducing facts from scientific theories. For if mathematics is a mere fiction, then perhaps some of the laws and scientific propositions that can be derived using mathematics together with scientific theories would be false. Field responds to this worry by formulating a requirement that any mathematical theory must be *conservative* with regard to nominalized scientific theories. A mathematical theory is conservative with regard to nominalized scientific theories if and only if it does not contradict any consistent nominalized theory N. Suppose, for example, that N is a consistent scientific theory and that M is a conservative mathematical theory. Let p be a proposition that cannot be derived from N and logic alone. Then the theory N together with the proposition "not-p" is also consistent. Since M is a conservative mathematical theory, it is consistent with both N and $N + p$. If M together with N allowed the derivation of p, then M would be not be consistent with $N + p$. In other words, adding the mathematical theory does not add any new content to a scientific theory. It only makes proving things in the theory easier (Field 1980: 11–13).

We can see why Field also thinks that he has avoided the metaphysical and epistemological problems that affect Platonism. His theory is reasonably moderate in terms of the entities that it postulates and it is clear that we have access to fictions, since we invent them.

10.8 Intuitionism

Now we turn to a very different sort of anti-realism: intuitionism. Intuitionism holds that mathematical objects are completely accessible to us because we *construct* them. In addition, intuitionists do not have a problem with the inaccessibility of mathematical truth. They think that what is true about mathematics is a subsidiary notion. Intuitionist mathematics deals instead with what can be proved. Thus, in order to understand intuitionism we will have to understand what intuitionists mean by "construction" and what they mean by "proof". We divide intuitionists into two camps: psychological intuitionists and non-psychological intuitionists. We shall discuss psychological intuitionism first.

The father of intuitionism, L. E. J. Brouwer, was a psychological intuitionist. According to Brouwer, mathematics is an activity of the mind. The objects of mathematics are mental constructs. The properties of these objects are those that can be proved of them, at least in principle.

Intuitionist mathematics takes proof to be determined by a means for proving logically simple statements (such as "2 + 2 = 4") and methods for proving logically complex statements (statements that include logical particles, such as "and", "or", "not", "all", "some" and "if, then"). The proof of a simple statement requires a method that can be specified in terms of a sequence of simple steps. As we shall see, some contemporary intuitionists interpret this in terms of the sorts of methods we can program a computer to do. Proofs of logically complex statements follow a set of canons of intuitionist proof, one for each of the logical particles.[20]

We shall not present the intuitionist interpretation of the logical particles in detail, but merely note a few differences between it and the standard, or "classical", interpretation of the logical particles. According to intuitionism, to prove a statement of the form "*A* or *B*", we must provide either a proof of *A* or a proof of *B*. This is a much stronger condition than the classical condition. In classical mathematics we can show that "*A* or not-*A*" is always true, even if we have no way of showing either *A* or its negation. In intuitionist logic that is not the case. As we saw in §6.6, they claim that the law of excluded middle, "*A* or not-*A*", sometimes fails to be true.[21] To prove a statement of the form "There is something that is *F*" in intuitionism we need to find an intuitionist method for finding a particular thing that has the property *F*. This is also a very demanding requirement. As we shall see below, in classical mathematics, we can sometimes show that there is something that has a given property without having a clue with regard to which particular thing has that property.

Psychological intuitionism has two virtues. One virtue is its ontological economy. It does not postulate the existence of anything outside the mind. The other virtue is epistemological. We can understand mathematics and its objects by reflecting on the operation of the human mind.

At the heart of psychological intuitionism is the notion of a mental construction. When Brouwer describes constructions, he often uses rather mystical language. This is in part because he thinks of the mathematical process as an activity that does not occur in language. When we construct mathematical objects, according to Brouwer, we do so without language. Thus, he has the problem of using language to describe a languageless process. For example, he talks about constructing "the twoity" in the mental construction of the natural number two (1981: 4). But his basic idea is not that mysterious. Brouwer adopts from Kant the idea that we have an internal intuition of time (see Chapter 5). From this intuition, we get an idea of an ongoing series. We can think of numbers as elements in such a series.

By treating mathematics as an essentially mental activity, psychological intuitionism psychologizes mathematics (see §10.2.1) Psychologism about mathematics may be an unattractive view if we want to be realists about science. As we have seen, many of our current scientific theories refer to mathematical objects. If these objects are mere mental constructions, then it would seem that these theories are not about subatomic particles or whatever, but are about our minds. Moreover, if the laws of mathematics are about the workings of our minds, rather than about some extra-mental reality, then it would seem that our use of these laws to derive laws in science makes derived scientific laws about the workings of human minds.

But there are also non-psychological interpretations of intuitionist mathematics. Dummett, for example, adopts a version of intuitionism that is "stripped of its psychologistic guise" (1978b: 200). Dummett treats intuitionism about mathematics as a form of verificationism (see Chapter 6). The key to non-psychological interpretations of intuitionism is the notion of a step-by-step procedure. Suppose that we want to construct the sequence of natural numbers. Intuitionists, like structuralists, do not think that there must be a unique series of natural numbers. They may take a series of natural numbers to start with a blank space followed by |, || ||| and so on. It is very easy to describe a method for producing the next number, the number after that and so on.[22] The key here is that each step is something simple that we know how to do (e.g. make a mark on a piece of paper) and that we are given a method for moving on to the next step after each step and the method tells us when, if ever, to stop.

Thus, the notion of a construction is no longer a purely psychological concept. These step-by-step instructions can be given to machines, such as computers. In fact, many people now take intuitionist constructions merely to be computer programs. Thus, non-psychological intuitionism's constructions can be taken to be mind-independent entities.

A mathematical object for intuitionists is something that we can construct using a step-by-step method. For example, a set is said to exist if there is a procedure that tells us when a thing belongs to that set. Consider, for example, the collection of even natural numbers. If we can divide a number by two, then we can include it in this set. Moreover, we can construct a step-by-step method that tells us of any given number that it can be divided by two. Thus, intuitionists think that there is a set of even natural numbers.

This brings us to the intuitionist theory of infinity. There is no step-by-step procedure that at any finite time allows us to have an infinite collection of, say, natural numbers. But these step-by-step procedures might be endless. For example, our procedure to find the even numbers can go on forever. This set is infinite for intuitionists. Their infinity is what is sometimes called a "potential infinity". A potential infinity is to be contrasted with an actual or complete infinity. A completely infinite set has, as it were, an infinite number of members all at one time. A potentially infinite set at any time is incomplete: at no stage of the construction is it finished. Moreover, for intuitionists, potential infinity is the only sort of infinity there is.

Although the entities of non-psychological intuitionism are mind-independent it is still a form of anti-realism. First, the boundaries on what can count as a mathematical object are established by what a human mind can do in principle and what counts as a mathematical act depends on what in principle we can prove. Secondly, intuitionism rejects the vast majority of objects postulated by standard mathematics. For example, it says that transfinite sets do not exist and our statements about them are false (or, for some intuitionists, even meaningless).

Non-psychological intuitionism has certain virtues. It gives us straightforward access to mathematical objects through constructions that can be described in terms of a sequence of simple steps. Thus, intuitionists not only avoid the epistemological problem of the access to Platonic objects, but also avoid the structuralists' commitment to a theory of mathematical abstraction.

One of the most interesting features of intuitionism is that it is a revisionist theory of mathematics: it is a revolutionary form of anti-realism. It does not claim to capture all of standard mathematics, nor does it claim to explain the practices of ordinary mathematicians; instead, it says that much of ordinary mathematics is epistemologically suspect or even meaningless. As we have seen, intuitionists reject the hierarchy of transfinite sets. They also reject certain sorts of alleged proofs that mathematicians standardly give. For example, mathematicians sometimes claim to prove the existence of some object with a particular property without having a means for finding out which object has that property. Intuitionists think that such "proofs" are not proofs at all. In order to prove that something of a particular sort exists, we need a means for finding at least one example of that sort.

Some mathematicians and philosophers think that the rejection of classical "existence proofs" creates a serious problem for intuitionism. We cannot, for example, prove the *intermediate value theorem* in intuitionist maths. Suppose that f is a continuous function on the real numbers between and including 0 and 1. To say that a function is continuous means, roughly, that if we draw a graph of it there are no breaks in the line of the graph. Also suppose that $f(0)$ is a value below 0 and $f(1)$ is greater than 0. The intermediate value theorem says that there is a point x between 0 and 1 such that $f(x) = 0$. This seems obvious: if we draw a continuous line starting below the x-axis and ending up above the x-axis we must go through the x-axis at some point. But we cannot prove this in intuitionist mathematics. Intuitionists, by and large, are happy to live with limitations such as the inability to prove the intermediate value theorem.

But the failure of theorems like this explains to a large extent why intuitionism is not more popular among mathematicians.

Intuitionists think that intuitionism gives us all the mathematics that we really need. They try to show that all scientific applications are catered for within intuitionism. This claim has been challenged by Geoffrey Hellman (1993), who has claimed that intuitionistic mathematics is not powerful enough for some branches of modern science. In particular, he has argued that intuitionist mathematics does not allow us to prove everything we need to do quantum mechanics. Douglas Bridges (1995) has argued in reply that Hellman is wrong on this point, but even if Hellman is right, the intuitionist has at least two responses.[23] First, she can point out that scientists formulate their theories with classical mathematics in mind. If they were constrained to work with intuitionist mathematics, they might come up with quite different but nevertheless empirically adequate theories. Secondly, she can admit that more work is needed: that intuitionists need to construct new structures for use in contemporary physics.

In sum, we can say that intuitionism offers us a trade-off. It gives us a very clear epistemology of mathematics but cannot yield all of classical mathematics. Whether this trade is a good deal is a question that we leave to the reader.

10.9 Response-dependence

Philip Kitcher (1984) sets out a response-dependent theory of mathematics. Like intuitionism, it takes mathematics to be an idealization of our own mathematical abilities. But Kitcher takes the idealization much further than the intuitionists do. In so doing, he attempts to give a philosophical justification for everything that the average mathematician takes to be mathematics. That is, he attempts to justify all of classical mathematics.

The only constraints on the idealization come from the development of mathematics itself. Mathematics expands sometimes because of the demands of science, but also because mathematicians themselves further generalize existing branches of mathematics. When mathematicians invent a new field or type of mathematical object – for example, the negative or complex numbers – they introduce new sorts of processes that they in effect attribute to the ideal mathematician (*ibid.*: 177). Clearly, this ideal mathematician has extraordinary abilities. He or she must be able not only to make collections of arbitrary finite size, but also amass collections of any transfinite number of things.

The postulation of an ideal mathematician avoids the specific epistemological and metaphysical problems that arise for Platonism, but it has epistemological and metaphysical problems of its own. First, it postulates a mathematician with god-like powers. We are supposed to understand what it is like to be this mathematician-god by abstracting and generalizing from our own abilities. Our own collecting activity takes place in time; we never can get to the end of a process of making an infinite collection. Yet Kitcher asks us to imagine an agent who can make collections of any infinite size. Secondly, there is the metaphysical problem of the status of the ideal mathematician.[24] Does this ideal mathematician exist in another possible world? Is it a fictional object? Whether these problems can be overcome or are overridden by the virtues of the theory, we leave as a problem for the reader.

Further reading

There are some good general books and collections on the philosophy of mathematics: Paul Benacerraf and Hilary Putnam (eds), *Philosophy of Mathematics*, 2nd edn (Cambridge: Cambridge University Press, 1983); Arend Heyting, *Intuitionism: An Introduction* (Amsterdam: North Holland, 1956); Michael Potter, *Set Theory and its Philosophy: A Critical Introduction* (Oxford: Oxford University Press, 2004); Matthias Schirn (ed.), *The Philosophy of Mathematics Today* (Oxford: Oxford University Press, 1998); Stewart Shapiro, *Philosophy of Mathematics: Structure and Ontology* (Oxford: Oxford University Press, 1997); and Mary Tiles, *The Philosophy of Set Theory: An Historical Introduction to Cantor's Paradise* (Oxford: Blackwell, 1989).

11 Possible worlds

Whether or not one is a realist about numbers, subatomic particles, moral properties or secondary qualities, it is easy to see the motivation for adopting a realist stance towards such purported entities. But some philosophers are realists of a more radical kind. According to them there are ghosts, goblins, witches, warlocks, angels, archangels, devils and demons. There are little green men who walk around with toast and jam on their heads six days of the week (on Sundays they wear crumpets and honey). There are swans that smoke cigars and monkeys that fly. Such entities are not of our own manufacture: they are real and exist independently of us. And such entities are not mere abstractions: they are concrete entities with a precise spatiotemporal location. What is truly unfortunate, however, is that we shall never become acquainted with these strange and exotic creatures. Why? They exist in a parallel universe – other worlds – spatially, temporally and causally discontinuous with ours.

This somewhat fantastic idea is put forward by David Lewis (1986). The suggestion is made in the context of discussions about modality and related issues. But it is important to stress that these claims are not modal claims. They are merely assertions about what is real. Perhaps, then, we should spell out in a little more detail some of the ontological commitments made by Lewis before we can evaluate his reasons for claiming that such entities are real.

1.1 Modal realism

Modal realism is roughly the conjunction of seven tenets: five onto-logical theses and (at least) two conceptual theses. The *ontological theses* can be stated as follows:

- *Minimal realism.* There are other worlds and other individuals that occupy those worlds.
- *Mind-independence.* The other worlds and individuals are not of our own making. They do not depend on us, our minds, our linguistic practices or our conceptual schemes. They would exist no matter what we thought or said.
- *Parity.* The other worlds are of the same kind of thing as our universe.[1] There is an ontological parity between this world and the other worlds. The individuals that occupy the alternative worlds vary in kind, just as they do in this world.
- *Isolation.* No single world has spatiotemporally disconnected parts. No two worlds are spatiotemporally continuous with one another. Two individuals are part of the same world if and only if there is some spatiotemporal relation that holds between them.
- *Plenitude.* For any collection of individuals, or parts of individuals, from any number of worlds, there is a single world containing any number of duplicates of each, and in any arrangement (so long as the individuals are not too large, or too numerous, or shaped too awkwardly to fit).

On its own, Lewis's ontological thesis is an outrageously implausible hypothesis. The impetus behind the proposal, though, is that it provides a useful way of analysing a diverse range of philosophical notions.[2] This, it is supposed, is good reason to believe it true. Consider the following:

> Logical space is a paradise for philosophers. We have only to believe in the vast realm of *possibilia* and there we find ... the wherewithal to reduce the diversity of notions we must accept as primitive, and thereby to improve the unity and economy of the theory that is our professional concern – total theory, the whole of what we take to be true. What price paradise? If we want the theoretical benefits that talk of *possibilia* brings, the most straightforward way to gain honest title to them is to

accept such talk as the literal truth. It is my view that the price
is right ... the benefits are worth their ontological cost.

(Lewis 1986: 4)

Possible worlds do provide a veritable paradise for philosophers. Lewis is right when he says that the hypothesis is serviceable. Talk of *possibilia* has at the very least clarified various modal
notions, including possibility, contingency and necessity, as well as
an impressive number of other related notions, including counterfactual conditionals, verisimilitude, properties, propositions, causation, determinism and supervenience. Furthermore, *possibilia*
provide us with the necessary tools to *reductively* analyse these
notions; to analyse modal terms without recourse to any primitive
modal component in the *analysandum*. The analysis *is* elegant and
unified. Modal realism, then, has a further component. Let us call
these remaining theses *conceptual theses*:

- *Possibility*. The worlds are *possible* worlds. The worlds of which
  we are not a part are the other ways the world might have been;
  the *merely possible* worlds. All individuals that occupy those
  worlds are *counterparts* of things in other worlds.
- *Actuality*. This world is the *actual* world. The other worlds are
  non-actual worlds. But every world is actual at itself. "Actuality" is an indexical term that serves to pick out the world in
  which its utterance occurs.

The ontological theses and the conceptual theses, taken together,
allow Lewis to make a series of interesting and important reductive
claims. Modal statements and their cognates are to be analysed in
terms of what is true in these worlds or what is true of these possible
individuals. Possibility and necessity, for example, are analysed in
terms of quantification over possible worlds. The proposition that
swans smoke cigars is possible if and only if swans smoke cigars
in some world; it is necessary if and only if swans smoke cigars in
all worlds. Moreover, *de re* modality is to be analysed in terms of
quantification over possible individuals. George Bush is essentially
a politician if and only if all of his counterparts are politicians; Bush
is accidentally a politician if and only if he is a politician but some
of his counterparts are not.

The ontological and conceptual theses, then, form the backbone of the Lewisian hypothesis. Lewis coins his hypothesis "modal realism", but to our minds the title is hardly appropriate. It does not capture what is truly distinctive about the programme. There are realists about modality (modal realists?) who make no reference to any entities that might deserve the name "possible world". Such theorists are committed to the view that there really are modal facts, but their commitment stops there.

Nor would it have done for Lewis to call his thesis "realism about possible worlds". Such a title would have distinguished it from the thesis stated above. The name, though, is inappropriate for other reasons. The realist thesis is, according to Lewis:

> simply the thesis that there are other worlds, and individuals inhabiting these worlds … It is an existential claim, not unlike the claim I would be making if I said that there were Loch Ness monsters, or Red moles in the CIA, or counter examples to Fermat's conjecture, or seraphim. (Lewis 1986: viii)

But this is nothing to write home about. Many modal theoreticians believe in the existence of worlds. Indeed, it seems to be the orthodoxy.

What *is* distinctive about Lewis's thesis is the claim that there is nothing exceptional about the actual world: that the other worlds are of exactly the same kind as ours. They are not only real but often concrete. Hence, Lewis advocates what might more fittingly be called "concrete realism about possible worlds and individuals" and it is this thesis that is truly astounding.[3]

However, Lewis's name for his theory is too well known, and our quibble too small, to warrant a change in terminology. It is worth noting, though, that Lewis himself regretted using the label. His reasons, though, were quite different. Lewis wanted to distance himself from present-day discussions of realism, discussions emanating from philosophers such as Dummett, Putnam and Davidson. Lewis writes:

> my modal realism is simply the thesis that there are other worlds, and individuals inhabiting these worlds …. It is *not* a thesis about our semantic competence, or about the nature of truth, or about bivalence, or about the limits of our knowledge.

> For me the question is about the existence of [merely possible] objects – not the objectivity of a subject matter. (*Ibid.*: viii)

He goes on to assert that "the worlds are not of our own making .. We make languages and concepts and descriptions and imaginary representations that apply to worlds ... But none of these things are the worlds themselves" (*ibid.*: 3). Lewis is therefore a realist about possible worlds and objects in *our* sense of the term "realism".

A number of criticisms have been levelled against Lewis's thesis. Most have been adequately (although not decisively) answered by Lewis (1986). Of those that remain, we shall be concerned with one in particular: the objection from parsimony. The objection, as the name suggests, makes an essential appeal to Ockham's razor. Ockham's razor, it will be recalled, is roughly the principle that one should not multiply kinds of entities without more than compensating explanatory advantage. Considerations of parsimony, then, should be balanced against explanatory power. The objection is that despite Lewis's protestations to the contrary, he fails to strike the right balance. The objection, of course, is a difficult one to make stick. But if the objection is to have any force at all, it must first be demonstrated that modal realism is an unparsimonious theory. Perhaps it might be thought that this premise is uncontroversial. It has, however, been controverted by Lewis himself. Lewis's response relies on the distinction between qualitative and qualitative parsimony. He writes:

> I subscribe to the general view that qualitative parsimony is good in a philosophical or empirical hypothesis; but I recognize no presumption whatever in favour of quantitative parsimony. My realism about possible worlds is merely quantitatively, not qualitatively, unparsimonious. You believe in our actual world already. I ask you to believe in more things of that kind, not in things of some new kind. (1973: 87)

Lewis's point is well taken. As was noted in Chapter 2, even if quantitative parsimony is a theoretical desideratum – and that really is controversial – the anti-realist cannot rely on such considerations to motivate her anti-realism. Moreover, the parity thesis guarantees that other possible worlds are of the same kind of thing as this world – something we are already and independently committed to – so if Lewis's overall theory is qualitatively unparsimonious, it is not because it posits a multitude of worlds.

Nonetheless, Lewis's response is too quick, for he is not only committed to a plurality of other worlds, he is also committed to a plurality of possible *individuals*. Lewis admits that "there are differences of kind between things that are parts of different worlds – one world has electrons and another has none, one has spirits and another has none" (1986: 2). While Lewis's worlds are of the same kind as this world, many of the possible individuals that occupy those worlds are qualitatively distinct from anything that exists at the actual world. How many different kinds of things exist? According to Lewis, there are as many as there could possibly be. It is hard to imagine how a theory could be more qualitatively unparsimonious![4]

But this observation does not, *by itself*, pose any real threat to modal realism. The envisaged objector must do something more; she must show that the analytic benefits are not enough to compensate for the Lewisian ontology. One decisive way this could be done would be to show that every single benefit had by Lewis can be had for less. Lewis himself thinks the prospects of an alternative analysis of modality are bleak, but others disagree. In the next few sections we shall look at alternative proposals and evaluate each in quite general terms.

11.2 Ersatz realism

Perhaps we can adopt an alternative less extravagant ontology that will enable us to enjoy the same conceptual benefits had by Lewis. Such is the aim of the ersatz modal realist.[5] Ersatz realism, though, is not a single unified thesis. Its tenets are many and varied. What unifies them is their denial of the ontological thesis, and their retention of the conceptual thesis – almost.

The ersatzer does not deny the ontological thesis outright. All ersatzers adopt an ontology of *possibilia*, and thus accept the minimal realism and mind-independence theses. What they deny is the parity thesis. Possible worlds are not like the actual world. They are something quite different. Unlike the concrete world, they are abstract entities. The ersatzer will want to tell us more about the nature of these abstract entities. But it is here that opinions diverge radically. Some suggest that a world is a construction out of word types in a natural or artificial language. Others say that a world is a set of propositions. Others still might say that a world is a kind of picture, something like a scale model of the world. One thing all ersatzers agree on, though, is that the worlds somehow represent the actual world. Most misrepresent it: only one represents it accurately.

If the ersatzer is an actualist, she will deny the isolation thesis. Possible worlds, it will be maintained, are not individuated spatiotemporally. Given that the ersatz worlds are abstract, it would not be unreasonable to suggest that they have no spatiotemporal location whatsoever. Thus, the parts of the worlds and the possible individuals contained therein (if worlds *contain* possible individuals at all) will not bear any spatiotemporal relation to one another. But they will be *represented* as bearing such a relation. If, on the other hand, the ersatz worlds do have a particular spatiotemporal location, *all* possible worlds and individuals will thus be spatiotemporally related to one another, and so cannot be individuated on the basis of lacking any such relation to one another.

The ersatzer need not accept the plenitude thesis. Many ersatzers have found reasons to reject it. For example, many religious philosophers believe that there is a necessary existent: a being that exists in *all* possible worlds.[6] The ersatzer who wanted to accommodate this possibility would have to deny the plenitude thesis, at least as it is stated by Lewis. The principle is roughly that for any number of individuals from any number of worlds, there is a single world containing *any number* of duplicates of each. If one of the numbers Lewis is quantifying over is 0, there can be no necessary existents.

There are, however, less esoteric reasons for rejecting the plenitude thesis. Consider an argument against concrete realism put forward by Peter Forrest and David Armstrong (1984). Forrest and Armstrong show that there is no set, nor is there an aggregate, of all possible worlds. The argument is put by Lewis as follows:

> Start with all the possible worlds. Each one of them is a possible individual. Apply the unqualified principle of recombination to this class of possible individuals. Then we have one big world which contains duplicates of all our original worlds as

non-overlapping parts. But we started with all the worlds; so our big world must have been one of them. Then our big world is bigger than itself; but no matter how big it is, it cannot be that.

(1986: 102)

Lewis avoids the paradox by adding a restriction to his principle: "size and shape permitting". This caveat implies that there is some unknown upper limit to the number of non-overlapping objects that inhabit the most populous worlds. Moreover, there must be some unknown geometric and topological restrictions on such objects in such worlds. Such a restriction might still seem somewhat arbitrary. The ersatzer, if she felt the need to adopt a principle of recombination at all, may quite reasonably prefer to adopt a different version of the principle that required no restrictions whatsoever.[7]

The ersatzer is unlikely to retain the conceptual thesis in its entirety, although she will accept something very close. She will probably eliminate all reference to counterparts, allowing for the possibility of trans-world identity. Moreover, applying the theory to an analysis of modality, the ersatzer's understanding of the modifier "at W" will be very different. For Lewis this means literally "is a part of W"; for the ersatzer, though, it will mean roughly "according to W".

The actuality thesis will also require some modification. The ersatzer invariably asserts that everything is actual (if only because it is a thesis of common sense). Thus, there are no non-actual worlds. Modal statements are analysed in terms of quantification over these *actual* worlds. But there is one and only one such world that accurately represents *the concrete universe*; it alone is *actualized*. All other worlds are unactualized. The ersatzer will have to distinguish between the one and only concrete world and the one and only accurate representation of the concrete world. Which one is picked out by the "actual world" will be important, and the conceptual thesis advocated by the ersatzer will have to make that clear. The ersatzer can adopt something like the indexical analysis of actuality proposed by Lewis, thus distinguishing her semantic thesis from her metaphysical thesis. She might well suggest that actuality is a property possessed by each world at itself; that every ersatz world is actualized *according* to itself; that each ersatz world is such that it *represents* itself as correctly representing the actual world. But, as Lewis (1986: 138) points out, relative actuality and actualization will always be accompanied by absolute actuality and actualization. On any such theory, there will be one world that is actualized absolutely, that is, one world that does not *misrepresent* itself as accurately representing the concrete world. The ersatzer can therefore draw an important distinction between the ontological status of that world and the others.[8]

Lewis mounts a concerted attack against the various forms of ersatzism. A variety of objections are made, but the objections differ depending on the particular variety of ersatzism under consideration. So, for example, an ersatz possible world may be something like a set of sentences (or propositions) describing, often inaccurately, the universe. But there are inconsistent sets of sentences, so we need a primitive understanding of consistency to distinguish the sets of sentences that count as *possible* worlds from those that do not. Unfortunately, consistency is also a modal notion. A set of sentences is consistent if and only if its members *could* all be true. So an ersatzer of this kind cannot claim to reduce talk of modality to talk of worlds.

Alternatively, consider the position Lewis calls "pictorial ersatzism". It maintains that a possible world is a kind of model of the world. It represents a possibility by picturing it. If a world is to represent the world precisely, it must represent it *isomorphically*. But, Lewis asks, isomorphic with what? They cannot be isomorphic with the actual universe, otherwise all worlds would represent the very same possibility. It seems the best we can say is that *if* the concrete world *had been* such and such a way, then some pictorial world *would have* represented it. But that is itself a modal claim. Worse still, it seems that the pictorial ersatzer cannot rid herself of an unwelcome ontology. Pictures represent by having much in common with what they represent. The more precise the representation is, the closer the ontology is to that adopted by the modal realist.

There is, of course, much more to be said about Lewis's objections to ersatz theories. Lewis himself does this admirably. But one cannot help feeling that the objections are not decisive. Why? Because the objections are directed at very specific theories about the nature of possible worlds, and a limited collection of views about the ways worlds represent. Perhaps Lewis's list is exhaustive; Lewis certainly thinks it is. But one cannot help feeling that perhaps there is an alternative that Lewis has not considered. It is for this reason that it is worth considering more *general* objections to the project of analysing modal terms and their cognates in terms of possible worlds. It is to this task that we now turn.

11.3 Two attitude problems

The first objection is put forward by Kripke against modal realism. Kripke objects to Lewis's account of *de re* modality. For Kripke, a *de re* modal claim such as "Humphrey might have won the election" is a claim about Humphrey *himself*; it is not about anyone else. For Lewis, however, such claims are to be analysed in terms of facts about Humphrey's counterparts: numerically distinct individuals who bear salient similarities to Humphrey. Kripke puts the objection as follows:

> The counterpart of something in another possible world is never identical with the thing itself. Thus, if we say "Humphrey might have won the election ..." we are not talking about something that might have happened to *Humphrey* but to someone *else*, a "counterpart." Probably, however, Humphrey could not care less whether someone else, no matter how much resembling him, would have been victorious in another possible world. Thus, Lewis's view seems to me even more bizarre than the usual notions of transworld identity that it replaces. (1980: 45)

Do not be distracted by Kripke's minor misconstrual of Lewis. *Pace* Kripke, Lewis does not identify what might have happened to Humphrey with what *might* have happened to Humphrey's counterparts. For Lewis, the modal facts about Humphrey are to be explained instead in terms of what *does* happen to his counterparts. Making the relevant changes, then, we can appreciate the force of the objection. Presumably Humphrey cares a great deal that he might have won the 1968 American Presidential election. Dwelling on this possibility presumably was the occasion for getting emotionally worked up, a cause of significant depression and regret. But Humphrey is hardly likely to have the same emotional attachment to *others* in relevantly similar situations, and is unlikely to get passionate about *their* plight. And Humphrey is not unusual in this respect.

The objection presents a difficulty for Lewis, but it is not decisive against his view. Many philosophers, on Lewis's behalf, have outlined potential solutions to the problem of concern. Perhaps the right lesson to learn from Kripke's observations is that modal realists should believe in overlap of worlds: that Humphrey is literally present in many different worlds. In some he wins; in others he does not (cf. McDaniel 2004). Or perhaps we should conclude not that counterpart theory is false, but rather that a revision to our patterns of concern is called for, in light of our discovery that counterpart theory is true (cf. Rosen 1990: 350–51). Or, finally, one might challenge the premises of the argument, suggesting that there is no genuine asymmetry between our emotional responses towards our counterparts on the one hand, and the modal facts on the other. Richard Miller (1992), for example, defends such an answer, pointing out that the concern we have for ourselves and others is often comparative. I might care more about the fact that I have more (or less) than someone else than I do about the fact that I have the amount I do. If Miller is right, perhaps we are not indifferent to the fate of our counterparts after all. We are already deeply concerned about the *extrinsic* facts about those in similar situations to our own, even if we are not so concerned about the corresponding *intrinsic* facts. Thus, it is supposed, no revision to our patterns of concern is necessary after all.

Whatever one makes of these responses to Kripke's problem, though, it is interesting to note that Lewis himself does not officially endorse any of them. Instead, he simply proffers the following *tu quoque* retort:

> I think counterpart theorists and ersatzers are in perfect agreement that there are other worlds (genuine or ersatz) *according to* which Humphrey – he himself! (stamp the foot, bang the table) – wins the election. And we are in equal agreement that Humphrey – he himself – is not *part* of these other worlds … Counterpart theory does say (and ersatzism does not) that someone else – the victorious counterpart – enters into the story of how it is that another world represents Humphrey as winning, and thereby enters into the story of how it is that Humphrey might have won. Insofar as the intuitive complaint is that someone else gets into the act, the point is rightly taken.

But I do not see why that is any objection, any more than it would be an objection against ersatzism that some abstract wotnot gets into the act.
(1986: 196)

The response draws attention to the fact that the problem of concern is a more general problem than Kripke acknowledges in the passage cited above. Every currently popular analysis of the modal facts in terms of possible worlds and individuals – whether they are concrete counterparts or abstract entities of some kind – seems vulnerable to attack on the same grounds. Interestingly, Lewis believes this is a way of dodging trouble, perhaps reckoning that a problem for everyone is not a genuine problem for anyone. We believe, however, that Kripke and Lewis have uncovered an attitude problem for all realists about possible worlds and individuals.[9] The problem might be stated as follows.

The problem of concern
(P1) We care deeply about the modal facts.
(P2) We do not care about other worlds and individuals.
(C) Therefore, modal facts are not reducible to facts about other worlds and individuals.

Of course, just as Kripke's more restricted version of the problem is not decisive against Lewis's counterpart theory, neither is this problem decisive against realist theories in general. But if there is a genuine asymmetry in our emotional responses identified here, the problem does call attention to an unacknowledged need for some revision to our modal theory and practice.

There is, however, another attitude problem that must be answered by any realist about *possibilia*, a problem at least as famous as Kripke's problem of concern. The worry mirrors Benacerraf's problem for the mathematical Platonist (see §10.2). Realists about possible worlds and individuals aim to provide an analysis of modality. And any successful analysis of modality must meet two separate conditions of adequacy: first, it should provide the meaning and truth-conditions for modal statements and, secondly, it should provide some account of how it is that we come to have modal knowledge. As many have pointed out, although the realist meets the first constraint admirably, it is not at all obvious how she could meet the second requirement.[10]

For the realist of any stripe, possible worlds and individuals are causally impotent with respect to individuals in the actual (concrete) world, perhaps because they are spatiotemporally isolated from us, or perhaps because they are abstract objects occupying no region of spacetime. But, runs the objection, it is a necessary condition of someone's having knowledge about a certain domain that there be a causal connection of an appropriate kind between the knower and that which is known. The realist violates this condition, at least when it comes to our knowledge of the merely possible truths. We might express the worry as follows.

The epistemic argument
(P1) We have abundant knowledge of the modal facts (including knowledge of mere possibilities).
(P2) We do not have knowledge of other worlds and merely possible individuals.
(C)   Therefore, modal facts are not reducible to facts about other worlds and individuals.

Some philosophers have attempted to avoid the problem by pointing out that the difficulty carries over to other domains. Indeed, Lewis does just that. After making explicit the analogy with Benacerraf's worry, he suggests that "Our knowledge of mathematics is ever so much more secure than our knowledge of the epistemology that seeks to cast doubt on mathematics. So mathematics will serve as a precedent [in the modal case]" (1986: 109). The response is fair, as far as it goes. Lewis's objection certainly shows that there is something wrong with the epistemic argument against realist reductions of modality. But it provides no diagnosis of what the problem really is or where the fallacy lies.

Realists in search of a solution to the problem have three options: (i) they can challenge the claim that the premises support the conclusion; (ii) they can undermine the first premise; or (iii) they can deny the second premise. The first option is unattractive, because the motivation for (P2) appeals to the (supposed) fact that there is a causal constraint on our knowledge of any domain. Because this constraint is not met in the *possibilia* case, knowledge of that domain is not merely lacking, it is denied to us altogether. If the causal theory of knowledge is basically correct, we do not just fail to have knowledge of the other worlds and individuals, we *could not possibly* have such knowledge. And this is inconsistent with (P1). The second option is also unappealing. Although there are many sceptics about modality (cf. n. 21), such philosophers do not base their scepticism on the ultimate untenability of a realist analysis of it. Moreover, the motivation for such realist reductions presupposes the truth of (P1); otherwise talk of *possibilia* would be utterly dispensable.

The realist, therefore, will reject (P2). She will seek to account for our knowledge of *possibilia* on the assumption that we cannot become causally acquainted with such entities. The first step will involve a denial of any causal constraint on knowledge. The challenge will then be to explain what justifies our beliefs about this domain. Maybe we learn about this modal realm by way of a special faculty of intuition, a faculty akin to that postulated by Moore and Gödel to detect moral and mathematical properties respectively. Or perhaps we can justify our beliefs about *possibilia* on pragmatic grounds, by showing how a commitment to this domain is essential to a systematic and useful theory of the world. Alternatively, our knowledge about merely possible objects might be grounded in the fact that our beliefs about that domain are reliable, despite the fact that we lack any causal contact with the domain. Or perhaps we can justify our modal judgements in some other way completely. It is not obvious how such a story might be fleshed out, however. Suffice it to say, it is this problem, the epistemic problem, that is the stumbling block of all realist theories. It is not surprising, therefore to see a burgeoning literature devoted to solving this problem. We leave it to the reader to evaluate the myriad of responses to the difficulty, something we cannot hope to do here.

11.4 Anti-realism about possible worlds and individuals

Those who have qualms about the realist's ontology, then, have some motivation to look elsewhere for an analysis of modality. If her analysis is successful, she will be in a position to deny outright that worlds, concrete or abstract, exist. Such a position would be radically anti-realist. Forbes elaborates:

> An anti-realist says that [merely possible] worlds do not exist, and thus he is an actualist of a more radical kind than any

reductive realist. For an anti-realist, any possible worlds sentence which has an existential quantifier over [merely possible] worlds as its main connective must be strictly and literally false ... So the anti-realist ... cannot say that possible world sentences exhibit the real meanings of modal sentences in a peculiarly perspicuous way.

(1985: 75–6)

It is important to note that Forbes's articulation of the anti-realist thesis is not simply intended to be a denial of the ontological thesis, a rejection of an ontology of worlds. Consider a position that might intelligibly be held by a fatalist. The fatalist might agree that there are no worlds other than the one of which we are a part. She might still maintain, though, that modal statements are to be analysed in terms of quantification over worlds. This world is indeed the actual world, but because there are no others, actuality, possibility and necessity are conflated. Such a theorist is *not* an anti-realist in the sense prescribed above.

In addition to her denial of the ontological thesis, the anti-realist will deny the conceptual thesis, suggesting that modal notions and their cognates can be analysed adequately without making any literal reference to possible worlds. Many of the advantages of possible world talk, it will be maintained, can be had without the ontological cost.

Like the ersatzer, the anti-realist will not deny the ontological thesis entirely (although she will take issue with the realist at entirely different junctures). She will of course deny the minimal realism and mind-independence theses: that other worlds exist independently of us. The parity thesis, suitably interpreted, says that all the worlds there are, are of the same kind as this world. Given that the anti-realist accepts that this world is a world, the parity thesis is trivially true.[11] She will also accept the isolation thesis. If this world does not consist of spatiotemporally disconnected regions, the isolation thesis is true.[12] Given her attitudes to each of these tenets, it follows as a consequence that the anti-realist will deny the plenitude thesis. Instead she embraces a principle of paucity: there is just one world (this one, the actual world).

In this connection it is worth noting that Forbes, after articulating the principle of paucity, goes on to suggest that the anti-realist *"will hold the non-existence of worlds to be necessary"* (1985: 76, emphasis added). We suspect this is because he believes it is a modal consequence of the principle of paucity. But it is important to recognize that it is not. The anti-realist has severed the connection between the ontological and conceptual theses. As a consequence other worlds – other regions of spacetime – should have nothing to do with modality. Moreover, Einstein's general theory of relativity permits spacetimes with disconnected regions. And Ockham's razor at best counsels us to favour hypotheses according to which worlds do not exist; it gives us no reason for thinking that their existence is impossible. Forbes's suggestion, then, that the anti-realist is committed to the *necessary* non-existence of worlds is not compulsory, and we suggest that it be resisted. [13]

Before we can assess the merits of the anti-realist's alternative, though, we must hear more about her account of the nature of modality. Given that she denies the realist's conceptual thesis, she is under some obligation to spell out an alternative. What might it be? In the next two subsections we shall consider two very different anti-realist responses to this request for further theoretical elaboration.

11.4.1 Modalism

Perhaps the most popular anti-realist position is the view Forbes calls "modalism". Modalism is roughly the view that modal operators should not be analysed as quantifiers over possible objects, but should instead be taken as primitive (cf. Forbes 1985, 1989). The modalist thus refuses to answer the realist's challenge to provide some sort of reductive explanation of modality.

Modalists accept that there are objective modal facts, and that there are true and substantial propositions expressed by sentences containing modal operators. Modalists are therefore not anti-realists about the modal facts, but they are anti-realists about merely possible worlds and individuals (the supposed reductive base of these modal facts). Modalists are not error theorists about possible worlds and individuals, for while they do not believe that such things exist, they do not think any of us have any pre-theoretic commitment to a realm of *possibilia*. There is thus no widespread mistake to be corrected.

The modalist is aware of the impressive advantages of the possible worlds framework. She knows how possible worlds can be used to evaluate the validity of arguments containing modal premises or conclusions, and how they can aid in the articulation of various important modal theses. But such advantages, claims the modalist, are not reasons to embrace any form of realism about *possibilia*. Instead, we should think of possible worlds and individuals as mere heuristic devices. Accepting the realist's theory of possible worlds and individuals is thus perfectly legitimate wherever modal inferences need to be made and modal theses need to be articulated clearly. But, suggests the modalist, justified acceptance of realism is not the same as justified belief in it. Talk of possible objects is literally false. Modalism, then, is a form of instrumentalism about possible worlds. Indeed, because the modalist thinks that all talk of possible worlds involves a kind of useful pretence, she is a non-cognitive fictionalist about possible worlds.

Now it should be clear that modalism is *not* ideologically on a par with modal realism. Modal realism has one major advantage over modalism, and the modalist is upfront about this: the modalist's "theory" requires modal primitives; the modal realist's does not. But when modalists address this issue they point to other desiderata, which are supposed, on balance, to vindicate their view. In particular, it is noted that modalism is more parsimonious than any version of realism about possible objects, whether genuine or ersatz. Moreover, any ideological advantage modal realism has over modalism *appears* to be lost in the contrast between ersatz realism and modalism. Why? Because both ersatzism and modalism are theories that appeal to a primitive modal component, and so neither theory can claim to give a fully reductive analysis of modality. This appearance, though, is deceptive.

If Lewis's objections to ersatzism are sound, the ersatzer's theory – one way or another – must contain a primitive modal component. The ersatzer cannot therefore claim to have provided a fully reductive explanation of modality. Despite this, though, she has provided an impressive explanation of an assortment of modal notions in terms of just one. No such claim can be made by the modalist, whose modal primitives are the operators "□" (necessarily) and "◊" (possibly). To see why, consider the following plausible modal claim M.

(M) It is possible that everything actually red is shiny.

This particular example was first considered by Crossley and Humberstone (1977), but similar examples are discussed in Hazen (1976). The interesting point about M – a modal claim expressible in natural language and easily expressible in the language of possible worlds[14] – is that it eludes translation into the modalist's language. And a little reflection on the inadequacies of some potential translations should reveal as much. Consider the following :

(M1) $\Diamond(\forall x)(Rx \to Sx)$

M1 says that it is possible that all red things are shiny. But that is not an adequate gloss on M because M1 might be true in virtue of there being a world in which nothing is red or shiny; such a world, though, has no bearing on the truth or falsity of M.

(M2) $(\forall x)(Rx \to \Diamond Sx)$

M2 says that all red things are such that they might be shiny. But that is not an adequate gloss on M because M2 might be true in virtue of the red things all being shiny at some world or other, but never all at the same world, something required for M to be true.

(M3) $(\forall x)\Diamond(Rx \to Sx)$

M3 says that all things are such that it is possible that if they are red, they are shiny. But that is not an adequate gloss on M because M3 might be true in virtue of there being a world in which every actual object is neither red nor shiny; such a world, though, has no bearing on the truth or falsity of M.[15]

Such examples might tempt the modalist to supplement her language with an additional modal operator "A" to correspond with the English modifier "actually".[16] Such an extension would considerably increase the expressive power of the language. M, for example, could naturally be translated as follows:

(M4) $\Diamond(\forall x)(ARx \to Sx)$

But this addition to her modal vocabulary does not save the modalist from all trouble. There are an impressive number of modal idioms expressible in natural language *and* the language of possible worlds that are inexpressible even in this extended modal language. Here are just a few:

- *Counterfactuals*: If you had jumped off the top of the Empire State building, you would not have survived.
- *Numerical quantification*: There are at least two different ways John could come to Wellington.
- *Modalized comparatives*: A red thing could resemble an orange thing more closely than a red thing could resemble a blue thing.
- *Supervenience*: There could be no difference of one sort without differences of another sort.[17]

We hope it is clear that those who take the view that the fundamental modal idioms are the operators "possibly" ($\lozenge$), "necessarily" ($\square$) and "actually" (**A**) are going to have trouble paraphrasing such claims. Extensions will always be possible. The modalist can, for example, add a primitive counterfactual conditional, and indexed modal operators to her vocabulary.[18] In this way, she will be able to provide a respectable gloss on the various modal idioms mentioned above. But such a proliferation of modal primitives is undesirable. We will have come a long way from our starting-point: a theory of modality that contains only *one* primitive modal component (the ideological equivalent of ersatz realism, without the ontological baggage that goes with it). And if we share Lewis's desire "to reduce the diversity of notions we must accept as primitive, and thereby to improve the unity and economy of the theory [of everything]", we are motivated to look elsewhere for another alternative to realism about *possibilia*, an alternative that seeks to give an analysis of our modal idioms.

11.4.2 Prefix fictionalism about possible worlds and individuals

A different anti-realist strategy has been proposed by Rosen (1990). Unlike the modalist, Rosen proffers a genuine analysis of modal notions.[19] His analysis is not fully reductive; it does inherit a primitive modal component. But unlike the modalist, Rosen suggests "a way of reducing a wide variety of modal notions to one" (1990:

45). Unlike the realist, Rosen tells us that possible worlds do not exist. Rosen is therefore committed to finding an analysis in terms of something other than quantifiers over possible worlds. Rosen's view best seen as a version of prefix fictionalism about possible worlds.[20] Rosen's idea is to exploit an analogy with standard accounts of a general analysis of truth in fiction and apply it to the modal case. Statements such as "There is a detective that lived at 221b Baker Street" and "There are possible worlds other than our own" are true but should not be taken at face value. They must instead be understood as elliptical for longer sentences explicitly about a story. The reason we assent to their truth is because the context of utterance is such that they can only be interpreted as sentences beginning with a silent operator, "According to such and such fiction ...". Thus, we are not committed to the existence of any entities quantified over within its scope, despite an appearance to the contrary.

Once the operator has been recognized, Rosen claims that we are in a position to see how useful it is. By treating the realist's theory as a fiction, the prefix fictionalist analyses a wide variety of modal claims cashing in on the realist's analysis. For example, she can say that it is possible that there are blue swans if and only if *according to the hypothesis of a plurality of possible worlds* (PW), there is some world containing blue swans. Certainly, we can, as Rosen does, put the proposal more generally:

> ... let P be an arbitrary modal proposition. The modal realist will have ready a non-modal paraphrase of P in the language of possible worlds; call it P*. The realist's assertions about possible worlds are guided by explicit adherence to the schema P iff P*. The fictionalist's parasitic proposal is therefore to assert every instance of the schema: P iff according to the hypothesis of the plurality of worlds (PW), P*. Like modal realism, the theory would seem to provide truth conditions for modal claims in a systematic way. (Rosen 1990: 332–3)

For Rosen, then, the correct analysis of our modal idioms is to be given in terms of the content of a story rather than in terms of what is going on in some disconnected region of spacetime.

There are a number of objections that have been levelled against prefix fictionalism, and we shall mention just two. Neither objection is decisive, but they each give a flavour of the difficulties this kind of view faces.

From prefix fictionalism to realism[21]

The first objection is that prefix fictionalism – an apparently anti-realist theory about possible worlds – entails realism (or so it seems). In order to see why, consider first the proposition that all triangles have three sides. The proposition is necessary, and the fictionalist will give the truth-conditions in the following way:

(FT)   It is necessary that triangles have three sides if and only if according to PW, at all worlds, triangles have three sides.

It is important to notice two things. First, the prefix fictionalist is committed to the view that the proposition on the left-hand side of the biconditional affirms a modal fact, a *real* modal fact. This is because the proposition on the right-hand side of the biconditional affirms a real fact, a fact to the effect that a story – PW – has a certain content (more on this in Chapter 12). Furthermore, by using the weak modal axiom "$\Box p \rightarrow p$" we can derive the *non*-modal fact that triangles have three sides. Secondly, the proposition on the left-hand side of the biconditional does not quantify over worlds. Quantification over worlds does occur on the right-hand side of the biconditional, but the quantifier occurs within the scope of the fictionalist's prefix and therefore is not existentially committing.

The trouble comes when we consider the proposition that there is a plurality of possible worlds. The prefix fictionalist should say that it is false. The realist, on the other hand, will not only say that it is true, but that it is true necessarily. Let us see why.

(i)   Most of us agree that there are other ways the world might have been. The realist, though, says something more: every way the world might have been is a way that some world is.
(ii)   In order to account for the truth of some of the weakest modal axioms, the realist should say that "There is a plurality of possible worlds" is true at all worlds.

The prefix fictionalist, then, has a problem. Consider the following:

FW) It is necessary that a plurality of worlds exist iff according to
     PW, it is true at every world that a plurality of worlds exist.

It has already been established that the right-hand side of the biconditional is true. Thus, if the analysis is correct, the left-hand side of
the biconditional will also be true. This is not a good consequence
for the fictionalist. By using the axiom "$\Box p \rightarrow p$" we can derive the
non-modal proposition that a plurality of worlds exists. The prefix
fictionalist, it seems, is committed to an ontology of possible worlds:
worlds that are independent of us in every way. And if that is right,
prefix fictionalism about possible worlds is a form of realism.[22]

Attitude problems

If prefix fictionalism entails realism, it cannot claim to be a parsimonious alternative to realism. Nor can it claim to be ideologically
on a par with genuine modal realism, as the prefix fictionalist concedes that her theory does not provide the resources for a complete
reduction of the modal to the non-modal. Worse still, perhaps, it
seems the prefix fictionalist faces further difficulties analogous to
those faced by the realist. In particular, the view faces roughly the
same suite of attitude problems.

Recall that the realist of any stripe must answer the problem of
concern: we care about the modal facts, but we do not care – at least
not in the same way – for individuals with which we are not in any sort
of causal contact. These two theses are in tension with all varieties of
modal realism. Likewise, the prefix fictionalist faces a similar problem:
we care about the modal facts, and we do not have the same kind of
concern for the content of any mere fiction. How can the prefix fictionalist reconcile this with her view that these are just two descriptions of
the very same kind of fact? Rosen illustrates the problem as follows:

> Humphrey cares that he might have won. Perhaps he regrets
> some decision because he thinks that had he acted differently,
> he might have won. Now imagine that Humphrey comes
> to embrace the fictionalist view of the content of his modal
> thoughts. He comes to believe that the fact that he might have
> won just is the fact that, according to the story PW, there is
> a world in which someone rather like him – his counterpart
> – does win. Could this pattern of concern conceivably survive

> this identification? ... [A] lucid fictionalist must have the same attitude towards both.
> (Rosen 1990: 351)

Now, of course this is not an objection to the coherence of prefix fictionalism; it does not bring out any kind of inconsistency in the view. But it does point to certain unpalatable consequences of the view. And in this respect, prefix fictionalism is in a perfectly analogous position to the realist.

Another attitude problem for the realist was the *epistemic problem*. The upshot of that objection was that a robustly realist conception of the truth-conditions for modal claims made it seem remarkable that we could know any of the modal facts. Lewis, by way of giving a partial response to this objection, writes the following:

> In the mathematical case, the answer is that we come by our opinions largely by reasoning from general principles that we already accept ... I suppose the answer in the modal case is similar. I think our everyday modal opinions are, in large measure, consequences of a principle of recombination ... One could imagine reasoning rigorously from a precise formulation of it, but in fact our reasoning is more likely to take the form of imaginative experiments. We try to think how duplicates of things already accepted as possible – for instance, because they are actual – might be arranged to fit the description of an alleged possibility. Having imagined various arrangements – not in complete detail of course – we consider how things might aptly be described.
> (1986: 113–14)

Thus, Lewis quite plausibly puts forward an account of the role imagination plays when we reason about the modal facts. But Rosen poses a problem for the realist swayed by Lewis's rhetoric.

We find the realist making two claims. First, the modal facts are identical to facts about a domain of worlds. Secondly, the principles that guide our imagination are true of that domain. Rosen's point is that it is at best contingent that both of these propositions are true together. Given this, it seems a surprising coincidence that our imaginative capacities coincide so perfectly with the modal facts, particularly when we have had no acquaintance with (most of) the worlds. Consider the following:

This line of response ought to seem profoundly puzzling ... a striking conjecture. We may ask: is it just a coincidence that the principles which guide our imaginations truly describe a domain of objects with which human beings had absolutely no contact when those principles were being shaped ... there might have been creatures whose imaginative principles were quite out of step with the distribution of worlds in modal space. ... The only point I want to stress is that no analogous problem arises for the fictionalist. If the realist is right ... then when we engage in imaginative experiments, the least we discover is what is true according to PW. But for the fictionalist, that is enough. Modal facts are just facts of that kind.　　　　(Rosen 1990: 340)

Rosen is partially right here. If we adopt prefix fictionalism over realism, there is no longer any mystery as to why we can trust our imagination as a guide to discovering what the modal truths are. This is certainly an advantage the prefix fictionalist has over the realist. But there is another epistemic worry in the close vicinity. It must be addressed before we can conclude that prefix fictionalism, unlike realism, makes plausible epistemological claims.

When we ask the prefix fictionalist "How can we come to know what the modal truths are?", it might seem that she has at hand a particularly straightforward answer: just read the book (PW). But if that were the only answer the prefix fictionalist could proffer, we could not be blamed for feeling more than a little unsatisfied. *On the Plurality of Worlds* was not published until 1986, yet we all had strong modal opinions, and could justifiably claim to know what the modal truths are, well before 1986. Indeed, it would not be unreasonable to suppose that people had justified modal beliefs well before human beings could communicate such sophisticated ideas to one another.

One requirement of any philosophical analysis (of the form P iff P^*) is that the biconditional be knowable *a priori*. It seems that the problem at hand arises because the prefix fictionalist's biconditional is only ever known *a posteriori* and so cannot count as an *analysis* of modality. An analogy might help here. Suppose there was an extraordinarily complete biography of the life of George Bush – called *The Life and Times of Bush* – written by a non-deceitful, omniscient and omnipotent god. Knowing of the existence of such a book, we could justifiably claim that Bush was sworn in for a second term as President of the United States on 20 January 2005 if and only if it said so in *The Life and Times of Bush*. Be that as it may, no one would be tempted to conclude from this fact that the biconditional gave us an account of the *meaning* of propositions about Bush. And if that is right, no one should be tempted to conclude that the prefix fictionalist's biconditional gives us an account of the meaning of modal claims.

Two responses are possible. Perhaps the prefix fictionalist will not pretend to be offering a modal analysis. Rosen (1990), at certain points, seems to be toying with something more modest than that. Alternatively, if the prefix fictionalist does aim to provide an analysis of modal terms, she seems committed to asserting that PW existed long before Lewis wrote it down. PW, on this account, is something like an abstract set of principles or postulates that existed prior to and independently of any written work of Lewis's. Such postulates have been accessible to anyone at any time. Lewis, therefore, cannot be credited with being the author of *On the Plurality of Worlds*. Nor can he be credited with being the first to discover it, because every competent user of modal idioms throughout history is, on this account, well aware of the details of the story. At best, Lewis can be credited with being the first to articulate the theory explicitly and taking the time to write it down. We shall have more to say about this latter response in Chapter 12. For now, it is enough to note that either position will be uncomfortable.[23]

Further reading

For book-length overviews of modal metaphysics, we recommend: Charles Chihara, *The Worlds of Possibility: Modal Realism and the Semantics of Modal Logic* (Oxford: Clarendon Press, 1998); John Divers, *Possible Worlds* (London: Routledge, 2002); Graham Forbes, *The Metaphysics of Modality* (Oxford: Clarendon Press, 1985); Rod Girle, *Possible Worlds* (Chesham: Acumen, 2003); David Lewis, *On the Plurality of Worlds* (Oxford: Blackwell, 1986); and Joseph Melia, *Modality* (Chesham: Acumen, 2003).

2 Fictional characters

It is a commonplace that fictional characters such as Sherlock Holmes are not real. If you ask a non-philosopher whether or not Holmes really exists, you will be told either that he does not, or that he exists "in our minds". However, a number of philosophers defend a position at odds with common sense, and in recent times this number has been growing. According to these philosophers, if a story of pure fiction tells us that an individual exists, then there really is such an individual. According to these realists about fictional characters, "Sherlock Holmes", "Scarlett O'Hara", "Charlie Brown", "Sonic the hedgehog", "Batman", "Superman", "Tweedledum" and "Tweedledee" are not denotationless terms, but names that refer to individuals who exist "outside" our minds.

12.1 Realism about fictional characters

Although they differ on many details, all realists about fictional characters accept the following two theses:

- *Ontological thesis*: There are fictional characters. A fictional character is an individual (or role) picked out by a name or description that (i) is first introduced in a work of fiction, and (ii) does not pick out a concrete individual in the actual world.
- *Objectivity thesis*: Fictional characters do not depend on anyone's attitudes, linguistic practices or conceptual schemes. Fictional characters would continue to exist (or be) even if there was nobody to think or talk about them.[1]

The ontological thesis does three important things. First, it tells us that fictional characters are referred to through a work of fiction; reference to them occurs by way of writing or telling a story. Secondly, it helps us individuate fictional characters from other kinds of things. For example, it rules out Napoleon or Duncan counting as fictional characters just because they are referred to respectively in Tolstoy's *War and Peace*, and Shakespeare's *Macbeth*. (These fictions refer to the real flesh-and-blood monarchs Napoleon and Duncan, although a make-believe story is told about them in each case.) Finally, it commits us to the first part of any realist position, what we call minimal realism: the view that there are fictional characters. The objectivity thesis commits the minimal realist to the further claim that fictional characters exist independently of us in the sense that is important for any kind of robust realism.

The realist position is one that needs to be supported by argument; the realist must demonstrate that there is some reason for embracing an objective realm of *fictionalia*. The realist attempts to provide us with such an argument. It is her view that there are quite ordinary claims, unhesitatingly taken to be true by the folk, which seem to commit us to the reality of fictional characters. If we are to be faithful to common-sense opinion, the realist claims, we must embrace an ontology of fictional objects.

In order to appreciate the realist's argument, it will be useful to distinguish between two kinds of statement, both of which seem, *prima facie*, to make reference to fictional characters: fictional statements and critical statements. Somewhat roughly, we might put the distinction as follows: fictional statements are claims about the content of a particular work of literary fiction; critical statements – statements that might be made in the context of literary criticism – are not claims *about* the content of a literary fiction, yet are true *in virtue* of the content of a work of literary fiction in the sense that, were those fictions not to exist, the relevant critical statements would not be true. Consider the following examples:

Fictional statements:
(1)   There is a famous detective living at 221b Baker Street.
(2)   Heathcliff was haunted by a ghost on the windy moors.
(3)   Scarlett O'Hara is a woman.

Critical statements:

(4) Scarlett O'Hara is a fictional character.

(5) Romeo has been discussed by many Shakespeare scholars.

(6) Holmes is admired by many members of the British police force.

(7) Holmes would not have needed tapes to get the goods on Nixon (Lewis).

(8) Holmes symbolizes mankind's ceaseless striving for truth (Lewis).

(9) Anna Karenina is less neurotic than is Katerina Ivanovna (Howell).

(10) The character Odysseus who occurs in the *Odyssey* is identical to the character who occurs in *Inferno*, Canto 26, under the name "Ulysses" (Howell).

(11) There are characters in some nineteenth-century novels that are presented with a greater wealth of physical detail than is any character in any eighteenth-century novels (van Inwagen).

(12) Since nineteenth-century English novelists were, for the most part, conventional Englishmen, we might expect most novels of the period to contain stereotyped comic Frenchmen or Italians; but very few such characters exist (van Inwagen).

(13) A certain fictional detective is more famous than any real detective (Parsons).

(14) Things would be better if certain politicians who (unfortunately) exist only in fiction, were running this country instead of the ones we now have (Parsons).

The realist's case starts by noting that fictional statements such as (1)–(3) seem *prima facie* to require the existence of a fictional character – Heathcliff, Scarlett O'Hara and a famous fictional detective – if they are to count as true. The realist concedes, however, that the anti-realist has at her disposal a way of interpreting such statements that avoids any such ontological commitment: any inclination we have to suppose that sentences such as (1)–(3) are true is to be explained by the fact that we implicitly understand them as elliptical for longer sentences explicitly about a fiction. We assent to their truth because the context of utterance is such that they can only be interpreted as sentences beginning with a silent prefix "*According to such and such fiction*", or something of the sort; the embedded sentence is false, but the compound sentence is true. The important point to note here is that the complex sentence in no way commits us to the existence of fictional characters.

The realist, though, has a more impressive argument against the anti-realist. The realist asks the anti-realist to focus not on fictional statements, but rather critical statements (such as sentences (4)–(14)) that appear to make reference to fictional characters. It should be obvious that there is a sense in which an utterance of any of sentences (4)–(14) above would be true. But, suggests the realist, the anti-realist is not in a position to paraphrase away such sentences in order to capture this sense. Certainly, she cannot avoid a commitment to the fictional characters mentioned therein by adopting the prefixing strategy outlined above. Such statements are not about the content of the stories in which the relevant names are introduced. Consider the following:

> Such truths about Holmes are not abbreviations of prefixed sentences, and also are not true just because "Holmes" is denotationless
> (Lewis 1978: 263)

> There is a group of difficulties that ... [the anti-realist's] approach faces. The group of difficulties arises from the fact that we – commonsense readers and literary critics alike – frequently make and hold to be in some sense actual-world truths ... fictional-object-involving facts which do *not* obtain within those fictional situations or worlds that are indicated by the works of fiction themselves.
> (Howell 1979: 152)

> [Critical] sentences seem to be true, not truth-valueless [or false] and they seem to commit us to there being fictional objects. They are problematic because they cannot be analyzed as containing an implicit prefix, "According to the relevant body of literature."
> (Parsons 1982: 83)

> [Critical] sentences are not presented as part of a story with standard illocutionary forces suspended yet nor do they seem to be paraphrasable into sentences containing the intensional

operator "In the fiction (novel)" ... [Such sentences], however,
seem to be true and able to be asserted.   (Lamarque 1983: 63)

There are kinds of sentences [namely critical sentences] in
which fictional names occur for which ... [an anti-realist] has
not provided intuitively correct truth-conditions. If we treat
them at face value, they come out false ... Yet we cannot sat-
isfactorily treat them as occurring within the scope of the [fic-
tional] operator F.   (Currie 1990: 171)

Such remarks cannot be prefixed by "in the story," and their
truth conditions are not the contents of the story but empirical
reality.   (Crittenden 1991: 95)

This assertion – that the anti-realist cannot avoid a commitment to
the existence of fictional characters presupposed in any utterance of
a *critical* statement by adopting the prefixing strategy – occurs over
and over again in the literature. There is something right about this
suggestion. The anti-realist cannot paraphrase away critical statements in *exactly the same way* as she paraphrases fictional statements. According to the anti-realist, sentence (1) is an abbreviation
of a sentence prefixed by "According to the Conan Doyle stories".
Yet we cannot understand sentences (6)–(8) as being abbreviations
for sentences so prefixed; understood in this way, such sentences
would all be false.

One might be tempted to conclude from this fact that no paraphrase whatsoever is available to the anti-realist, in which case the
realist's case against the anti-realist would be very strong indeed.
But such a conclusion would be too strong. It is certainly possible
to paraphrase (at least some) critical statements by variants of the
prefixing strategy. Consider the following:

(4*)   Scarlett O'Hara does not exist but there is some fiction
       according to which Scarlett O'Hara exists.
(9*)   According to the novel *Anna Karenina*, Anna Karenina
       is neurotic to degree x and according to the novel *The
       Brothers Karamazov*, Katerina Ivanovna is neurotic to
       degree y and $x < y$.
(12*) Since nineteenth-century English novelists were, for the

most part, conventional Englishmen, we might expect that according to most novels of the period, there are stereotypically comic Frenchmen or Italians; but this is true of very few nineteenth-century novels.

(14*) Things would be better if certain actual politicians were not running this country and instead (some salient parts of) certain novels – according to which there exist certain politicians worthy of admiration running this country – were true.

Sentences (4*), (9*), (12*) and (14*) might reasonably be proffered as candidates for anti-realist paraphrases for sentences (4), (9), (12) and (14).[2] Perhaps such paraphrases are not available for all critical statements. But presumably the realist will not want to base her case on such a claim, for the realist has given us no *principled* reason for supposing that such paraphrases cannot always be given. Nonetheless, the realist notes that there is something particularly unsatisfying about this way of approaching the problem. Consider the following:

> [W]hy should anyone bother to try to construct such paraphrases? It would probably be very difficult to do this, and the paraphrases would probably be long and messy if they could be got at all.   (Van Inwagen 1977: 304)

> [T]here is a strong reason to require that semantic theories of our claims about fiction should give to these claims the same sort of treatment, in terms of scope, comprehensiveness, and systematic organization, that semantic theories of our actual-object-concerning claims give to those claims. Of the latter such semantic theories, however, we nowadays rightly require treatments that proceed in a comprehensive, uniform manner; we do not aim merely at a handful of disconnected, hit-or-miss analyses of a few of our claims about actual objects. Hence, we should impose the same requirement on our semantic theories of our claims about fiction.   (Howell 1979: 153)

> [When] evaluating other theories, such as scientific theories, the need to constantly adjust the theory with a series of ad

hoc tinkerings to avoid apparent counter-examples would be taken as a sign of the theory's failure and need to be replaced. The issue is not whether one can devise some analysis of language that avoids reference to fictional objects, but what the best theory of language is, and whether it is one that accepts or denies that there are fictional objects referred to by fictional terms. It might be hoped that a smoother, more adequate, and less ad hoc analysis of language could be offered by admitting that there are fictional objects to which we can refer.

(Thomasson 1999: 99–100)

Such is the case for embracing some variety of realism about fictional characters. If we are to proffer a plausible theory of fiction, then our theory must provide an account of the semantics of critical statements that is systematic; it must provide a smooth and uniform handling of all claims about fictional characters. The realist theory seems to satisfy this desideratum. The prospects for an anti-realist theory doing the same seem dim.

12.2 Error theory about fictional characters

There is something odd about the realist's argument. Realists about other domains tend to argue by way of an indispensability argument, claiming that the distinctive postulates of the domain in question are indispensable to our best scientific theories. No such claim is made by the realist about fictional characters, and understandably so. Perhaps fictions themselves are essential for our scientific theorizing – perhaps, for example, science needs to postulate *idealized laws* – but the natural sciences have no need for fictional *entities* (cf. Chapter 9). The case for fictional characters is thus based on the apparent sincere assertions made by the folk.[3]

This dependence on common-sense opinion to buttress the realist position is problematic. Why so? Not so much because common-sense opinion is in general fallible, which of course it is, but rather because on this question – the question as to whether fictional characters exist – common sense is quite equivocal. The realist is right that some of the things we say seem to commit us to the existence of fictional characters. But this is only part of the story. Other assertions are made quite explicitly to distance ourselves from such commitments. When a desire to tell the truth trumps our desire to maintain the fantasy, we tell our children there is no Santa Claus. Likewise, in our more helpful moments, we might inform someone looking for Holmes on Baker Street that Holmes does not exist. Such assertions (if that they be) are inconsistent with any sincere assertion of a critical statement. But we are prepared to make both kinds of claims at the drop of a hat. Certainly, we might deny the existence of Santa and Sherlock, and *in the very same breath* say things such as "which is a shame, because children the world over love Santa" or "Holmes is in fact only a fictional character". If we take all such claims at face value, the folk must be mistaken about the nature of fictional characters; their thought and talk about them is hopelessly muddled and inconsistent. Far from supporting a realist position about *fictionalia*, then, we should conclude that the folk are guilty of making a massive mistake. And because there is no further evidence in support of an objective realm of fictional objects, we should conclude – using Ockham's razor – that there are no such things.

Before acquiescing to such a diagnosis, however, we should look for a more charitable way of understanding the various different claims made about fictional characters: a way of understanding such talk that does not commit ordinary language-users quite generally to incoherence. Realists of every stripe have risen to this challenge by suggesting that (i) sincere utterances of negative existentials can never be taken at face value, whether or not we are realists about the entities we are disavowing, and (ii) the right paraphrase of such claims will be compatible with a full-fledged realism about fictional characters. Thus, it is suggested, our assertions about fictional characters – when taken as a whole – presuppose realism. Let us look at each stage of the argument in turn.

Negative existentials such as "Ebenezer Scrooge does not exist" and "Holmes does not exist" appear, *prima facie*, to be saying *of* an individual – Sherlock Holmes and Ebenezer Scrooge respectively – that *he* does not have the property of existing or, alternatively, that there is nothing identical to *him*. But, of course, this is doublespeak. Everything exists; everything is identical to itself. And so, these claims – if taken to express *true* propositions – *must* be given a non-literal gloss.

The realist's point can be put in argument form as follows:

P1) Negative existentials are grammatically of subject–predicate form. For example, the sentence "Ebenezer Scrooge does not exist" has the subject expression "Ebenezer Scrooge" and the predicate expression "does not exist".

P2) Hence, *if negative existentials are taken at face value*, the propositions expressed by such sentences are logically of subject–predicate form (i.e. they have the same structure as the sentences that express them).

P3) A proposition that has the same structure as a subject–predicate sentence that expresses it will be true just in case the subject expression refers to an object (or objects) that has (have) the property expressed by the predicate.

P4) No object has the property of not existing. If there are entities that the subject expression refers to, then such entities exist.

C) Therefore, if negative existentials are taken at face value, there can be no true negative existentials.

But if negative existentials are not to be taken at face value, how are we to understand them? The realist's answer to this question will vary depending on what kind of realism is adopted. Realism about fictional characters comes in two broad varieties: concrete and abstract realism.

In addition to the two theses stated above, the concrete realist embraces the following two theses:

- *Concreteness thesis*: Just as real-world individuals vary in kind, so too do fictional characters. Some fictional characters – such as Scarlett O'Hara and Robin Hood – are concrete. Other fictional characters – such as the unit set of Scarlett O'Hara, and Little John's particular loyalty to Robin Hood – are abstract.[4]
- *Non-actualism*: Fictional characters exist, but they are not actual individuals. Here the concrete realist is making a distinction (unnoticed by most of us) between existence and actuality. She maintains that "there exists" is a quantifier, while "is actual" is a predicate that acts to restrict the domain of quantification.

Such a view has been advanced by Lewis (1986) and Parsons (1980).[5] Concrete realism comes in two varieties. According to the first variety, defended by Parsons, this difference between existence and actuality marks a significant ontological difference between objects. Actual objects are of an entirely different kind to non-actual objects. According to the second variety of concrete realism defended by Lewis, the difference between actual and non-actual objects is not a difference in kind between those objects. Instead "actuality" is treated as an indexical term that serves to pick out the world at which its utterance occurs (cf. Chapter 11).

Now consider the sentence "Sherlock Holmes does not exist". According to the concrete realist, if this sentence is taken literally it expresses a *false* proposition. Nonetheless, the concrete realist can leave room for a sense in which it is true. More often than not the context of such an utterance should force us to understand such quantification as implicitly restricted. If I tell you that there is no food, you should interpret my utterance as implicitly restricting the domain of quantification to everything *around here*; I am not telling you that there is no food *anywhere*. Likewise, when I tell you that Sherlock Holmes does not exist, there is a sense in which I speak truly, but you must interpret me as implicitly quantifying only over everything that *actually* exists.

Concrete realism is not a parsimonious theory. As a consequence, some realists have proffered a more conservative realism about fictional characters: abstract realism. In contrast to the concrete realist, the abstract realist embraces the following two alternative theses:

- *Abstractism*: Fictional characters are all abstract entities of some kind or another. Bill Clinton, Kate Moss and New York are entities of a fundamentally different kind from Sherlock Holmes, Scarlett O'Hara and Wuthering Heights.
- *Actualism*: Everything is actual; it is an analytic truth that there are no non-actual or nonexistent individuals. Hence, if there are fictional characters, these characters must *actually* exist.[6]

Abstract realism, like concrete realism, tends to come in two broad varieties. The first (most popular) view, which we shall call "individual realism", is the view that fictional characters are abstract individuals. Abstract individuals, according to this view, are of roughly the same kind as ersatz possible individuals, although fictional characters, unlike possible individuals, may be impossible and incomplete objects. We believe this view was first put forward by Mally (1912), and counts Kripke (1973), Castañeda (1974), van Inwagen (1977), Howell (1979), Zalta (1983), Emt (1992), Levinson (1993) and Salmon (1998) among its adherents. The second variety of abstract realism, which we shall call "role realism", is the view that fictional characters are not individuals at all, but rather abstract roles defined or constituted by certain sets of properties. Such roles may be occupied by many different possible individuals. This view has been defended by Wolterstorff (1980), Lamarque (1983) and Currie (1990).

Because the abstract realist is an actualist, she is not required to explain the distinction between being and existence, or existence and actuality. Unlike the concrete realist, the abstract realist does *not* make a distinction where common sense tells us there is none. This concession to common sense, however, might seem to come at a cost. If there is no ambiguity to be exploited in our apparent idioms of quantification, it seems that there will be little room for the abstract realist to give a sense in which sentences such as "Sherlock Holmes does not exist" are true. Like the concrete realist, though, the abstract realist suggests that such claims should not be taken at face value. Instead we should interpret someone who utters such a sentence as asserting something like the proposition that there is nothing that has all the properties ascribed to Holmes, or the proposition that there is nothing that occupies the Holmes role.

12.3 The social construction of fictional characters

Let us suppose, then, that the realist's response to the error theorist is satisfactory. Is realism about fictional characters compulsory in light of the linguistic evidence presented in §12.1? Not according to Amie Thomasson (1999). Thomasson points out that all of the arguments for realism support the ontological thesis alone. Absolutely nothing is said in defense of the objectivity thesis. It is a presupposition of both realism and anti-realism that if fictional characters exist at all, they exist objectively, independently of our minds and social institutions. Thomasson believes the assumption remains unquestioned and undefended not because of any obviousness that it is true, but rather because of a general prejudice against socially constructed entities. But, she argues, once the best theory of fictional characters is fleshed out, it will be discovered that this prejudice is in fact misguided.

Thomasson outlines and defends a theory she calls the "artifactual theory of fictional characters" (AT). AT is the view that fictional characters are contingently existing abstract artifacts. That is, fictional characters exist, but they are not concrete entities that have a spatial location. Nor do they exist necessarily; they might not have existed and, indeed, did not always exist. Instead, fictional characters are artifacts: products of intelligent design.

Why does Thomasson believe AT? The answer is that it is the only theory consistent with *creationism*, the intuitive thesis that fictional characters are created by the authors of the novels in which they first appear.[7] Writing a fiction, suggests Thomasson, is a creative act rather than an act of discovery or selection. But if fictions are created, and fictional characters depend for their continued existence on the fictions in which they appear, then fictional characters are also created by the authors of such fictions. The view is an intuitive one. But it is inconsistent with all previously defended philosophical theories of fictional characters, views that place such individuals outside our sphere of causal influence, whether as immutable abstract entities that exist eternally, or as concrete entities that exist in an isolated region of spacetime.

Thomasson thinks it is very important that we appreciate the points of similarity between fictional characters and other artifacts. Understanding how fictional characters fit into our ontology will help us understand how artifacts in general do the same. More importantly, however, the analogy helps dispel the image of fictional characters as a bizarre and exotic kind of entity quite unlike anything else, for artifacts are of a kind with tables, chairs, coffee mugs, wine glasses, screwdrivers and washing machines: objects that one and all exist uncontroversially. The main difference between fictional characters and the rest is that the former are abstract, and the latter are concrete. But this, she claims, is not a reason to banish fictional characters from our ontology.

Because artifacts are the products of the practices and intentional acts of human beings, they are all socially constructed. But this, *all by itself*, should not tempt us to deny their reality. Only some social constructions are "unreal"; only some are mind-dependent in the relevant

nse. Recall that tables, tools and televisions all *causally* depend on
minds for their existence; without minds they would not have come
to being. But they do not *metaphysically* depend on minds – they
would continue to exist even if all minds were to go out of existence
and so tables, tools and televisions are as real as rocks, planets and
stars. Laws, nations, wars and dollar bills, on the other hand, are less
than fully real, because not only do they causally depend on the intentional thoughts and actions of human beings, but they also metaphysically depend on us for their continued existence.

What kind of dependence do fictional characters have on minds
according to AT? At first blush it might seem that the dependence
is merely causal, for, although such entities "come into existence
only through the mental and physical acts of an author ... once
created, clearly a fictional character can go on existing without the
author or his or her creative acts" (Thomasson 1999: 6–7). So, for
example, James Bond was created by Ian Fleming and, fortunately
for us, Bond survives the demise of his creator, and has taken on a
life of his (its?) own. Thus, the dependence of fictional characters
on the mind of an author is merely causal – it is not metaphysical
– and so to that extent the social construction of the fictional poses
no real threat to a robust realism.

But AT is also the only theory that implies (or, indeed, is even
consistent with) another thesis: *destructionism*. Destructionism is
the view that fictional characters are not only created, they can
also be destroyed. Thomasson thinks this is an advantage of her
theory, even though destructionism is not clearly a thesis of common sense, and even though many philosophers think it is false.
Thomasson notices that fictional characters metaphysically depend
for their existence on either a token copy of some work of fiction or
other in which the character appears as a protagonist.[8] Moreover,
fictional characters also depend for their continued existence on
a competent readership: at least one individual who can interpret
the work in the language in which it was written. And so, because
all token works of any given fiction can go out of existence, and
also because human beings might (and most likely will) become
extinct, fictional characters will be destroyed with them. And this
kind of metaphysical dependence on a competent readership is the
hallmark of the kind of mind-dependence that puts it in conflict
with a robustly realist conception of fictional characters.[9]

Whatever the merits of AT, it is vulnerable to an objection that can be mounted against *any* minimal realist theory of fictional characters: the theory is either unparsimonious, or it fails, *by its own lights*, to meet a condition of adequacy for any theory of fictional characters. The objection is easiest to make out against the concrete realist. It is a consequence of concrete realism that hobbits and elves and ghosts and goblins exist. Moreover, each of these exotic things is a distinct kind of thing. Ockham's razor tells us this is undesirable and that we should look elsewhere for an alternative, less profligate theory of fiction. If one is available that meets all of our theoretical needs as well as the concrete realist theory, we should reject concrete realism. Many such theories are available (or so it is often claimed) so concrete realism must be rejected.

Abstract theories, whether they be realist or constructivist in flavour, claim to have an advantage over the concrete realist on this score. For according to abstractism, fictional characters are all of the same kind: they are abstract objects. Moreover, creatures of fiction are in the same category as other kinds of things we are independently committed to: stories, plots and so on. Theories that quantify over fictional characters but construe them as abstract entities are therefore ontologically conservative in a way that concrete theories simply cannot be.

Nonetheless, abstract theories face a very different problem. Recall that the original motivation for claiming that fictional characters exist rested on a view about the best analysis of critical statements. It was a prerequisite that our theory provides a smooth and uniform semantic treatment of such statements. Our analysis or paraphrase of such claims should *not* be "long and messy", and must, as far as possible, respect the surface structure of such claims. It was this condition of adequacy that made (minimal) realism about fictional objects seem so attractive. It is unclear, though, that the abstract realist can meet this condition.

Of course, the abstract realist can take many critical claims at face value. But she cannot take them all at face value. She must paraphrase many critical claims away, and her paraphrase is long and messy in a way that the concrete realist's is not. To illustrate, consider again the following critical claim:

(7)   Holmes would not have needed tapes to get the goods on Nixon.

We take claims like (7) to be true. But, according to abstractism, Holmes is an abstract object, and no abstract object is in a position to "get the goods on Nixon". Those who take fictional characters to be abstract objects, therefore, cannot take (7) at face value. It must therefore be paraphrased away. The adherent of abstractism will presumably put something like the following gloss on such statements:

7*) Holmes is ascribed (or partly constituted by) certain properties, and anyone who had such properties would not have needed tapes to get the goods on Nixon.

The point to be noticed in the present context, though, is that this gloss is no simpler or less *ad hoc* than an alternative paraphrase that might be given by any anti-realist; abstractism does not provide a significantly more straightforward account of this statement, and nor does it provide a more systematic treatment of critical claims generally. Consider again the following critical claims:

(6)   Holmes is admired by many members of the British police force.
(9)   Anna Karenina is less neurotic than is Katerina Ivanovna.
(14) Things would be better if certain politicians who (unfortunately) exist only in fiction, were running this country instead of the ones we now have.

The problem with taking such claims at face value is that they all presuppose that fictional characters have a mental life of their own, something an adherent of abstractism simply cannot accept. Presumably if Holmes really were admired, he would be admired for attributes such as his deductive abilities. But no abstract object can deduce anything. Likewise, abstract objects cannot be neurotic to any degree. So, if Anna and Katerina were both abstract objects, neither would be less neurotic than the other. Finally, abstract objects cannot make decisions, enact legislation or show any kind of leadership at all. So if abstract objects were running the country there would be total anarchy: presumably a state far worse than we are in now. All such claims must therefore be paraphrased away.[10]

We could go on, soliciting more and more examples, but the point should by now be clear: construing fictional characters as abstract objects does not provide any significant analytic advance over theories that deny the existence of fictional characters altogether. It is therefore worth examining the prospects of a different kind of anti-realism, one that denies that fictional characters exist.

12.4 Prefix fictionalism about fictional characters

Because it is agreed on all sides that fictional statements need not be ontologically committing, those who claim there are no fictional characters often attempt to understand critical statements on the same model as fictional statements. The proposals we consider in the remainder of this chapter all share this feature, although the model for understanding fictional statements is different in each case.

The first anti-realist strategy of this kind is the prefix strategy (cf. Brock, 2002). A prefix fictionalist about fictional characters claims that fictional and critical statements are (often) true, and are (often) used assertorically. Neither kind of statement, though, should be taken at face value. How, then, are they to be paraphrased away? The answer is that both kinds of assertion should be understood as implicitly containing a story prefix. Fictional claims contain a prefix of the form "According to such-and-such *literary* fiction"; critical claims, on the other hand, are prefixed with the operator "*According to the realist's theory of fictional characters*". So, for example, we might take (4) quite straightforwardly as elliptical for the longer sentence "According to the realist's theory of fictional characters, Scarlett O'Hara is a fictional character". In this way the prefix fictionalist provides an intuitively plausible interpretation of critical claims, yet avoids committing herself to a realm of fictional entities. The prefix fictionalist's theory thus provides a smooth and fairly uniform anti-realist treatment of all claims about fictional characters.

There is, however, an objection to this kind of proposal that has been raised by Kendall Walton (1990: 391ff.), among others. The objection might be expressed as follows. Apart from the occasional idiomatic exception (e.g. "Bob's your uncle", "It is not for every Tom, Dick, and Harry", "Borrowing from Peter to pay Paul") the proposition expressed by an assertoric use of a declarative sentence containing a proper name is determined compositionally, that is, it is established by the meaning of its parts and the manner in which they are combined. Each part of the sentence plays some role in determining which proposition is expressed by that sentence. Thus, such a sentence expresses a proposition only if each of its parts has some meaning. But, according to one popular philosophical tradition, Millianism, the meaning of a name just is its referent (i.e. the object to which it refers). And if this view is right, sentences containing an occurrence of a non-referring name express no proposition at all.

Such an argument presents no problem for the realist. For her, all fictional names have a referent. But according to the prefix fictionalist, fictional names are non-referring terms. And so because they have no denotation, they have no meaning. And because they have no meaning, any sentence containing an occurrence of such a name fails to express a proposition. This is a consequence the prefix fictionalist will not want to embrace, for according to her, the fictional and critical claims (1)–(14) are all true (when suitably prefixed). But if the argument considered here is sound, the prefix fictionalist's gloss on such statements renders them not true; in fact they are utterly meaningless.

The prefix fictionalist will have to answer this objection if her theory is to count as a credible alternative to realism. She will, of course, have a plethora of responses available to her. She may deny that the meaning of a sentence is determined compositionally; perhaps they are all idiomatic expressions. Or she may claim that the proposition expressed by a simple subject–predicate sentence varies depending on whether it stands alone or occurs within the context of a fictional operator. Or she may deny that the meaning of a proper name is its referent. Or she may deny that a term with no semantic value occurring in a declarative sentence precludes an utterance of that sentence from expressing a proposition: perhaps it expresses a special kind of gappy proposition. All of these alternatives have been canvassed and defended by some very able philosophers of language. But every one of the alternatives is uncomfortable to embrace. We are thus motivated to look elsewhere for a satisfying theory of our thought and talk about fiction, in both fictional and critical contexts: a theory that makes no ontological commitment to fictional characters.

12.5 Non-factualism and non-cognitive fictionalism about fictional characters

A very different kind of anti-realism starts, like prefix fictionalism, from the assumption that fictional statements are of primary importance in understanding fiction. In order to fully appreciate what is going on when we make critical claims, we must first understand what we are doing when we utter fictional statements. But this is where the agreement with the prefix fictionalist ends. According to Ralph Clark (1980) and Walton (1990), when we make a sincere utterance of a fictional statement we are not making an assertion, and what we say is not the object of belief. So what are we doing when we sincerely utter a fictional statement? We are performing a speech act quite unlike an assertion.

According to Clark, "works of fiction … consist of sentences and phrases that are best understood to express implicit imperatives" (1980: 342). Thus, when we say "Holmes lived at 221b Baker Street" we are not making an assertion despite the sentence being in declarative form. Instead we are *commanding* our audience to make-believe that Holmes lives there. And because imperatives are not truth-apt, our utterance does not directly express a proposition, and is neither true nor false. Clark is therefore a non-factualist about fictional characters.

A related, but importantly different, idea is developed by Walton. Walton is a non-cognitive-fictionalist about fictional characters. According to Walton, when I utter the sentence "A cocaine-addicted detective lives at 221b Baker Street" as part of telling a story, I am not expressing something that I believe. If pressed, I would deny that I know anyone who lives at that address. Of course, I may agree that *according to the Conan Doyle stories, a cocaine-addicted detective lives at 221b Baker Street*, but this is not what I was asserting. I was telling a story, not describing the content of that story, and the two speech acts are very different. The former involves *assertion*; the latter involves a kind of *pretence*. When I tell a story I am pretending to report something about the real world – or pretending to actually take part in these events – rather than really reporting something about a fictional world. And this is why I might have an air of disdain in my voice when I make mention of Holmes's propensity to use cocaine, and why I might "put on" different voices when I speak the parts of Watson, Holmes and

[M]oriarty. Such things are inexplicable on the assumption that I am making an assertion.

Both Walton and Clark believe that we should understand critical statements on the same model as fictional statements. Utterances of critical statements involve no direct assertions. When (minimal) realists claim that fictional characters must exist if we are to make sense of what people tend to say in critical contexts, they are mistaking the serious pretence of referring to fictional characters, or the imperative to imagine something about them, for genuine ontological commitment. Likewise, when prefix fictionalists get themselves in a muddle about how critical statements could be used to express a proposition of any kind if fictional names have no referent, their mistake is to think of such statements as vehicles for making assertions and nothing more. In fact, such statements are usually made to perform another speech act entirely.

One natural objection that should be made against this kind of non-cognitivist construal of critical claims is that it just seems implausible to think of such statements as vehicles to make commands or to engage in acts of pretence, for unlike fictional statements, we often use critical statements in a sober way to inform the listener of important literary information. Clark and Walton agree that this is so, but suggest that we can do this in addition to issuing a command or engaging in an act of pretence. To illustrate, consider the act of *asking the question* "Can you pass the salt?". The speech act performed here is obvious to all. Clearly an assertion is not being made, and so no proposition is directly expressed. Nonetheless, as a listener, we can infer the truth of certain propositions on hearing the question, even though they were not directly expressed. For example, I can infer *that the speaker wants the salt passed*. In fact, it is crucial that I infer this proposition if the speaker is to succeed in achieving the end to which her act aims, namely, getting me to pass the salt. It would be an unhappy consequence if I merely answered "Yes" and left it at that. Likewise, it is maintained, I can command or pretend, and thereby inform the listener (or reader) of important information; in fact, it may be crucial for my purposes that such information is pragmatically imparted.

Now, the question will be asked, what information can we infer when a speaker utters a fictional or critical statement? Consider first a fictional statement such as (2): "Heathcliff was haunted by ghost on the windy moors". According to Clark, we can infer tha *the speaker is instructing us to imagine that* "Heathcliff was haunte by a ghost on the windy moors" expresses a true proposition. An he would be right if the utterance was an imperative. According t Walton, on the other hand, we can infer that *the speaker is pretend ing that* "Heathcliff was haunted by a ghost on the windy moors expresses a true proposition. And Walton would be right if th utterance was part of an act of pretence.

In fact, Walton thinks we can infer a lot more than just that. H notes that in such contexts, while we are pretending to assert (o commanding the listener to imagine) something, we are also usin a fiction as a prop. Thus, he believes we can also infer importan information about the content of the fiction itself, and its func tion in certain authorized contexts. So, for example, we might als pragmatically infer from an utterance of (2) that in any authorizec game of the appropriate kind using *Wuthering Heights* as a prop it will be appropriate to pretend to assert a true proposition by uttering "Heathcliff was haunted by a ghost on the windy moors". (A similar claim could, *mutatis mutandus*, be made by Clark. Bu from here we focus only on what Walton says about such cases, leaving it up to the interested reader to make the relevant changes on Clark's behalf. We do this partly to avoid needless repetition, and partly because Clark never explicitly develops his theory in this way.)

Recognizing this much gives us the clue we need to appreciate how we can use critical statements, in the spirit of pretence, to convey pragmatically a lot of information. According to Walton, utterances of critical statements involve pretence just as utterances of fictional claims do, it is just that the pretence is not author- ized. Our act of make-believe is non-standard and unofficial. To illustrate, consider again the following critical claim proffered by Howell that is meant to pose a difficulty for any anti-realist theory:

(1) Anna Karenina is less neurotic than is Katerina Ivanovna.

Walton suggests that whenever we pretend to assert something by making this utterance, we impart the following information:

b) In a "combination" game, using *Anna Karenina* and *Crime and Punishment* as props, it will be appropriate to pretend to assert a true proposition by uttering "Anna Karenina is less neurotic than is Katerina Ivanovna".[11]

In fact Walton generalizes his view by suggesting that for every critical statement C we pretend to assert using a fiction (or set of fictions) F as a prop, we pragmatically convey the following information: in any game of a certain salient sort, to pretend to assert C is fictionally to speak truly. Such paraphrases are complicated, and require further elaboration regarding the kind of game we are playing. As a consequence it might seem that Walton's account fails to meet the realist's condition of adequacy outlined in §12.1. To his charge, Walton answers as follows:

> Some readers will be distressed by the complexity of my paraphrases of what appear to be simple, everyday utterances. They need not worry. If what … [we mean] by (1), made explicit, is as complicated as (1b), this is a good reason to have the simpler way of saying it. One would expect the language to devise a manageable equivalent of (1b) just because (1b) is so awkwardly complex. (1990: 404)

Walton, then, is an instrumentalist of sorts. Our thought and talk apparently about fictional characters is not true, but it is useful: it enables us pragmatically to convey information in a relatively simple way that would be much more difficult to do if we had to convey the information more directly by way of an assertion.

At this point, we leave it to the reader to decide whether Walton's non-cognitivist fictionalism (or Clark's non-factualism) adequately characterizes our thought and talk about fictional characters. Obviously the views have their merits. But they are put forward in a hermeneutic (as opposed to a revolutionary) spirit. The reader thus needs to ask the question: does Walton (or Clark) capture what *I and other ordinary speakers* of English tend to mean when we utter critical statements? Our suspicion is that the answer is not as clear as Walton and Clark make out.

Further reading

It is surprisingly difficult to find any general introductions to the literature on the metaphysics of fictional characters. What literature there i
tends to be biased towards a particular viewpoint. Keeping this in mind
we recommend that the interested reader consult the following: Charle
Crittenden, *Unreality: The Metaphysics of Fictional Characters* (Ithaca, NY
Cornell University Press, 1991); Amie Thomasson, *Fiction and Metaphys-
ics* (Cambridge: Cambridge University Press, 1999); Peter van Inwagen
"Existence, Ontological Commitment, and Fictional Entities", in *Oxford
Handbook of Metaphysics*, Michael Loux (ed.), 131–57 (Oxford: Oxford
University Press, 2003); and Kendall Walton, *Mimesis as Make-Believe*, pt
IV (Cambridge, MA: Harvard University Press, 1990).

Notes

1. Introduction
1. We do not mean to suggest that the epistemic and semantic theses are the only tenets that might reasonably be added to the characterization of realism. Compare, for example, §2.2.2.

2. Local realism and anti-realism: the existence axis
1. See D. Lewis, "Noneism or Allism?", *Mind* 99 (1990), 23–31. Similar expressions can also be found in R. Routley, *Exploring Meinong's Jungle and Beyond: An Investigation of Noneism and the Theory of Items* (Canberra: Australian National University Press, 1980).
2. We shall not get involved in the controversy over the reliability of abduction here. For an argument against the use of abduction see B. C. van Fraassen, *Laws and Symmetry* (Oxford: Oxford University Press, 1989) §6.4 and for defences of it see P. Lipton, *Inference to the Best Explanation* (London: Routledge, 1991) and T. Day and H. Kincaid, "Putting Inference to the Best Explanation in its Place", *Synthese* 98 (1994), 271–95.
3. There is a problem, however, if we follow Quine, and regiment to a first-order logic, for among the entities for which philosophers divide along realist–anti-realist lines, we find *properties*. Unless properties are to be replaced by proxy objects, such as sets, this will (*pace* Quine) require *second-order* regimentation. For ease of exposition, we shall ignore this complication in what follows.
4. We can, of course, look for the ontological commitments of a theory elsewhere. *Pace* Quine, there is no reason to insist that the ontological commitments of a theory can be found only by looking for the bound variables of the regimented theory. The ontological commitments of a theory are to be found wherever there is a referring term: an indexical, a pronoun, a proper name and so on.
5. Perhaps not every existential theorem of a regimented theory should count as an ontological commitment of that theory. Suppose such a theory is inconsistent. Should we say it is ontologically committed to everything? Or suppose that a consistent theory makes no explicit reference to something that exists necessarily. Is such a theory ontologically committed to its existence anyway? To get around this problem, we suggest the use of relevant logic or paraconsistent logic, which do not allow the derivation of every proposition from a contradiction.

See E. D. Mares, *Relevant Logic: A Philosophical Interpretation* (Cambridge: Cambridge University Press, 2004) and G. Priest, *In Contradiction: An Essay on the Transconsistent* (Dordrecht: Nijhoff, 1987).

6. For an argument against the use of the substitutional interpretation of the quantifiers, see P. van Inwagen, "Why I don't Understand Substitutional Quantification", *Philosophical Studies* 39 (1981), 281–6.

7. Whether or not any formulation of this important epistemic principle should be attributed to William of Ockham is unclear. For an interesting discussion about the history of the razor, see W. M. Thorburn, "The Myth of Occam's Razor", *Mind* 27 (1918), 345–53.

8. See also G. Schlesinger, "Induction and Parsimony", *American Philosophical Quarterly* 8 (1971), 179–85, for a justification of induction using the principle of parsimony.

9. A close reading of J. P. Burgess and G. Rosen, *A Subject with No Object: Strategies for Nominalistic Interpretations of Mathematics* (Oxford: Oxford University Press, 1998) will reveal that this is not quite the distinction they had in mind. Nonetheless, it is commonly believed to be. See, for example, R. Joyce, "Moral Fictionalism", in *Fictionalist Approaches to Metaphysics*, M. Kalderon (ed.), 287–313 (Oxford: Oxford University Press, 2005), M. Kalderon, *Moral Fictionalism* (Oxford: Clarendon Press, 2005), and J. Stanley, "Hermeneutic Fictionalism", *Midwest Studies in Philosophy: Figurative Language* 25 (2001), 36–71.

3. Local realism and anti-realism: the independence axis

1. For those sceptical of the claim that we are essentially psychological kinds it is worth reflecting on the fact that none of the paradigm cases of what we call psychological constructions would continue to exist if, for example, we all collectively became permanently comatose.

2. Kukla believes that psychological constructions divide into three different subspecies, depending on whether the constructions are constituted by, supervene on or are causally maintained by facts about us; see A. Kukla, *Social Constructivism and the Philosophy of Science* (London: Routledge, 2000), 21–2. We believe, however, that the most interesting psychological kinds do not fit neatly into any of these categories.

3. See M. Johnston, "Dispositional Theories of Value", *Proceedings of the Aristotelian Society*, supp. vol. 63 (1989), 139–74, and "Objectivity Refigured: Pragmatism Without Verificationism", in *Reality, Representation, and Projection*, J. Haldane and C. Wright (eds), 85–103 (Oxford: Oxford University Press, 1993); C. Wright, *Truth and Objectivity* (Cambridge, MA: Harvard University Press, 1992) and *Realism, Truth, and Meaning* (Oxford: Blackwell, 1993); and P. Pettit, "The Reality of Rule Following", *Mind* 99 (1990), 1–21, and "Realism and Response-Dependence", *Mind* 100 (1991), 587–626. The idea, though, is developed in a different way by each author. Our formulation is closest to the presentation in Johnston's papers.

4. For Johnston, this is merely a sufficient condition for response-dependence. This special class of response-dependent concepts are what he calls the "response-dispositional concepts". According to Johnston, "a concept is *response-dependent* just in case it is either a response-dispositional concept or a truth-functional or quantificational combination of concepts with at least one non-redundant element being a response-dispositional concept" ("Objectivity Refigured", 103). This added complication can, however, be ignored in what follows. It is also

important to note in this context that the extension of the concept F is everything that has the property F-ness.

. One might be tempted to insist that the mark of a response-dependent concept
is to be found in the fact that there is a basic equation appealing to the concept
that is *necessarily true* (rather than knowable *a priori*). But to insist on this would
make too many concepts ineligible for response-dependent status.

5. Although, of course, Pettit himself places less significance on these differences,
and attempts to explain some of them away. We leave it to the reader to make
a judgement about how successful he is.

7. This is an oversimplification of Wright's view. Wright's considered view is in fact
that our concept of an intention *is* response-dependent after all (cf. C. Wright,
"Wittgenstein's Rule-Following Considerations and the Central Project of Linguistics", in *Reflections on Chomsky*, G. Alexander [ed.], 233–64 [Oxford: Blackwell, 1989] and J. Edwards, "Best Opinion and Intentional States", *Philosophical
Quarterly* 42 [1992], 21–33). Wright argues that we can delete the offending no
self-deception clause from the C-conditions, thereby making the basic equation
non-trivial, and taking the equation to be not *a priori* invariably true, but *a priori*
positive presumptive. He argues that this is enough to allow, *ceteris paribus*, that
a subject's responses determine the extension of her intensions. We leave it to the
reader to decide how successful Wright's arguments are, and whether this should
cause us to worry about the reality of our own mental states.

4. Idealism

1. See, for example, Vere Chappell (ed.), *Cambridge Companion to Locke* (Cambridge: Cambridge University Press, 1994) for a more modern interpretation
of Locke.

2. We can say that Stu is thinking about this llama in the thin sense of §10.2.2.

3. Conceptual realism is a watered-down version of what Margaret Wilson, *Ideas
and Mechanism: Essays on Early Modern Philosophy* (Princeton, NJ: Princeton
University Press, 1999), 229, calls "phenomenal realism". This is the claim that
things are as we perceive them to be. Berkeley is certainly a perceptual realist,
but we do not want to go into his arguments for that position. For our purposes, it will do merely to attribute the weaker position of conceptual realism
to him.

5. Kantianism

1. This is the way Kant's works are usually cited. The A and B numbers refer to
pages in the first and second editions of the *Critique of Pure Reason*.

2. In fact, Euclid's axiomatization was incomplete in the sense that the axioms
alone do not entail all of the propositions that Euclid thought that he could
prove. Euclidian geometry was only properly axiomatized in the nineteenth century. On the nature of mathematical knowledge in Kant, see M. Friedman, *Kant
and the Exact Sciences* (Cambridge, MA: Harvard University Press, 1992).

3. Universal response-dependent theorists – philosophers who hold that all concepts are response-dependent – are also Kantians. They think that what we
experience and understand of the world is at least partially due to the input of
our minds. See P. Pettit, *Rules, Reasons, and Norms* (Oxford: Oxford University
Press, 2002).

4. Mereology was first developed in 1916 by the Polish logician Stanislaw
Leśniewski.

5. For the concept of a possible world, see Chapter 11.
6. Of course we could have a collie–chihuahua cross. To avoid this complication let us read "is a collie" and "is a chihuahua" as "is a pure-bred collie" and "is a pure-bred chihuahua".
7. In fact, as long as D is infinitely large, any size of infinity will do. For the notion of different sizes of infinity, see Chapter 10. The Löwenheim–Skolem theorem for first-order logic says that any set of sentences that has an infinite model also has a model of size k for each infinite cardinal k.

6. Verificationism

1. Tyler Burge, "Frege on Knowing the Third Realm", *Mind* 101 (1992), 633–50 and Bob Hale, *Abstract Objects* (Oxford: Blackwell, 1987) are among Frege' defenders.
2. An epitome of the trend against which the Logical Positivists were fighting is the work of the German philosopher G. W. F. Hegel. Here is a quotation to illustrate the point: "The onward movement of the notion is no longer either a transition into, or a reflection on something else, but Development. For in the notion, the elements distinguished are without more ado at the same time declared to be identical with one another and with the whole, and the specific character of each is a free being of the whole notion" (*Logic*, W. Wallace (trans.) [Oxford: Oxford University Press, 1975], 224). Do not worry if you do not understand this; that is our whole point!
3. Our paradigm Logical Positivist is Rudolf Carnap, who was very liberal about linguistic frameworks. Not all Positivists were as liberal (or, to our minds, as consistent in this regard).
4. If there are any other canonical means of verifying the statement, they too will be part of its content.
5. In his earlier writings, Dummett merely says that there must be some means to verify the statement (e.g. "his assertion is correct if there is some means of verifying it"; *The Seas of Language* [Oxford: Oxford University Press, 1993], 78). It would seem, however, that Dummett's view that only the canonical means of verifying a statement make up its meaning entails that the statement's being right means that there is a canonical means of verifying it. At any rate, it would seem that if there is a non-canonical verification there could have been a canonical verification of the same statement.
6. The view that the meaning of a sentence consists in a structure that has the referents of the phrases that make up the sentence as constituents is called the theory of "direct reference" and originated with the work of David Kaplan, although it has antecedents in the work of Ruth Barcan Marcus and Saul Kripke.
7. Dummett does not say that the law of excluded middle is false, for this would mean that he asserts its negation; that is, for some sentence A, $\neg(A \vee \neg A)$. In intuitionist logic, which Dummett accepts, this formula is a contradiction, that is, it can be proved false. So, rejection of a sentence and the acceptance of its negation are not the same thing. Every logician who accepts a non-classical theory of negation must also distinguish between rejection and the assertion of a negation. See Edwin Mares, "Even Dialetheists should Hate Contradictions", *Australasian Journal of Philosophy* 78 (2000), 503–16.
8. Tarski avoids the paradoxes by creating a hierarchy of languages. No language contains its own truth predicate, on his view. Thus, the expression "this sentence is false" is not a meaningful sentence for Tarski. There is no language that contains it.

Colour

1. See, for example, F. Jackson and R. Pargetter, "An Objectivist's Guide to Subjectivism About Color", *Revue Internationale de Philosophie* **160** (1987), 129–41 and F. Jackson, "The Primary Quality View of Color", *Philosophical Perspectives* **10** (1996), 199–219.

2. See, for example, M. Matthen, "Biological Functions and Perceptual Content", *Journal of Philosophy* **85** (1988), 5–27; D. Lewis, "Naming the Colours", *Australasian Journal of Philosophy*, **75** (1997), 325–42; M. Tye, *Consciousness, Color, and Content* (Cambridge, MA: MIT Press, 2000); and A. Byrne and D. Hilbert, "Color Realism and Color Science", *Behavioral and Brain Sciences* **26** (2003), 3–21.

3. See, for example, G. Evans, "Things Without the Mind", in *Philosophical Subjects: Essays Presented to P. F. Strawson*, Z. Van Straaten (ed.), 76–116 (Oxford: Oxford University Press, 1980); C. McGinn, *The Subjective View: Secondary Qualities and Indexical Thoughts* (Oxford: Oxford University Press, 1983); J. McDowell, "Values and Secondary Qualities", in *Morality and Objectivity*, T. Honderich (ed.), 110–29 (London: Routledge, 1985); and M. Johnston, "How to Speak of the Colors", *Philosophical Studies* **68** (1992), 221–63.

4. See, for example, P. M. S. Hacker, *Appearance and Reality* (Oxford: Blackwell, 1987); J. Westphal, *Colour: A Philosophical Introduction* (Oxford: Blackwell, 1991); J. Campbell, "A Simple View of Colour", in *Reality, Representation, and Projection*, J. Haldane and C. Wright (eds), 257–68 (Oxford: Oxford University Press, 1993); C. McGinn, "Another Look at Color", *Journal of Philosophy* **93** (1996), 537–53; and M. Johnston, *The Manifest*, forthcoming. It is interesting to note that both Johnston and McGinn change their minds about the nature of colour properties.

5. See, for example, P. Boghossian and D. Velleman, "Colour as a Secondary Quality", *Mind* **98** (1989), 81–103; E. Averill, "The Relational Nature of Color", *Philosophical Review* **101** (1992), 551–88; C. L. Hardin, *Color for Philosophers: Unweaving the Rainbow* (Indianapolis, IN: Hackett, 1993); and B. Maund, *Colors: Their Nature and Representation* (Cambridge: Cambridge University Press, 1995).

6. Such a restriction might be seen to unfairly favour physicalism about colour. After all, one objection to physicalism is that its reduction of the colours to microphysical or reflectance properties *of surfaces* seems to imply that the sky, rainbows, light sources, volumes and after images are not coloured. But see D. Hilbert, *Color and Color Perception* (Stanford, CA: Centre for Studies in Language and Information, 1987) for an extension of the physicalist idea to these tricky cases.

7. It is controversial whether or not the phenomenology of colour experience is identical to its representational content; cf. S. Shoemaker, "The Inverted Spectrum", *Journal of Philosophy* **79** (1982), 357–81 and C. Peacocke, *Sense and Content: Experience, Thought and Their Relations* (Oxford: Oxford University Press, 1983). Fortunately we do not need to take a stand on this debate here.

8. Although none of the original works of Democritus (c.460–370 BCE) survive, this quote has been attributed to him by ancient sources, including Sextus Empiricus; see J. Barnes, *Early Greek Philosophers* (Harmondsworth: Penguin, 1987).

9. See §8.4.2 for a similar argument.

10. Such an account, for example, does not explain why we experience objects and their after-images as having different colours. Nor does it explain why we can experience mixtures of some hues – such as blue and red hues (purple), and red and yellow hues (orange) – but not others – such as yellow/blue or red/green

mixtures. The need to explain such data led to the development of the current popular opponent-process theory of colour vision. See Hardin, *Color for Philosophers*, and A. Byrne and D. Hilbert, *Readings on Color*, volumes I and (Cambridge, MA: MIT Press, 1997), for a scientifically informed discussion opponent-process theory aimed at philosophers.

11. This view is also known in the literature variously as "the primary quality view" "objectivism", "materialism" and "reductive realism".

12. The two objections outlined here are simplified versions of arguments against the physicalist presented in P. Boghossian and D. Velleman, "Physicalist Theories of Color", *Philosophical Review* 100 (1991), 67–106; Johnston, "How to Speak of the Colors"; and Maund, *Colors*.

13. This is not the only possible response. See Boghosian and Velleman, "Physicalist Theories of Color", for a functionalist alternative.

14. Interestingly, it is not *because* the cape is *red* that a bull is angered. Bulls, it turns out, are colour blind, and see red things as grey.

15. These examples, and the problems they present for the physicalist, were first raised by Boghosian and Velleman, "Physicalist Theories of Color".

16. This view is also known in the literature variously as "the secondary quality view", "subjectivism" and "dispositionalism".

17. This worry for the response-dependent theorist is introduced by Boghossian and Velleman, "Colour as a Secondary Quality", and developed in McGinn, "Another Look at Color".

18. This example is taken directly from Johnston, "How to Speak of the Colors". Johnston credits the idea to Charlie Martin.

19. This objection was first put forward by Jackson and Pargetter, "An Objectivist' Guide to Subjectivism". For a response to this argument, see Johnston, "How to Speak of the Colors". It is interesting to note that to the extent that the argument is successful against its target, it will also be successful against reflectance physicalism. See Lewis, "Naming the Colours", 341ff. for a physicalist's response to this objection.

20. This view is also known in the literature variously as "primitivism", "impressionism" and "the simple view".

8. Morality

1. This version of the distinction is not just of historical interest. It is adopted, for example, by A. Miller, *Introduction to Contemporary Metaethics* (Cambridge: Polity, 2003), 4.

2. Plato suggests that our souls mingle with the forms before we are born and during our lives we recollect their natures (*Meno* 80d–86c). Plato does clearly think that we have innate knowledge of the forms, but it is arguable that even in Plato the story about our souls mingling with forms is a suggestive myth.

3. J. L. Mackie writes: "'a special sort of intuition' is a lame answer, but it is one to which a clear-headed [non-reductivist] objectivist is compelled to resort" (*Ethics: Inventing Right and Wrong* [Harmondsworth: Penguin, 1977], 39).

4. See F. Jackson, *From Metaphysics to Ethics: A Defence of Conceptual Analysis* (Oxford: Oxford University Press, 1998), ch. 5.

5. More exactly, moral properties supervene *globally* on descriptive properties.

6. The divine command theory is an odd form of realism, since it makes moral facts in a sense dependent on the opinions of God. But the divine command theory's moral facts – if they exist – are certainly independent of any human being's opinions.

7. For an attack on the technique of using the causal theory of reference in this way, see S. Darwall, A. Gibbard and P. Railton, "Toward *Fin de siècle* Ethics: Some Trends", *Philosophical Review* **101** (1992), 115–89.

8. We interpret N. Sturgeon, "Moral Explanations", in *Morality, Reason, and Truth: New Essays on the Foundations of Ethics*, D. Copp and D. Zimmerman (eds), 49–78 (Totowa, NJ: Rowman and Allanheld, 1985) as giving an argument of this sort.

9. Here an atomic sentence is a sentence that does not contain any logical particles such as "and", "not", "or" or "if ... then", for example, "Zermela is barking".

10. David Brink has responded to this argument on behalf of externalism. Brink distinguishes between *motivating* and *justifying* reasons for an action. Suppose that Ed asks Stu why he did a particular action. Stu could answer: (i) "I felt like it"; or (ii) "It is the right thing to do". Answer (i) is a motivating reason; it gives us an explanation of why Stu did what he did. Answer (ii) is a justifying reason. If Ed is asking Stu to defend his action, the latter statement might be used to warrant what he did. Brink claims that moral facts give us justifying reasons but not motivating reasons for actions (*Moral Realism and the Foundations of Ethics* [Cambridge: Cambridge University Press, 1989], 39–40). Brink has another argument against the internalist. He claims that internalism is empirically false, since sociopaths can judge something to be morally good but feel no relevant motivation (*ibid.*: 46–9). He could claim that non-sociopaths are conditioned to desire to do what they judge to be good, try to become good people and so on, and so feel the relevant emotional pull of moral judgements even if that motivational force is not intrinsic to moral judgements. At any rate, we shall leave the debate between internalists and externalists (as we do with all other debates) to the reader to explore further.

11. Of course, sociopaths could lack the "morality gene" or some other mechanism used to pass on or activate the moral sense.

12. Peter Railton, "Moral Realism", *Philosophical Review* **95** (1986), 163–207, and "Moral Realism: Prospects and Problems", in *Moral Knowledge? New Readings in Moral Epistemology*, W. Sinnott-Armstrong and M. Timmons (eds), 49–81 (Oxford: Oxford University Press, 1996) constructs a different response-dependence theory of morality, in which this identification of morality and rationality is rejected. Railton thinks that in deciding what one morally should do, we should think about what the *community* of idealizations of people who will be affected by the decision would decide. In this way, we can get a "balancing of interests" of the people affected. A worry about Smith's view is that our "better selves" may be quite selfish, and would not be what is normally considered moral.

13. In this connection we should not forget John Rawls, *A Theory of Justice* (Cambridge, MA: Harvard University Press, 1971), who uses an idealizing technique to help argue for his principles of justice. It would be inappropriate to label Rawls either as a factualist or non-factualist, since he does not think of himself as doing metaethics.

14. The method originated in F. P. Ramsey, "Theories" [1929], reprinted in his *Philosophical Papers*, D. H. Mellor (ed.), 112–36 (Cambridge: Cambridge University Press, 1990), and was developed into the form that Jackson uses by David Lewis, "How to Define Theoretical Terms", *Journal of Philosophy* **67** (1970), 427–46 (reprinted in Lewis, *Collected Papers* [Oxford: Oxford University Press, 1983], volume 1, ch. 6).

15. Jackson allows even for infinitely long disjunctions of properties (and infinitely long conjunctions). He uses these to give a general argument that any moral property can be reduced to a descriptive property. Here is Jackson's method. We

take a moral property, for example, the property of being forbidden. Then we select a possible world. In that world, we look at all the actions that we consider forbidden. Then we look at one of these actions. We list all of its descriptive properties. Let us call these properties $P1$, $P2$, ... Then we take another event that we consider forbidden and list all of its properties $Q1$, $Q2$, ... Now we create a "superproperty", $(P1$ and $P2$ ...) or $(Q1$ and $Q2$ ...), that incorporates all the properties of all the objects that we consider forbidden in that world. Then we do the same for every other possible world, and disjoin all the super-properties from all the worlds. This disjunction of conjunctions fits all the same actions in every possible world as the property of being forbidden. For Jackson, any two properties with the same extension in every possible world are in fact the same property. Thus, we have a general method of reducing moral proper-ties to descriptive properties (*From Metaphysics to Ethics*: 122–3).

9. Science

1. In fact, for any set of data, in principle we can come up with infinitely many theories to explain them.
2. Fine claims that the methods used to study science should be more rigorous than those used by scientists. This view is rejected by proponents of naturalized epis-temology. Instead of becoming embroiled in this debate, we have reconstructed Fine's argument in terms of what methods are allowed for use in the dialogue between realists and anti-realists.
3. We are grateful to Oliver Schulte for telling us about Stanford's paper.
4. It might seem odd to call van Fraassen a fictionalist when he does not believe that scientific theories are literally false. But consider an example of a person who tells a story that he or she has made up but that just happens to be true. Most of us, we think, would call such a story fiction. Mark Kalderon, for exam-ple, agrees with our categorization, when he says "Modern fictionalism emerged in 1980 with the publication of Hartry Field's *Science without Numbers* and Bas van Fraassen's *The Scientific Image*" (*Fictionalist Approaches*, 1).
5. For a recent defence by van Fraassen of his view of epistemic communities, see van Fraassen, "The Day of the Dolphins: Puzzling over Epistemic Partnership", in *Mistakes of Reason*, A. Irvine and K. Peacock (eds), 111–13 (Toronto: Uni-versity of Toronto Press, 2005).
6. Of course, as we have seen, it is also the predictable behaviour of microscopes that assures us about the existence of human eggs, according to the experimental philosophers.
7. http://planetquest.jpl.nasa.gov/SIM/new_worlds.cfm (accessed January 2007).
8. At least according to I. Hacking, *The Social Construction of What?* (Cambridge, MA: Harvard University Press, 1999), 97.

10. Mathematics

1. More recently a mathematical theory has emerged that may not be able to be reduced to set theory: category theory. There is an active debate on the philo-sophical status of category theory and its relationship to set theory (see Solomon Feferman, "Categorical Foundations and the Foundations of Category Theory", in *Logic, Foundations of Mathematics and Computability Theory*, R. Butts and J. Hintikka (eds), 149–69 (Dordrecht: Reidel, 1977), J.-P. Marquis, "Category Theory and the Foundations of Mathematics: Philosophical Excavations", *Syn-these* 103 (1995), 421–47 and "Category Theory", in *Stanford Encyclopedia of*

Philosophy (Spring 2006), E. N. Zalta (ed.), http://plato.stanford.edu/entries/category-theory/ (accessed January 2007).

2. In the nineteenth century, a set was treated as an arbitrary collection, but this led to paradoxes. Now we think of a set as a collection that obeys certain restrictions, which have been codified in a mathematical theory called "set theory".

3. It is not clear whether any form of the supervenience problem affects Platonism about mathematics.

4. Our version of Benacerraf's complaint is due to H. H. Field, *Science without Numbers* (Princeton, NJ: Princeton University Press, 1980) and P. Maddy, *Realism in Mathematics* (Oxford: Oxford University Press, 1990).

5. The sort of logicism that we describe here is a simplified version of Gottlob Frege's view. Bertrand Russell was also a logicist, but he thought that certain mathematical truths (in particular, that there are an infinite number of numbers) are empirical. And Russell was not a Platonist in the usual sense. He thought that sets are fictional objects ("logical fictions" or "logical constructs").

6. Gödel showed that every sentence in a logical language (that includes arithmetic) can be assigned a number. Moreover, he constructed what has become known as a "diagonal operator", which allows sentences in effect to talk about themselves, and a predicate, which we can call "P", such that Px means "x is provable". This process is known as the "arithmetization of syntax" of a logical language. He then was able to construct a formula that in effect says "this formula is not provable". Let this sentence be "G". If G is provable, then we will also be able to prove Pg, where g is the number assigned to G. But G is logically equivalent to $\neg Pg$, so we would be able to prove both Pg and $\neg Pg$. Hence our system would be inconsistent. Thus, if the system is consistent, then the sentence G cannot be proved. But it says exactly this: that it cannot be proved. So, intuitively it is true although not provable.

7. Later in this chapter we shall discuss ways of generating the natural numbers. But simply put, the idea is that there is a rule that we can state in a finite amount of time and a finite space.

8. We include Stewart Shapiro, *Foundations without Foundationalism: A Case for Second Order Logic* (Oxford: Oxford University Press, 2000) and Jaakko Hintikka, *The Principles of Mathematics Revisited* (Cambridge: Cambridge University Press, 1996), as well as Crispin Wright and Bob Hale, *The Reason's Proper Study: Essays Towards a Neo-Fregean Philosophy of Mathematics* (Oxford: Oxford University Press, 2004) in this list. We are not sure that Shapiro and Hintikka would agree to the label of logicism for their views, but certainly they have defended the use of non-computable logics for the foundations of mathematics.

9. At least they have limited value in this context. A relative consistency proof can be useful if there is a theory (e.g. a set theory) that has been used a great deal and another newer theory is shown to be consistent relative to that older theory. In this case, the fact that a theory has been well used without showing a contradiction may give us reason to believe that it is consistent. Then the relative consistency proof will give us reason to believe that the newer theory is also consistent.

10. Actually, she has since rejected this view. See Penelope Maddy, *Naturalism in Mathematics* (Oxford: Oxford University Press, 1997). To make matters worse, Maddy refers to what we call her "naturalism" as "Platonism" and to her later view as "naturalism". We apologise for whatever confusion results, but we want to keep our categorization consistent from field to field and we found that our changes of terminology from hers were necessary.

11. One might think that what we perceive is a fact that can be expressed as $\exists x \exists y \exists z (\neg x = y \ \& \ \neg x = z \ \& \ \neg y = z \ \& \ \text{InFridge}(x) \ \& \ \text{InFridge}(y) \ \& \ \text{InFridge}(z)$ $\& \ \text{Egg}(x) \ \& \ \text{Egg}(y) \ \& \ \text{Egg}(z) \ \& \ \forall w((\text{InFridge}(w) \ \& \ \text{Egg}(w)) \to (w = x \lor w = y \lor w = z))$. But note the use of negation in this formula. It seems implausible, at least to many philosophers, to suggest that we perceive negative facts.

12. Maddy in fact gives a hybrid realist version of her view as well in which there are pure sets.

13. For Lewis's theory of possible worlds, see Chapter 11. In fact, his mereological treatment of mathematics depends on his realism about merely possible entities. For his theory to work, he must assume that there are a very large number of things, more things than can possibly fit into a single possible world (if they are material).

14. There are some structuralists, such as Geoffrey Hellman (*Mathematics Without Numbers: Towards a Modal-Structural Interpretation* [Oxford: Oxford University Press, 1989], who are not hybrid realists.

15. Sometimes structuralists talk as if there is no unique series that is the natural numbers or sometimes they talk of individual numbers as "positions in patterns". See M. D. Resnik, *Mathematics as a Science of Patterns* (Oxford: Oxford University Press, 1997).

16. Here we have Hilbert's formalist programme in mind. Hilbert's programme was to show that arithmetic could be formalized completely and be shown (using finitary means only) to be consistent. The point is that we have certain mathematical abilities in which we are confident. These are the abilities to carry out "finitary" processes. We know that we can count and that we can do addition and subtraction in ways that are reliable and accord with the way the world works. According to the programme, mathematical theories are formal games that allow us to derive things about the world elegantly and relatively briefly. The formal systems are acceptable on Hilbert's programme if and only if they do not prove statements in finite mathematics that could not have been proved (perhaps at much greater length in very awkward ways) using our finite combinatorial intuitions. The importance of consistency is that inconsistent theories (at least in classical logic) entail every statement. Thus, in order to show that a theory does not entail any incorrect statement of finite mathematics, we need to know that it is consistent. Gödel showed that (i) no finite formal system could produce all the truths of arithmetic and (ii) that no computable theory of arithmetic can prove itself to be consistent. Most mathematicians and philosophers of mathematics have taken Gödel's theorems to have shown Hilbert's programme to be untenable. Michael Detlefsen, *Hilbert's Program: An Essay on Mathematical Instrumentalism* (Dordrecht: Reidel, 1986), however, has defended Hilbert's programme.

17. Hilbert's appeal to finite combinatorial intuitions is precisely meant to connect mathematics with the physical world.

18. That is, in formal logic $\exists x \exists y (\text{Ard}(x) \land \text{Ard}(y) \land \neg x = y \land \text{InSH}(x) \land \text{InS}(y) \land \forall z((\text{Ard}(z) \land \text{InS}(z)) \to (z = x \lor z = y)))$.

19. M. Resnik, "How Nominalist is Hartry Field's Nominalism?", *Philosophical Studies* 47 (1985), 163–81, objects that these are as abstract as sets, numbers and other traditional Platonic entities.

20. These interpretations of the logical operators is called the "Brouwer–Heyting–Komolgorov interpretation" after Brouwer, Arend Heyting (who first developed intuitionist logic) and the great Russian mathematician A. N. Komolgorov.

21. As we saw in §6.6 above, intuitionists do not claim that the law of excluded middle is false, but rather that it merely fails to be true.

22. Not all of the rules for these constructions need be fully deterministic. This

means we do not always need a rule that will specify what the next step is in all of its detail. A rule can say that, for example, to determine the next entity in the sequence we can make a random choice (e.g. by flipping a coin). A sequence of such random choices is called a "free-choice sequence". See M. Dummett, *Elements of Intuitionism* (Oxford: Oxford University Press, 1977).

3. These responses were given to us by our colleague, Neil Leslie.

4. Like all response-dependent theorists, Kitcher needs to tell us about the status of his ideal agent. Kitcher says that he is not committed to the existence of an ideal agent. Unfortunately, he draws from the nonexistence of his ideal mathematician the conclusion that statements of mathematics "turn out to be vacuously true" (*The Nature of Mathematical Knowledge* [Oxford: Oxford University Press, 1994], 117 n.18). This means that all statements of mathematics, including statements such as "2 + 2 = 5" and "There are no even numbers", are in fact true! In effect, Kitcher takes the idealization to be a heuristic: it merely describes what mathematicians are doing when they do mathematics. It does not give truth-conditions for statements of mathematics. But the nonexistence of the ideal mathematician and the vacuousness of mathematical truth are not integral to the response-dependent theory of mathematics and so we ignore this unattractive aspect of Kitcher's view here.

1. Possible worlds

1. "World" is an ambiguous term. Sometimes we use it to refer to the entire universe, but at other times to mere planets. In this context, it is important to keep in mind that Lewis means to use the term in the former sense.

2. There are, of course, other reasons Lewis puts forward for adopting his ontology. Consider the following (in)famous argument: "I believe, and so do you, that things could have been different in countless ways. But what does this mean? Ordinary language permits the paraphrase: there are many ways things could have been besides the way they actually are. On the face of it, this sentence is an existential quantification. It says that there exist many entities of a certain description, to wit 'ways things could have been' ... taking the paraphrase at its face value, I therefore believe in the existence of entities that might be called 'ways things could have been'. I prefer to call them 'possible worlds'" (Lewis, *Counterfactuals* [Oxford: Blackwell, 1973], 84). Whatever one makes of this argument, though, at best it only provides support for the first of the ontological theses: *minimal realism*. This thesis is comparatively uncontroversial. It does not support any of the other interesting ontological theses.

3. Regarding this Lewis says the following: "doubtless you will expect me to say that possible worlds and individuals are concrete, not abstract. But I am reluctant to say that outright. Not because I hold the opposite view, but because it is not at all clear to me what philosophers mean when they speak of 'concrete' and 'abstract' in this connection" (*On the Plurality of Worlds* [Oxford: Blackwell, 1986], 81). While we appreciate the qualm Lewis raises here, it is enough to say that, *in this context*, what we mean when we say of a world that it is concrete is merely that it is of the same kind as this world. Likewise, when we say of a world that it is abstract, we mean that it is *not* of the same kind as this world.

4. This point is made by J. Melia, "A Note on Lewis's Ontology", *Analysis* 52, (1992), 191–2.

5. The name was coined by Lewis, *Counterfactuals*.

6. See, for example, A. Plantinga, *The Nature of Necessity* (Oxford: Blackwell, 1974).

7. Whatever that alternative principle is, however, it seems likely that the concrete realist could take it on board. Consider Lewis's comments on an alternative combinatorial principle proffered by D. Armstrong, *A Combinatorial Theory of Possibility* (Cambridge: Cambridge University Press, 1989): "The range of possibilities question is everyone's question. It can be framed in different ways to suit different views about the nature of possibilities; and no matter how we frame it, we can, if we like, borrow Armstrong's answer. We can say that for any way of recombining all or some of the universals that are found within our actual word, there is another 'concrete' world wherein these constituents are thus recombined; or there is an 'abstract' ersatz world that represents these universals as being thus recombined; or it is primitively possible, without benefit of any entities to play the role of possible world, that they might have been thus recombined" (D. Lewis, "Critical Notice: Armstrong, D. M. *A Combinatorial Theory of Possibility*", *Australasian Journal of Philosophy* 70 [1992], 211). It seems to us, then, that while some principle of recombination may be required to determine the range of possibilities, the principle one finally selects will be available to all. We might conclude, therefore, that the plenitude thesis is inessential to the Lewisian hypothesis. Moreover, the Forrest–Armstrong objection is an objection not so much to Lewisian realism, but rather to *any* modal theorist who adopts the *unrestricted* principle to specify the range of possibilities.

8. See A. Hazen, "One of the Truths About Actuality", *Analysis* 39 (1979), 1–3, for a discussion of the metaphysical and semantic theses about "actuality".

9. Indeed, it is arguable that Kripke himself thought of the problem of concern as a general problem for all forms of reductive realism. In the preface to *Naming and Necessity* (Cambridge, MA: Harvard University Press, 1980), he says "I do not think of 'possible worlds' as providing a *reductive* analysis in any philosophically significant sense, that is, as uncovering the ultimate nature, from either an epistemological or a metaphysical point of view, of modal operators, propositions, etc., or as 'explicating' them" (*ibid.*: 19 n.14, original emphasis).

10. This problem was first raised specifically as an objection to Lewis's modal realism. See T. Richards, "The Worlds of David Lewis", *Australasian Journal of Philosophy* 53 (1975), 105–18; B. Skyrms, "Possible Worlds, Physics and Metaphysics", *Philosophical Studies* 30 (1976), 323–32; Armstrong, *A Combinatorial Theory of Possibility*; and O. Bueno and S. Shalkowski, "A Plea for a Modal Realist Epistemology", *Acta Analytica* 15 (2000), 175–93. The problem is obviously generalizable, though, and some notable attempts at tackling the problem can be found in S. Yablo, "Is Conceivability a Guide to Possibility?", *Philosophy and Phenomenological Research* 53 (1993), 1–42; J. Hawthorne, "The Epistemology of Possible Worlds", *Philosophical Studies* 84 (1996), 183–202; and T. Gendler and J. Hawthorne (eds), *Conceivability and Possibility* (Oxford: Clarendon Press, 2002).

11. The anti-realist is in no position to deny the parity thesis. She may of course use the term "world" in a different way, perhaps to "refer" to some nonexistent abstract entities, but Lewis is perfectly entitled to stipulate what *he* means by the term. The anti-realist is in a position only to assert that there is not a plurality of such entities.

12. It might be thought that it is possible for the anti-realist to accept the parity thesis and yet not accept the isolation thesis. But it seems to us that Lewis states his position a little too weakly. Lewis never defines what he means by the term "world", preferring to take it as a primitive. But he could define world (and his view often seems to require it) as a maximally extended region of continuous spacetime. Thus, the parity thesis could be replaced with this one principle of

maximal continuity. As a consequence, we take the isolation thesis to be a kind of analytic truth. Thus, the kind of anti-realism mentioned above would instead be a kind of agnosticism.

We do not mean to suggest, however, that someone who took issue with Lewis's conception of a "world", and yet felt that there are abstract entities that (closely enough) fill the role Lewis hopes his spatiotemporal regions fill, would be an anti-realist. An anti-realist must deny that there are any appropriate entities that could be quantified over in our explication of modal notions. Hence her denial of the conceptual thesis.

13. It should be noted, though, that there are other philosophers who believe that it is both necessary and *a priori* knowable that there are no disconnected spatiotemporal regions; and thus that there are no other worlds. Their arguments for this position are interesting in their own right. See, for example, Kant's *Critique of Pure Reason*, and, for a more guarded defence of this view, A. Rosenberg, "Is Lewis's Genuine Modal Realism Magical Too?", *Mind* 98 (1989), 411–21.

14. There is some world w, such that for all x, if x is red in @, then x is shiny in w.

15. One might worry that this kind of objection begs the question against the modalist who suggests that modality should not be analysed in terms of quantification over possible worlds. But remember, the modalist has no objection to philosophers' use of the possible worlds idiom, it is just that she thinks it is simply a heuristic device that can be used as an aid to modal reasoning ultimately explainable in terms of the modal operators.

16. See J. Crossley and L. Humberstone, "The Logic of 'Actually'", *Reports on Mathematical Logic* 8 (1977), 11–29, and M. Davies, *Meaning, Quantification and Necessity: Themes in Philosophical Logic* (London: Routledge & Kegan Paul, 1981) for the syntactic and semantic features of the actuality operator.

17. An extended discussion of most of these kinds of examples is given in Lewis, *On the Plurality of Worlds*, 13ff. For further examples, see A. Hazen, "Expressive Completeness in Modal Language", *Journal of Philosophical Logic* 5 (1976), 25–46.

18. An attempt to provide the appropriate extensions to express such sentences is given in G. Forbes, *The Metaphysics of Modality* (Oxford: Clarendon Press, 1985) and *Languages of Possibility* (Oxford: Blackwell, 1989) and C. Peacocke, "Necessity and Truth Theories", *Journal of Philosophical Logic* 7 (1978), 473–500. For a critique of such extensions see J. Melia, "Against Modalism", *Philosophical Studies* 68 (1992), 35–56.

19. Rosen is a little equivocal on this point. At the end of his paper, he toys with an alternative "timid" view of his theory according to which it is not an analysis of modal terms, but rather a set of rules, that license one moving from modal talk to possible world talk and back again. It should be clear, though, that this is not the view Rosen favours.

20. See Armstrong, *A Combinatorial Theory of Possibility*, for an alternative version of modal fictionalism.

21. This objection to fictionalism was first raised independently in S. Brock, "Modal Fictionalism: A Response to Rosen", *Mind* 102 (1993), 147–50, and G. Rosen, "A Problem for Fictionalism About Possible Worlds", *Analysis* 53 (1993), 71–81.

22. A number of philosophers have proposed amendments to fictionalism in response to this objection. See, for example, P. Menzies and P. Pettit, "A Defence of Fictionalism about Possible Worlds", *Analysis* 54 (1994), 27–36 and H. Noonan, "A Defence of the Letter of Fictionalism", *Analysis* 54 (1994), 133–9. But there is no widespread agreement about the success of these patches to the theory.

23. Of course, fictionalism and modalism hardly exhaust the anti-realist alternatives to realism. Due to limitations of space, we have not considered more extreme

234   REALISM AND ANTI-REALISM

(and less popular) varieties of anti-realism. Every position mapped out in this chapter presupposes realism about the modal *facts*. Anti-realists about the modal facts are also anti-realists about possible worlds and individuals; because there are no (real) modal truths, there is no need to postulate truth-makers for such truths. Many philosophers have defended an extreme version of modal anti-realism. W. V. Quine, in many writings, has defended a version of error theory about the modal facts. See J. Melia, *Modality* (Chesham: Acumen, 2003), ch, 3, for an excellent discussion of Quine's defence of modal error theory. Simon Blackburn, "Morals and Modals", in *Facts, Science, and Value*, C. Wright and G. McDonald (eds), 634–48 (Oxford: Blackwell, 1987) defends a version of non-factualism about the modal facts, and Peter Menzies, *Secondary Qualities Generalised, Monist*, special issue, 81(1) (1998), defends a response-dependent account of modality.

12. Fictional characters

1. The ontological and objectivity theses do not exhaust the points of similarity between all realist theories. For example, it could be argued that another crucial thesis held in common by all realists is a principle of plenitude, roughly that there is an abundance of fictional characters (cf. S. Brock, "Fictionalism about Fictional Characters", *Noûs* 36 [2002], 1–21).

2. Sentence (4*) was suggested in conversation by David Lewis, and (9*) is borrowed from R. Howell, "Fictional Objects: How They Are and How They Aren't", *Poetics* 8 (1979), 129–77, esp. 154.

3. P. van Inwagen, "Fiction and Metaphysics", *Philosophy and Literature* 7 (1983), 67–77, bases his case in support of the reality of fictional characters not so much on the commitments of the folk, but rather the commitments of literary critics. But there is a problem with such an argument, for literary critics are almost universally relativists of a quite radical kind, and so advocate a position at odds with any form of realism.

4. We do not pretend, merely by giving a short list of examples, to have adequately characterized the distinction between abstract objects and concrete objects. Indeed, one realist doubts that such a categorization can adequately be given at all. Regarding this issue, Lewis says the following: "doubtless you will expect me to say that ... [such] individuals are [sometimes] concrete, not abstract. But I am reluctant to say that outright. Not because I hold the opposite view, but because it is not at all clear to me what philosophers mean when they speak of 'concrete' and 'abstract' in this connection" (*On the Plurality of Worlds*, 81). We can only presume, though, that the abstract realist will have some such distinction in mind if her theory is to provide any contrast to the concrete realist's theory (as the philosophers who espouse such theories claim they do). We shall not attempt to guess how this distinction is to be made. We merely want to point out that however the abstract realist chooses to spell out this distinction, the realist will be committed to the view that some fictional objects are concrete, while others are abstract.

5. There is, of course, something unnatural about our suggestion that Parsons, who is influenced by the work of Meinong, defends the same kind of theory as Lewis, for neo-Meinongians are famous for their distinction between being and existence, rather than any distinction between actuality and existence. Parsons therefore offers an alternative to the non-actualist thesis: there are fictional characters, but they do not exist. Because Parsons also asserts that "there is" is a quantifier and "exists" is a predicate (rather than an alternative quantifier as suggested in Chapter 2) it is not clear to us that *this* difference between Lewis

and Parsons is anything more than a mere verbal difference. (That is not to say that there are no other substantive differences between the two views. For an interesting and detailed comparison of the Lewisian and neo-Meinongian theories, see B. Linsky and E. Zalta, "Is Lewis a Meinongian?", *Australasian Journal of Philosophy* 69 (1991), 438–53.

. Of course, there is nothing that compels the realist about fictional characters who embraces the abstractism thesis to be an actualist. Indeed, Howell ("Fictional Objects") suggests that fictional characters are non-actual abstract objects. But actualism is a very plausible thesis, and we should not want to give it up unless we have a good reason to do so. An abstract realist has no such reason. Thus, Howell subsequently retracted his commitment to the thesis that fictional characters are non-actual objects. See R. Howell, "Review of Parsons' *Nonexistent Objects*", *Journal of Philosophy* 80 (1983), 163–73, and "Review of Walton's *Mimesis as Make-Believe*", *Synthese* 109 (1996), 424–34.

. This thesis should not be confused with the theological thesis of the same name, according to which God is the creator of heaven and earth.

. Thomasson allows that a memory of such work may be enough to ensure the continued existence of a fictional character. We ignore this complication here, but note that this added wrinkle only makes it less likely (and not more) that fictional characters are mind-dependent objects.

. It is important to note that Thomasson's terminology differs from ours. She puts the idea as follows: "Clearly the dependence of a fictional character on the intentional acts of its creator or creators is a rigid historical dependence … The second immediate dependence of a fictional character is a generic constant dependence on some literary work about it [or memory of that work]" (*Fiction and Metaphysics* [Cambridge: Cambridge University Press, 1999]. 35–6). Thomasson's distinctions are more fine-grained than ours. The differences between her conceptualization and ours, though, need not concern us here.

. One way of constructing such a paraphrase, defended by E. Mally, *Gegenstandstheoretische Grundlagen der Logik und Logistik*, supplement to *Zeitschrift für Philosophie und philosophische Kritik* 148 (1912), H.-N. Castañeda, "Thinking and the Structure of the World", *Philosophia* 4 (1974), 3–40 and E. N. Zalta, *Abstract Objects* (Dordrecht: Reidel, 1983) and *Intensional Logic and the Metaphysics of Intentionality* (Cambridge, MA: MIT Press, 1988), is that there are two *ways* of having properties. Sherlock Holmes does not have his properties of being a detective, being human and so on, in the same way that the detectives in your local police station do. Rather, Holmes has these properties in a different sense. Our criticism of individual realism can be modified easily to apply to this view. It is not the "fact" that Holmes stands in this other relation to the property of being a clever detective that real detectives admire about Holmes, but it is because he supposedly has these properties in the normal sense that they admire him. Mally, Castañeda and Zalta have a reply to this problem. They hold that when we think of ordinary objects, we think of them in terms of abstract objects that have the properties that we think of them as having in this second sense. In this, these views are very close to Frege's theory of meaning (see §6.1). And they have the same problems as Frege's theory. They need to explain how we can grasp abstract objects when we think. Moreover, we claim the views of intentionality held by Mally, Castañeda and Zalta are counterintuitive and the complexities that they introduce are unwarranted by the problems that they are supposed to solve. We leave it to the reader to follow up this issue and decide whether they or we are right.

11. We have changed the numbers to correspond to Walton's quote below.

Bibliography

Allison, H. 1983. *Kant's Transcendental Idealism*. New Haven, CT: Yale Universit; Press.

Allison, H. (ed.) 1989. *Kant's Critical Philosophy*. *The Monist* 72(2).

Alston, W. 1958. "Ontological Commitments". *Philosophical Studies* 9, 8–17.

Alston, W. 1996. *A Realist Conception of Truth*. Ithaca, NY: Cornell Universit; Press.

Appiah, A. 1986. *For Truth in Semantics*. Oxford: Blackwell.

Armstrong, D. M. 1989. *A Combinatorial Theory of Possibility*. Cambridge: Cam bridge University Press.

Averill, E. 1992. "The Relational Nature of Color". *Philosophical Review* 101, 551- 88.

Ayer, A. J. 1932. *Language, Truth, and Logic*. Harmondsworth: Penguin.

Ayer, A. J. (ed.) 1959. *Logical Positivism*. London: Macmillan.

Baker, A. 2003. "Quantitative Parsimony and Explanatory Power". *British Journa; for the Philosophy of Science* 54, 245–59.

Balaguer, M. 1998. *Platonism and Anti-Platonism in Mathematics*. Oxford: Oxford University Press.

Barnes, B. & D. Edge (eds) 1982. *Science in Context: Readings in the Sociology of Science*. Milton Keynes: Open University Press.

Barnes, E. C. 2000. "Ockham's Razor and the Anti-Superfluity Principle". *Erken- ntnis* 53, 353–74.

Barnes, J. 1987. *Early Greek Philosophy*. Harmondsworth: Penguin.

Benacerraf, P. 1973. "Mathematical Truth". *Journal of Philosophy* 70, 661–80. Reprinted in Benacerraf & Putnam (1983), 403–20.

Benacerraf, P. & H. Putnam (eds) 1983. *Philosophy of Mathematics*, 2nd edn. Cambridge: Cambridge University Press.

Berkeley, G. 1965. *Principles, Dialogues, and Philosophical Correspondence*, C. Tur- bayne (ed.). Indianapolis, IN: Bobbs-Merrill.

Bigelow, J. 1988. *The Reality of Numbers*. Oxford: Oxford University Press.

Bigelow, J. & R. Pargetter 1990. *Science and Necessity*. Cambridge: Cambridge University Press.

Blackburn, S. 1984. *Spreading the Word*. Oxford: Oxford University Press.

Blackburn, S. 1987. "Morals and Modals". In *Facts, Science, and Value*, C. Wright & G. McDonald (eds), 119–41. Oxford: Blackwell.

Blackburn, S. 1993. *Essays in Quasi-Realism*. Oxford: Oxford University Press.

ackburn, S. 2005. "Quasi-Realism no Fictionalism". In *Fictionalism in Metaphysics*, M. Kalderon (ed.). Oxford: Oxford University Press.

oor, D. 1976. *Knowledge and Social Imagery*. London: Routledge.

ghossian, P. 2006. *Fear of Knowledge*. Oxford: Oxford University Press.

ghossian, P. & D. Velleman 1989. "Colour as a Secondary Quality". *Mind* 98, 81–103.

ghossian, P. & D. Velleman 1991. "Physicalist Theories of Color". *Philosophical Review* 100, 67–106.

oyd, R. 1988. "How to be a Moral Realist". In *Essays on Moral Realism*, G. Sayre-McCord (ed.), 181–228. Ithaca, NY: Cornell University Press.

oyd, R., P. Gasper & J. D. Trout (eds) 1991. *The Philosophy of Science*. Cambridge, MA: MIT Press.

ridges, D. 1995. "Constructive Mathematics and Unbounded Operators – A Reply to Hellman". *Journal of Philosophical Logic* 24, 549–61.

rink, D. O. 1989. *Moral Realism and the Foundations of Ethics*. Cambridge: Cambridge University Press.

roakes, J. forthcoming. *What is Colour?* London: Routledge.

rock, S. 1993. "Modal Fictionalism: A Response to Rosen". *Mind* 102, 147–50.

rock, S. 2002. "Fictionalism about Fictional Characters". *Noûs* 36, 1–21.

rouwer, L. E. J. 1981. *Brouwer's Cambridge Lectures on Intuitionism*. Cambridge: Cambridge University Press.

ueno, O. & S. Shalkowski 2000. "A Plea for a Modal Realist Epistemology". *Acta Analytica* 15, 175–93.

urge, T. 1992. "Frege on Knowing the Third Realm". *Mind* 101, 633–50.

urgess, J. P. & G. Rosen 1997. *A Subject with No Object: Strategies for Nominalistic Interpretations of Mathematics*. Oxford: Oxford University Press.

yrne, A. & D. Hilbert 1997. *Readings on Color*, volumes I and II. Cambridge, MA: MIT Press.

yrne, A. & D. Hilbert 2003. "Color Realism and Color Science". *Behavioral and Brain Sciences* 26, 3–21.

Campbell, J. 1993. "A Simple View of Colour". In *Reality, Representation, and Projection*, J. Haldane & C. Wright (eds), 257–68. Oxford: Oxford University Press.

Carnap, R. 1959. "The Old and New Logic". In *Logical Positivism*, A. J. Ayer (ed.), 133–46. London: Macmillan.

Carnap, R. 1963. "Carnap's Intellectual Autobiography". In *The Philosophy of Rudolf Carnap*, P. A. Schilpp (ed.), 1–84. La Salle, IL: Open Court.

Cartwright, N. 1983. *How the Laws of Physics Lie*. Oxford: Oxford University Press.

Cartwright, N. 1999. *The Dappled World: A Study of the Boundaries of Science*. Cambridge: Cambridge University Press.

Casati, R. & C. Tappolet (eds) 1998. *European Review of Philosophy: Response-Dependence*, volume 3. Stanford, CA: CSLI Publications.

Castañeda, H.-N. 1974. "Thinking and the Structure of the World". *Philosophia* 4, 3–40. Reprinted in Castañeda, *Thinking, Language, Experience*, ch. 13 (Minneapolis, MN: University of Minnesota Press, 1989).

Chappell, V. C. (ed.) 1994. *Cambridge Companion to Locke*. Cambridge: Cambridge University Press.

Chihara, C. 1998. *The Worlds of Possibility: Modal Realism and the Semantics of Modal Logic*. Oxford: Clarendon Press.

Churchland, P. M. & C. A. Hooker (eds) 1985. *Images of Science: Essays on Realism and Empiricism with Replies by Bas C. van Fraassen*. Chicago, IL: University of Chicago Press.

Clark, P. & B. Hale (eds) 1994. *Reading Putnam*. Oxford: Blackwell.

Clark, R. 1980. "Fictional Entities: Talking about Them, and Having Feelings about Them". *Philosophical Studies* 38, 341–49.

Coffa, J. A. 1991. *The Semantic Tradition from Kant to Carnap: To the Vienna Station*. Cambridge: Cambridge University Press.

Cohen, L. J. 1989. "Belief and Acceptance". *Mind* 98, 367–89.

Colyvan, M. 2001. *The Indispensability of Mathematics*. Oxford: Oxford University Press.

Copp, D. & D. Zimmerman (eds) 1985. *Morality, Reason, and Truth: New Essays on the Foundations of Ethics*. Totowa, NJ: Rowman and Allanheld.

Crittenden, C. 1991. *Unreality: The Metaphysics of Fictional Characters*. Ithaca, NY: Cornell University Press.

Crossley, J. & L. Humberstone 1977. "The Logic of 'Actually'". *Reports on Mathematical Logic* 8, 11–29.

Currie, G. 1990. "The Characters of Fiction". *The Nature of Fiction*. Cambridge: Cambridge University Press.

Darwall, S., A. Gibbard & P. Railton 1992. "Toward *Fin de siècle* Ethics: Some Trends". *Philosophical Review* 101, 115–89.

Davidson, D. 1974. "On the Very Idea of a Conceptual Scheme". *Proceedings and Addresses of the American Philosophical Association* 47, 5–20. See Davidson (1984), ch. 13.

Davidson, D. 1977. "Reality without Reference". *Dialectica* 31, 247–53. See Davidson (1984), ch. 15.

Davidson, D. 1984. *Inquiries into Truth and Interpretation*. Oxford: Oxford University Press.

Davidson, D. 1986. "A Nice Derangement of Epitaphs". In *Truth and Interpretation*, E. LePore (ed.), 433–46. Oxford: Blackwell.

Davidson, D. 1990. "The Structure and Content of Truth". *Journal of Philosophy* 87, 279–328.

Davidson, D. 2005a. *Truth, Language, and History*. Oxford: Oxford University Press.

Davison, D. 2005b. *Truth and Predication*. Cambridge, MA: Harvard University Press.

Davies, M. 1981. *Meaning, Quantification and Necessity: Themes in Philosophical Logic*. London: Routledge & Kegan Paul.

Day, T. & H. Kincaid 1994. "Putting Inference to the Best Explanation in its Place". *Synthese* 98, 271–95.

Detlefsen, M. 1986. *Hilbert's Program: An Essay on Mathematical Instrumentalism*. Dordrecht: Reidel.

Devitt, M. [1984] 1991. *Realism and Truth*. Oxford: Blackwell.

Divers, J. 2002. *Possible Worlds*. London: Routledge.

Dummett, M. 1977. *Elements of Intuitionism*. Oxford: Oxford University Press.

Dummett, M. [1969] 1978a. "The Reality of the Past". In *Truth and Other Enigmas*, 358–74. London: Duckworth.

Dummett, M. 1978b. *Truth and Other Enigmas*. London: Duckworth.

Dummett, M. 1981. *Frege: Philosophy of Language*, 2nd edn. London: Duckworth.

Dummett, M. 1991. *The Logical Basis of Metaphysics*. Cambridge, MA: Harvard University Press.

Dummett, M. 1993. *The Seas of Language*. Oxford: Oxford University Press.

Dummett, M. 2004. *Truth and the Past*. New York: Columbia University Press.

Edwards, J. 1992. "Best Opinion and Intentional States". *Philosophical Quarterly* 42, 21–33.

Emt, J. 1992. "On the Nature of Fictional Entities". In *Understanding the Arts: Con-*

temporary Scandinavian Aesthetics, J. Emt & G. Hermerén (eds), 149–76. Lund: Lund University Press.

Evnine, S. 1991. *Donald Davidson*. Cambridge: Polity.

Evans, G. 1980. "Things Without the Mind". In *Philosophical Subjects: Essays Presented to P. F. Strawson*, Z. Van Straaten (ed.), 76–116. Oxford: Oxford University Press.

Feferman, S. 1977. "Categorical Foundations and the Foundations of Category Theory". In *Logic, Foundations of Mathematics and Computability Theory*, R. Butts & J. Hintikka (eds), 149–69. Dordrecht: Reidel.

Field, H. H. 1980. *Science without Numbers*. Princeton, NJ: Princeton University Press.

Fine, A. 1986. *The Shaky Game: Einstein, Realism, and the Quantum Theory*. Chicago, IL: University of Chicago Press.

Forbes, G. 1985. *The Metaphysics of Modality*. Oxford: Clarendon Press.

Forbes, G. 1989. *Languages of Possibility*. Oxford: Blackwell.

Forrest, P. & D. Armstrong 1984. "An Argument Against David Lewis's Theory of Possible Worlds". *Australasian Journal of Philosophy* 62, 164–68.

Frege, G. 1984. "On Sense and Meaning". In *Frege, Collected Papers*, B. McGuiness (ed.), 157–77. Oxford: Blackwell.

Friedman, M. 1992. *Kant and the Exact Sciences*. Cambridge, MA: Harvard University Press.

Friedman, M. 2001. *The Dynamics of Reason*. Stanford, CA: Centre for Studies in Language and Information.

Gallois, A. 1974. "Berkeley's Master Argument". *Philosophical Review* 83, 55–69.

Gardiner, M. Q. 2000. *Semantic Challenges to Realism: Dummett and Putnam*. Toronto: University of Toronto Press.

Geach, P. 1964. "Assertion". *Philosophical Review* 74, 449–65.

Gendler, T. & J. Hawthorne (eds) 2002. *Conceivability and Possibility*. Oxford: Clarendon Press.

Gibbard, A. 1990. *Wise Choices, Apt Feelings*. Oxford: Oxford University Press.

Giere, R. 1988. *Explaining Science*. Chicago, IL: University of Chicago Press.

Giere, R. 1999. *Science without Laws*. Chicago, IL: University of Chicago Press.

Girle, R. 2003. *Possible Worlds*. Chesham: Acumen.

Gödel, K. 1947. "What is Cantor's Continuum Problem?". *American Mathematical Monthly* 54, 515–25. Reprinted in Benacerraf & Putnam (1983), 258–73.

Green, K. 2001. *Dummett: Philosophy of Language*. Cambridge: Polity.

Gunson, D. 1998. *Michael Dummett and the Theory of Meaning*. Aldershot: Ashgate.

Guyer, P. (ed.) 1992. *The Cambridge Companion to Kant*. Cambridge: Cambridge University Press.

Haack, S. 1978. *Philosophy of Logics*. Cambridge: Cambridge University Press.

Hacker, P. M. S. 1987. *Appearance and Reality*. Oxford: Blackwell.

Hacking, I. 1983. *Representing and Intervening*. Cambridge: Cambridge University Press.

Hacking, I. 1985. "Can We See Through a Microscope?". See Churchland and Hooker (eds) (1985), 132–52.

Hacking, I. 1999. *The Social Construction of What?* Cambridge, MA: Harvard University Press.

Haldane, J. & C. Wright (eds) 1993. *Reality, Representation, and Projection*. Oxford: Oxford University Press.

Hale, B. 1987. *Abstract Objects*. Oxford: Blackwell.

Hardin, C. L. 1993. *Color for Philosophers: Unweaving the Rainbow*. Indianapolis, IN: Hackett.

Hare, R. M. 1952. *The Language of Morals*. Oxford: Oxford University Press.

Hare, R. M. 1963. *Freedom and Reason*. Oxford: Oxford University Press.

Harman, G. 1977. *The Nature of Morality: An Introduction to Ethics*. Oxford: Oxford University Press.

Harman, G. & J. J. Thomson 1996. *Moral Relativism and Moral Objectivity*. Oxford: Blackwell.

Hawthorne, J. 1996. "The Epistemology of Possible Worlds". *Philosophical Studies* 84, 183–202.

Hazen, A. 1976. "Expressive Completeness in Modal Language". *Journal of Philosophical Logic* 5, 25–46.

Hazen, A. 1979. "One of the Truths About Actuality". *Analysis* 39, 1–3.

Hegel, G. W. F. 1952. *Philosophy of Right*, T. M. Knox (trans.). Oxford: Oxford University Press.

Hegel, G. W. F. 1975. *Logic*, W. Wallace (trans.). Oxford: Oxford University Press.

Hellman, G. 1989. *Mathematics Without Numbers: Towards a Modal-Structural Interpretation*. Oxford: Oxford University Press.

Hellman, G. 1993. "Gleeson's Theorem is not Constructively Provable". *Journal of Philosophical Logic* 22, 193–203.

Hempel, C. 1950. "The Empiricist Criterion of Meaning". *Revue Internationale de Philosophie* 4, 41–63. Reprinted in Ayer (1959), 108–29.

Heyting, A. 1956. *Intuitionism: An Introduction*. Amsterdam: North Holland.

Hilbert, D. 1987. *Color and Color Perception*. Stanford, CA: Centre for Studies in Language and Information.

Hintikka, J. 1996. *The Principles of Mathematics Revisited*. Cambridge: Cambridge University Press.

Horwich, P. (ed.) 1993. *World Changes: Thomas Kuhn and the Nature of Science*. Cambridge, MA: MIT Press.

Howell, R. 1979. "Fictional Objects: How They Are and How They Aren't". *Poetics* 8, 129–77.

Howell, R. 1983. "Review of Parsons' *Nonexistent Objects*". *Journal of Philosophy* 80, 163–73.

Howell, R. 1996. "Review of Walton's *Mimesis as Make-Believe*". *Synthese* 109, 424–34.

Hume, D. 1986. *A Treatise of Human Nature*. Oxford: Oxford University Press.

Irvine, A. (ed.) 1990. *Physicalism in Mathematics*. Dordrecht: Kluwer.

Jackson, F. 1980. "Ontological Commitment and Paraphrase". *Philosophy* 55, 303–15.

Jackson, F. 1982. "Epiphenomenal Qualia". *Philosophical Quarterly* 32, 127–36.

Jackson, F. 1989. "A Puzzle About Ontological Commitment". *Cause, Mind, and Reality: Essays Honouring C. B. Martin*, John Heil (ed.), 191–9. Dordrecht: Kluwer.

Jackson, F. 1996. "The Primary Quality View of Color". *Philosophical Perspectives* 10, 199–219.

Jackson, F. 1998. *From Metaphysics to Ethics: A Defence of Conceptual Analysis*. Oxford: Oxford University Press.

Jackson, F. & R. Pargetter 1987. "An Objectivist's Guide to Subjectivism About Color". *Revue Internationale de Philosophie* 160, 129–41.

Johnston, M. 1989. "Dispositional Theories of Value". *Proceedings of the Aristotelian Society*, supp. vol. 63, 139–74.

Johnston, M. 1992. "How to Speak of the Colors". *Philosophical Studies* 68, 221–63. Reprinted with postscripts in Byrne & Hilbert (1997), ch. 9.

Johnston, M. 1993. "Objectivity Refigured: Pragmatism Without Verificationism". In Haldane & Wright (1993), 85–130.

hnston, M. unpublished manuscript. *The Manifest*.

seph, M. A. 2004. *Donald Davidson*. Chesham: Acumen.

yce, R. 2001. *The Myth of Morality*. Cambridge: Cambridge University Press.

yce, R. 2005. "Moral Fictionalism". In *Fictionalist Approaches to Metaphysics*, M. Kalderon (ed.), 287–313. Oxford: Oxford University Press.

ılderon , M. (ed.) 2005a. *Fictionalist Approaches to Metaphysics*. Oxford: Oxford University Press.

ılderon, M. 2005b. *Moral Fictionalism*. Oxford: Clarendon Press.

ant, I. 1965. *Critique of Pure Reason*, N. Kemp Smith (trans.). London: Macmillan.

tcher, P. 1984. *The Nature of Mathematical Knowledge*. Oxford: Oxford University Press.

ripke, S. 1980. *Naming and Necessity*. Cambridge, MA: Harvard University Press.

ripke, S. 1973. "Reference and Existence". Unpublished manuscript, presented as the John Locke Lectures, 1973.

ripke, S. 1976. "Is there a Problem about Substitutional Quantification?". In *Truth and Meaning; Essays in Semantics*, G. Evans & J. McDowell (eds), 324–419. Oxford: Oxford University Press.

uhn, T. 1970. *The Structure of Scientific Revolutions*, 2nd edn. Chicago, IL: University of Chicago Press.

uhn, T. 1977. *The Essential Tension*. Chicago, IL: University of Chicago.

uhn, T. 1990. "Dubbing and Re-Dubbing: The Vunerability of Rigid Designation". In *Scientific Theories*, Wade Savage (ed.), 298–318. Minneapolis, MN: University of Minnesota Press.

uhn, T. 2000a. "A Discussion with Thomas Kuhn". In Kuhn (2000b), 255–99.

uhn, T. 2000b. *The Road Since Structure*. Chicago, IL: University of Chicago Press.

ukla, A. 2000. *Social Constructivism and the Philosophy of Science*. London: Routledge.

amarque, P. 1983. "Fiction and Reality". In *Philosophy and Fiction: Essays in Literary Aesthetics*, P. Lamarque (ed.), 52–72. Aberdeen: Aberdeen University Press.

ambert, K. 2002. *Free Logic: Selected Essays*. Cambridge: Cambridge University Press.

atour, B. & S. Woolgar 1979. *Laboratory Life: The Social Construction of Scientific Facts*. Beverly Hills, CA: Sage.

audan, L. 1981. "A Confutation of Convergent Realism". *Philosophy of Science* 48, 19–49.

epore, E. & K. Ludwig 2005. *Donald Davidson: Meaning, Truth, Language, and Reality*. Oxford: Oxford University Press.

evinson, J. 1993. "Making Believe". *Dialogue* 32, 359–74.

Lewis, D. 1970. "How to Define Theoretical Terms". *Journal of Philosophy* 67, 427–46. Reprinted in Lewis, *Collected Papers* (Oxford: Oxford University Press, 1983), volume 1, ch. 6.

Lewis, D. 1973. *Counterfactuals*. Oxford: Blackwell.

Lewis, D. 1978. "Truth in Fiction". *American Philosophical Quarterly* 15, 37–46. Reprinted with postscripts in Lewis, *Philosophical Papers* (Oxford: Oxford University Press, 1983), volume I, 261–80.

Lewis, D. 1984. "Putnam's Paradox". *Australasian Journal of Philosophy* 62, 221–36. Reprinted in Lewis, *Papers in Metaphysics and Epistemology* (Cambridge: Cambridge University Press, 1999), ch. 2.

Lewis, D. 1986. *On the Plurality of Worlds*. Oxford: Blackwell.

Lewis, D. 1990. "Noneism or Allism?". *Mind* 99, 23–31.

Lewis, D. 1991. *Parts of Classes*. Oxford: Blackwell.

Lewis, D. 1992. "Critical Notice: Armstrong, D. M. *A Combinatorial Theory of Po* sibility". *Australasian Journal of Philosophy* 70, 211–24.

Lewis, D. 1997. "Naming the Colours". *Australasian Journal of Philosophy*, 7. 325–42.

Lewis, D. 2005. "Quasi-Realism as Fictionalism". In *Fictionalist Approaches to Met. physics*, M. Kalderon (ed.), 314–21. Oxford: Oxford University Press.

Lewis, D. & S. Lewis 1970. "Holes". *Australasian Journal of Philosophy*, 48, 206 12.

Lipton, P. 1991. *Inference to the Best Explanation*. London: Routledge.

Linsky, B. & E. Zalta 1991. "Is Lewis a Meinongian?". *Australasian Journal of Ph. losophy* 69, 438–53.

Loar, B. 1987. "Truth Beyond All Verification". In *Michael Dummett: Contribution to Philosophy*, Barry Taylor (ed.), 81–116. The Hague: Nijhoff.

Locke, J. 1959. *An Essay Concerning Human Understanding*, 2 vols. New York Dover.

Mackie, J. 1977. *Ethics: Inventing Right and Wrong*. Harmondsworth: Penguin.

MacKinnon, C. 1989. *Toward a Feminist Theory of the State*. Cambridge, MA Harvard University Press.

Maddy, P. 1990. *Realism in Mathematics*. Oxford: Oxford University Press.

Mally, E. 1912. *Gegenstandstheoretische Grundlagen der Logik und Logistik*, supple ment to *Zeitschrift für Philosophie und philosophische Kritik* 148.

Marcus, R. B. 1962. "Interpreting Quatification". *Inquiry* 5, 252–9.

Mares, E. D. 2000. "Even Dialetheists should Hate Contradictions". *Australasian Journal of Philosophy* 78, 503–16.

Mares, E. D. 2004. *Relevant Logic: A Philosophical Interpretation*. Cambridge: Cam bridge University Press.

Marquis, J. P. 1995. "Category Theory and the Foundations of Mathematics: Philo-sophical Excavations". *Synthese* 103, 421–47.

Marquis, J. P. 2006. "Category Theory". In *Stanford Encyclopedia of Philosophy*, E. N. Zalta (ed.), http://plato.stanford.edu/entries/category-theory/

Matthen, M. 1988. "Biological Functions and Perceptual Content". *Journal of Phi-losophy* 85, 5–27.

Maund, B. 1995. *Colors: Their Nature and Representation*. Cambridge: Cambridge University Press.

Maund, B. 2002. "Color". In *Stanford Encyclopedia of Philosophy*, http://plato. stanford.edu/entries/color/

McDaniel, K. 2004. "Modal Realism with Overlap". In *Lewisian Themes: The Phi-losophy of David Lewis*, F. Jackson & G. Priest (eds), 140–55. Oxford: Oxford University Press.

McDowell, J. 1985. "Values and Secondary Qualities". In *Morality and Objectivity*, T. Honderich (ed.), 110–29. London: Routledge.

McDowell, J. 1994. *On Mind and World*. Cambridge, MA: Harvard University Press.

McGinn, C. 1983. *The Subjective View: Secondary Qualities and Indexical Thoughts*. Oxford: Oxford University Press.

McGinn, C. 1996. "Another Look at Color". *Journal of Philosophy* 93, 537–53.

Melia, J. 1992a. "A Note on Lewis's Ontology". *Analysis* 52, 191–2.

Melia, J. 1992b. "Against Modalism". *Philosophical Studies* 68, 35–56.

Melia, J. 2003. *Modality*. Chesham: Acumen.

Menzies, P. (ed.) 1988. *Secondary Qualities Generalised*, Monist, special issue, 81(1), 255–77.

Menzies, P. 1998. "Possibility and Conceivability: A Response-Dependent Account of Their Connections". In *European Review of Philosophy: Response-Dependence*, vol. 3, R. Casati & C. Tappolet (eds). Stanford, CA: CSLI Publications.

Menzies, P. & P. Pettit 1994. "A Defence of Fictionalism about Possible Worlds". *Analysis* 54, 27–36.

Merrill, G. H. 1980. "The Model-Theoretic Argument Against Realism". *Philosophy of Science* 47, 69–81.

Miller, A. 2002. "Realism". In *Stanford Encyclopedia of Philosophy*, http://plato. stanford.edu/entries/realism/

Miller, A. 2003a. *Introduction to Contemporary Metaethics*. Cambridge: Polity.

Miller, A. 2003b. "The Significance of Semantic Realism". *Synthese* 136, 191–217.

Miller, A. 2006. "Realism and Anti-Realism". In *Handbook of the Philosophy of Language*, E. Lepore & B. Smith (eds), 983–1005. Oxford: Oxford University Press.

Miller, R. 1992. "Concern for Counterparts". *Philosophical Papers* 21, 133–40.

Millikan, R. 1984. *Language, Thought, and other Biological Categories*. Cambridge, MA: MIT Press.

Misak, C. J. 1995. *Verificationism: Its History and Prospects*. London: Routledge.

Misak, C. J. 2004. *Truth and the End of Inquiry: A Peircean Account of Truth*, expanded edn. Oxford: Oxford University Press.

Moore, G. E. 1903. *Principia Ethica*. Cambridge: Cambridge University Press.

Nolan, D. 1997. "Quantitative Parsimony". *British Journal for the Philosophy of Science* 48, 329–43.

Nolan, D., G. Restall & C. West 2005. "Moral Fictionalism". *Australasian Journal of Philosophy* 83, 307–30.

Noonan, H. 1994. "A Defence of the Letter of Fictionalism". *Analysis* 54, 133–9.

Norris, C. 2002a. *Realism, Reason and the Uses of Uncertainty*. Manchester: Manchester University Press.

Norris, C. 2002b. *Truth Matters: Realism, Anti-Realism, and Response-Dependence*. New York: Columbia University Press.

Papineau, D. (ed.) 1996. *Philosophy of Science*. Oxford: Oxford University Press.

Pappas, G. S. 2000. *Berkeley's Thought*. Ithaca, NY: Cornell University Press.

Parsons, T. 1980. *Nonexistent Objects*. New Haven, CT: Yale University Press.

Parsons, T. 1982. "Fregean Theories of Fictional Objects". *Topoi* 1, 81–7.

Passmore, J. 1968. *A Hundred Years of Philosophy*. Harmondsworth: Penguin.

Peacocke, C. 1978, "Necessity and Truth Theories". *Journal of Philosophical Logic* 7, 473–500.

Peacocke, C. 1983. *Sense and Content: Experience, Thought and Their Relations*. Oxford: Oxford University Press.

Peirce, C. S. 1958. *Charles S. Peirce: Selected Writings (Values in a World of Chance)*. New York: Dover.

Pettit, P. 1990. "The Reality of Rule Following". *Mind* 99, 1–21.

Pettit, P. 1991. "Realism and Response-Dependence". *Mind* 100, 587–626.

Pettit, P. 2002. *Rules, Reasons, and Norms*. Oxford: Oxford University Press.

Pigden, C. 1993. "Naturalism". In *Companion to Ethics*, P. Singer (ed.), 421–31. Oxford: Blackwell.

Pinkard, T. 2002. *German Philosophy 1760–1960: The Legacy of Idealism*. Cambridge: Cambridge University Press.

Pitcher, G. 1977. *Berkeley*. London: Routledge.

Plantinga, A. 1974. *The Nature of Necessity*. Oxford: Blackwell.

Potter, M. 2004. *Set Theory and its Philosophy: A Critical Introduction*. Oxford: Oxford University Press.

Prawitz, D. 1987. "Dummett on a Theory of Meaning and Its Impact on Logic". In *Michael Dummett: Contributions to Philosophy*, B. Taylor (ed.), 117–65. The Hague: Nijhoff.

Priest, G. 1987. *In Contradiction: An Essay on the Transconsistent*. Dordrech Nijhoff.

Priest, G. 2003. *Beyond the Limits of Thought*, 2nd edn. Oxford: Oxford Universi Press.

Putnam, H. 1970. "Reply to Dummett's Comments". In *Meaning and Use*, A. Marga (ed.), 226–8. Dordrecht: Reidel.

Putnam, H. 1971. *Philosophy of Logic*. New York: Harper & Row.

Putnam, H. 1978. *Meaning and the Moral Sciences*. London: Routledge & Kega Paul.

Putnam, H. 1981. *Reason, Truth and History*. Cambridge: Cambridge Universi Press.

Putnam, H. 1987. *The Many Faces of Realism*. La Salle, IL: Open Court.

Putnam, H. 1990. *Realism with a Human Face*. Cambridge, MA: Harvard Univer sity Press.

Quine, W. V. O. 1953. *From a Logical Point of View*. Cambridge, MA: Harvar University Press.

Rachels, J. (ed.) 1998. *Ethical Theory I: The Question of Objectivity*. Oxford: Oxfor University Press.

Rae, A. I. M. 1992. *Quantum Mechanics*, 3rd edn. Bristol: Institute of Physics Pub lishing.

Railton, P. 1986. "Moral Realism". *Philosophical Review* 95, 163–207.

Railton, P. 1996. "Moral Realism: Prospects and Problems". In *Moral Knowledge: New Readings in Moral Epistemology*, W. Sinnott-Armstrong & M. Timmons (eds) 49–81. Oxford: Oxford University Press.

Ramberg, B. T. 1989. *Donald Davidson's Philosophy of Language: An Introduction* Oxford: Blackwell.

Ramsey, F. P. [1929] 1990. "Theories". Reprinted in F. P. Ramsey, *Philosophical Papers*, D. H. Mellor (ed.), 112–36 (Cambridge: Cambridge University Press, 1990).

Rawls, J. 1971. *A Theory of Justice*. Cambridge, MA: Harvard University Press.

Resnik, M. 1985. "How Nominalist is Hartry Field's Nominalism?". *Philosophical Studies* 47, 163–81.

Resnik, M. D. 1997. *Mathematics as a Science of Patterns*. Oxford: Oxford Univer sity Press.

Richards, T. 1975. "The Worlds of David Lewis". *Australasian Journal of Philosophy* 53, 105–18.

Ridge, M. 2003/2004. "Moral Non-Naturalism". In *Stanford Encyclopedia of Phi losophy*, E. Zalta (ed.), http://plato.stanford.edu/entries/moral-non-naturalism/

Rorty, R. 1965. "Mind–Body Identity, Privacy, and Categories". *Review of Meta physics* 19, 24–54.

Rosen, G. 1990. "Modal Fictionalism". *Mind* 99, 327–54.

Rosen, G. 1993. "A Problem for Fictionalism About Possible Worlds". *Analysis* 53, 71–81.

Rosen, G. 1994. "Objectivity and Modern Idealism: What is the Question?". In *Phi losophy in Mind: The Place of Philosophy in the Study of Mind*, M. Michael & J. O'Leary-Hawthorne (eds), 277–319. Dordrecht: Kluwer.

Rosenberg, A. 1989. "Is Lewis's Genuine Modal Realism Magical Too?" *Mind* 98, 411–21.

Ross, W. D. 1930. *The Right and the Good*. Oxford: Oxford University Press.

Routley, R. 1980. *Exploring Meinong's Jungle and Beyond: An Investigation of Non eism and the Theory of Items*. Canberra: Australian National University Press.

Ruse, M. 1995. *Evolutionary Naturalism*. London: Routledge.

Russell, B. 1912. *The Problems of Philosophy*. Oxford: Oxford University Press.

Salmon, N. 1998. "Nonexistence". *Noûs* 32, 277–319.

Sayre-McCord, G. (ed.) 1988. *Essays on Moral Realism*. Ithaca, NY: Cornell University Press.

Schirn, M. (ed.) 1998. *The Philosophy of Mathematics Today*. Oxford: Oxford University Press.

Schlesinger, G. 1971. "Induction and Parsimony". *American Philosophical Quarterly* 8, 179–85.

Shapiro, S. 1997. *Philosophy of Mathematics: Structure and Ontology*. Oxford: Oxford University Press.

Shapiro, S. 2000. *Foundations without Foundationalism: A Case for Second Order Logic*. Oxford: Oxford University Press.

Sharrock, W. & R. Read 2002. *Kuhn: Philosopher of Scientific Revolution*. Cambridge: Polity.

Shoemaker, S. 1982. "The Inverted Spectrum". *Journal of Philosophy* 79, 357–81.

Sinnott-Armstrong, W. & M. Timmons (eds) 1996. *Moral Knowledge? New Readings in Moral Epistemology*. Oxford: Oxford University Press.

Skyrms, B. 1976. "Possible Worlds, Physics and Metaphysics". *Philosophical Studies* 30, 323–32.

Smart, J. J. C. 1975. "On Some Criticisms of a Physicalist Theory of Colors". In *Philosophical Aspects of the Mind–Body Problem*, C. Cheng (ed.), 54–63. Honolulu, HI: University of Hawaii Press.

Smart, J. J. C. 1989. *Our Place in the Universe*. Oxford: Blackwell.

Smith, M. 1994. *The Moral Problem*. Oxford: Blackwell.

Smith, N. H. 2002. *Reading McDowell: On Mind and World*. London: Routledge.

Sober, E. 1981. "The Principle of Parsimony". *British Journal for the Philosophy of Science* 32, 145–56.

Stanford, K. 2000. "An Anti-Realist Explanation of Success". *Philosophy of Science* 67, 266–84.

Stanley, J. 2001. "Hermeneutic Fictionalism". *Midwest Studies in Philosophy: Figurative Language* 25, 36–71.

Stevenson, C. L. 1944. *Ethics and Language*. New Haven, CT: Yale University Press.

Stevenson, C. L. 1963. *Facts and Values*. New Haven, CT: Yale University Press.

Steiner, M. 1975. *Mathematical Knowledge*. Ithaca, NY: Cornell University Press.

Strawson, G. 1989. "Red and 'red'". *Synthese* 78, 193–232.

Sturgeon, N. 1985. "Moral Explanations". In *Morality, Reason, and Truth: New Essays on the Foundations of Ethics*, D. Copp & D. Zimmerman (eds), 49–78. Totowa, NJ: Rowman and Allanheld.

Tarski, A. [1931] 1983. "The Concept of Truth in Formalized Languages". Translated and reprinted in *Logic, Semantics, Metamathematics*, 152–278. Indianapolis, IN: Hackett.

Taylor, B. (ed.) 1987. *Michael Dummett: Contributions to Philosophy*. The Hague: Nijhoff.

Taylor, B. 2006. *Models, Truth, and Realism*. Oxford: Oxford University Press.

Taylor, C. 1975. *Hegel*. Cambridge: Cambridge University Press.

Thomasson, A. 1999. *Fiction and Metaphysics*. Cambridge: Cambridge University Press.

Thomasson, A. forthcoming. "Parsimony and Ontological Commitment". In *Ordinary Objects*. Oxford: Oxford University Press.

Thorburn, W. M. 1918. "The Myth of Occam's Razor". *Mind* 27, 345–53.

Tiles, M. 1989. *The Philosophy of Set Theory: An Historical Introduction to Cantor's Paradise*. Oxford: Blackwell.

Tipton, I. C. 1974. *Berkeley: The Philosophy of Immaterialism*. London: Methuen.

Tolliver, J. (ed.). 1992. *Papers on Colour*. Special issue, *Philosophical Studies* 63(3).

Tye, M. 2000. *Consciousness, Color, and Content*. Cambridge, MA: MIT Press.

van Brakel, J. 1993. "The Plasticity of Categories: The Case of Color". *British Journal for the Philosophy of Science* **44**, 103–35.

van Fraassen, B. C. 1980. *The Scientific Image*. Oxford: Oxford University Press.

van Fraassen, B. C. 1985. "Empiricism in the Philosophy of Science". In *Images of Science: Essays on Realism and Empiricism with Replies by Bas C. van Fraassen*, P. M. Churchland & C. A. Hooker (eds), 245–308. Chicago, IL: University of Chicago Press.

van Fraassen, B. C. 1989. *Laws and Symmetry*. Oxford: Oxford University Press.

van Fraassen, B. C. 2005. "The Day of the Dolphins: Puzzling over Epistemic Partnership". In *Mistakes of Reason*, A. Irvine and K. Peacock (eds), 111–13. Toronto: University of Toronto Press.

van Inwagen, P. 1977. "Creatures of Fiction". *American Philosophical Quarterly* **24**, 299–308.

van Inwagen, P. 1981. "Why I don't Understand Substitutional Quantification". *Philosophical Studies* **39**, 281–6.

van Inwagen, P. 1983. "Fiction and Metaphysics". *Philosophy and Literature* **7**, 67–77.

van Inwagen, P. 1998. "Meta-Ontology". *Erkenntnis* **48**, 233–50.

van Inwagen, P. 2003. "Existence, Ontological Commitment, and Fictional Entities". In *Oxford Handbook of Metaphysics*, M. Loux (ed.), 131–57. Oxford: Oxford University Press.

Walton, K. 1990. *Mimesis as Make-Believe*. Cambridge, MA: Harvard University Press.

Weiss, B. 2002. *Michael Dummett*. Chesham: Acumen.

Westphal, J. 1991. *Colour: A Philosophical Introduction*. Oxford: Blackwell.

Williamson, T. 1995. "Realism and Anti-realism". In *Oxford Companion to Philosophy*, T. Honderich (ed.), 746–8. Oxford: Clarendon Press.

Wilson, M. D. 1999. *Ideas and Mechanism: Essays on Early Modern Philosophy*. Princeton, NJ: Princeton University Press.

Winkler, K. P. 1989. *Berkeley: An Interpretation*. Oxford: Oxford University Press.

Wolterstorff, N. 1980. *Works and Worlds of Art*. Oxford: Clarendon Press.

Wong, D. 1984. *Moral Relativity*. Los Angeles, CA: University of California Press.

Wollheim, R. 1959. *F. H. Bradley*. Harmondsworth: Penguin.

Wright, C. 1989. "Wittgenstein's Rule-Following Considerations and the Central Project of Linguistics". In *Reflections on Chomsky*, G. Alexander (ed.), 233–64. Oxford: Blackwell.

Wright, C. 1992. *Truth and Objectivity*. Cambridge, MA: Harvard University Press.

Wright, C. 1993. *Realism, Truth, and Meaning*. Oxford: Blackwell.

Wright, C. & B. Hale 2004. *The Reason's Proper Study: Essays Towards a Neo-Fregean Philosophy of Mathematics*. Oxford: Oxford University Press.

Yablo, S. 1993. "Is Conceivability a Guide to Possibility?". *Philosophy and Phenomenological Research* **53**, 1–42.

Young, J. O. 1995. *Global Antirealism*. Aldershot: Ashgate.

Zalta, E. N. 1983. *Abstract Objects*. Dordrecht: Reidel.

Zalta, E. N. 1988. *Intensional Logic and the Metaphysics of Intentionality*. Cambridge, MA: MIT Press.

Index

CPSIA information can be obtained
at www.ICGtesting.com
Printed in the USA
FSHW021619050820
72686FS

9 780773 532397